ON APRIL 19, 1987, TWO DAYS BEFORE HIS WIFE WAS TO BE BRUTALLY STRANGLED AND LEFT FOR DEAD, WALKER RAILEY DELIVERED A RIVETING EASTER SERMON. . . .

"There is nothing about this morning that spares us from the grave. You will die someday. You and you—and you. And someday I will die as well. Everybody dies, and sometimes the ending of life on this earth is the most redemptive experience available. Sometimes death heals in a way that medicine cannot. Resurrection does not take away the inevitability of death at the end of life; Resurrection promises the reality of life at the end of death. . . .

"One day there will be no opening to a new episode in life. . . . It could be today. It might be tomorrow. Nobody knows. . . ."

THE DEMON INSIDE

BARBARA WEDGWOOD

POCKET BOOKS

New York London Toronto Sydney Tokyo Singapore

An *Original* Publication of POCKET BOOKS

POCKET BOOKS, a division of Simon & Schuster Inc.
1230 Avenue of the Americas, New York, NY 10020

ISBN: 0-671-67417-X

First Pocket Books printing February 1993

10 9 8 7 6 5 4 3 2 1

POCKET and colophon are registered trademarks of
Simon & Schuster Inc.

Cover photo by Judy Walgren/*The Dallas Morning News*

Printed in the U.S.A.

For My Husband
Hensleigh Cecil Wedgwood
in memoriam

There is a demon inside my soul. It has always been
  there.
My demon tries to lead me down paths I do not want
  to follow.
At times that demon has lured me into things I did not
  want to do.

—Walker L. Railey
May 1, 1987

Foreword

I was baptized in First United Methodist Church of Dallas. When I was eleven, I joined the Church with my father. Three of my closest friendships today began during my childhood at that Church.

Many years later, when I lived in England, my husband and I visited Dallas and heard the newly appointed young Reverend Walker L. Railey preach. We were favorably impressed. I remember feeling grateful that my parents had a minister who displayed such obvious brillance and caring concern for his congregation.

Five years ago the violent acts against members of the Railey family shocked me. Why had it happened to them? Why in Dallas? Why in *my* Church? And why, in the name of God, has this evil crime not been solved? In the Code of Criminal Procedures, it is stated that a prosecutor's duty is "not to convict but to see that justice is done." So far, justice has not been done.

The continuing fascination of the Railey case is like that of a classic Greek tragedy. If only we could see behind the masks, we might recognize the demons, theirs sins and their hypocrisies—but no one really knows what is in another person's mind.

FOREWORD

What follows are the amazing facts of a crime that destroyed a family, devastated a city and divided a church. This story could not have been told without the generous cooperation of countless kind and concerned people. Most specifically it could not have been written without the help of Peggy's lawyer and benefactor, A. W. Arnold, III, and her parents Bill and Billie Jo Nicolai.

Walker Railey declined requests to be interviewed, and Lucy Papillon did not answer letters or return my phone calls. Upon the advice of retired Bishop W. McFerrin Stowe, some of Walker's closest friends refused to talk to me about any aspect of this tragedy. Thus, because of an absence of response to those who did talk, this book will seem to present only one side of the story. This was not my intention, for, to this day, Walker Railey maintains his innocence.

I am especially indebted to Wayne Lee Gay for his assistance, research and encouragement. For her Herculean efforts in transcribing hand-written notes, placing them on a computer and then adding, subtracting, transposing and changing the typescript at least four or five times without ever losing her cheerfulness, I am indebted to Carol Lee South. Most of all I am indebted to my husband Hensleigh for his helpful critique, support and understanding throughout the ups and downs this book brought into four years of our lives.

Many people gave their valuable time in interviews for this story, some of them several times. It would be impossible to list them all, but special thanks go to members of the media for refusing to let this story be suppressed or fade away. Within the Church two men in particular stand out for their integrity and intelligence, lay leader Ralph Shannon and Dr. Gordon Casad whom Shannon described as "God's gift to the Church."

Others who deserve recognition for their help with this book include Assistant District Attorney Norman Kinne, Diane Yarrington, Maxie Hardin, Jane Buckner, Dede Casad, Joyce Meier, Marie Fisher, Vermelle Votteler, Pat Mills, Corinne Fields, Betty Baird, Diane Garvin, Susan

Hall, Mary Nash, Roberta Crowe, Rabbi Sheldon Zimmerman, Bishop O. Eugene Slater, Reverend Howard Grimes, Reverend James Reaves, Reverend Hal Brady, Karen Spencer and almost all of the staff of First United Methodist Church of Dallas. Many of the congregation of the Church, who shared their thoughts and feelings about this tragedy, have my gratitude and respect. I am also grateful to representatives of the Dallas Police Department, of the District Attorney and of the Dallas Office of the Federal Bureau of Investigation.

I thank my agents Ruth Nathan and Jane Cushman for their work, their support and their friendship. I also thank the editors and staff at Simon & Schuster and Pocketbooks, especially Elaine Pfefferblit, Jane Rosenman and Mary Anne Sacco for their patience and understanding.

All the people in this story are real. No names have been changed with the exception of three couples who are or were members of First Church and who requested that their real names *not* be used. In the story they are Will and Charlotte Lieber, Bobby and Betty Eubank and Charles and Ann Nichols. For the same reason Reverend Horace Hanley is also a fictitious name for a real person.

The dialogue in the story comes directly from sworn testimony, quotations from newspapers and magazines or the recollections of two observers of a scene or one of the participants in a dialogue. Without intending to deceive or distort, people sometimes recall conversations or descriptions of particular events differently. Usually the difference is of little consequence—such as whether on Easter Sunday Peggy wore a pink suit, a cream-colored suit or a lavender dress. Yet, wherever there have been variations in memory, I have chosen either what was remembered by the most people or else what appeared most probable.

Until August 25, 1992, it seemed unlikely that the Railey case, one of the most fascinating and haunting crimes in Dallas history, would ever be brought to trial. Over the past five years people voiced their suspicions that Walker Railey was involved in the attack on his wife, yet he was never charged or convicted of any criminal action.

FOREWORD

Prosecutor and Assistant District Attorney Norman Kinne answered criticisms by saying that all of the evidence was circumstantial and that Walker Railey's guilt could not be proven beyond a reasonable doubt.

In July of 1992, without making any public announcement, District Attorney John Vance took Kinne off the case and substituted Assistant District Attorney Cecil Emerson. To avoid media publicity, Emerson scheduled a grand jury to hear the case of the people versus John R. Doe, who was none other than Walker Railey. A felony indictment was returned. Railey was arrested in California, extradited and brought back to Texas by Dallas Police Detective Stan McNear, who had worked on this case from the beginning. Railey posted bail, consulted with his Dallas lawyer and, as of this writing, has returned to Los Angeles. Will he return to Texas again for his trial, wherever and whenever it may be?

In this book are some of the known facts, opinions and statements that can now be heard in a court of law. But, *will* they be heard? Nothing in this case has so far been logical or even rational. You, the readers of this book, may still be the only judge and jury.

—Barbara Wedgwood
September 1992

PART I

The Voice of the Shepherd

"My sheep hear my voice, and I know them, and they follow me."

John 10:4

1

∽ THE SUN ROSE BRIGHT AND GLORIOUS THAT EASTER, with as much hope and joy and mystery as on that morning nearly two thousand years ago when Mary Magdalene found the stone pushed aside and the tomb empty. A blinding white light rebounded from the dozen gold-mirrored, glass-and-chrome towers of the downtown Dallas business district, where skyscrapers crowd in a haphazard jungle of monuments to materialism and Mammon.

A square of white on the red carpet at First United Methodist Church caught the eye of Dr. Gordon Casad as he walked into his office an hour before the eleven o'clock service. The envelope had been slipped under the side door, the one he hardly ever used. He knew instantly what it contained. Picking it up carefully between his thumb and index finger, he touched it only on one corner but noted, as he had feared, that it was addressed to Reverend Walker L. Railey.

A police officer who sat in the central administrative office skillfully opened the envelope with a pencil and eraser. Carefully unfolding the paper, he read aloud: "On Easter

3

Christ arose from the dead. And on this day you are going down."

The first of these hate letters to the popular, young senior minister had arrived through the mail early in March, during Lent. The brief and poorly typed letter called Walker "a nigger lover" and ended with "you're not even a good preacher." It had been opened by Walker's secretary Karen Spencer, a calm, efficient woman far from the prudish stereotype of a minister's secretary. Karen showed the letter to Walker. They concurred that some crank or crackpot had written it. Neither of them took it seriously because all high-profile clergymen occasionally receive hate mail. Karen put the letter in a special file.

When the second letter came, looking and sounding much like the first, Walker and Karen informed Church members Ralph Shannon, Chairman of the Pastor-Parish Committee, Elizabeth Jasmine, a policewoman, and Susan Sanders, a young, single lawyer close to Walker. They all agreed that the letters were written by someone intelligent who was purposely using incorrect grammar. Walker took the letters to the F.B.I. and informed the police that he had received them. The next letter came to the Railey home. It not only threatened Walker but ended with, "What would your children say if they knew what an S.O.B. their father is?"

A week later a fourth letter arrived at the church. Each of the letters intensified in hostility and showed increasing knowledge of the Railey family's activities. On Good Friday a fifth sinister letter addressed to Walker came to his home. It read: "You have a beautiful home, a beautiful wife and two beautiful children—but not for long." Peggy Railey felt more angry than frightened, while Walker seemed convinced that someone really was "out to get him."

The door under which Dr. Casad found the sixth envelope this Easter morning usually remained locked. It opened onto a wide, heavily trafficked corridor where the hundred-member choir and six or seven ministers assembled for the processional. Before and after the processional, dozens, possibly even hundreds, of other people passed.

Police Officer Steve Torres, who took the envelope from Casad, immediately called the Intelligence Division to send more plainclothes reinforcements. He and two colleagues, Elizabeth Jasmine and Royce Massingill, members of the Church, had already agreed that Elizabeth should follow Peggy and the children, Ryan, aged five, and Megan, aged two, who would be driven from their house to the church. Elizabeth would be with Peggy when she took the children to the nursery. Then she'd accompany her to the sanctuary and remain with her during the service.

Half a dozen of the Church's large ministerial staff had gathered in Karen's office. They seemed as nervous and indecisive as the lost sheep about whom they had all so often preached. No one quite knew what to do.

The Reverend Susan Monts, thirty-four and the first woman ever appointed to the senior ministerial staff, begged Walker not to preach the next service, expressing the general feeling among the staff.

Energized by the threat, Walker stood in the doorway leading to his private suite of offices. He was not a physically impressive man; he was of slight build, less than five feet ten inches tall and balding. His beetling nose was often inflamed from colds or allergies. What remained of his sandy brown hair he wore long on the sides and turned under just above the collar. Children sometimes thought of a circus clown; some adults occasionally had old school book images of the neatly coiffed William Shakespeare; but most people saw an energetic young man attempting to blend the rebellious idealism of the 1960s with the materialistic lifestyle of the 1980s. He drove in the fast lane. A modern man of God who had created his own new image, the thirty-nine-year-old senior minister wore expensive custom-tailored suits and stiff-collared shirts with French cuffs and ostentatious gold cuff links. Now a flowing black gown hung from his shoulders, making him seem like a giant raven poised over his staff, most of whom were seated patiently. His changing eyes, sometimes green and sometimes gray-blue, fixed on a point on the opposite wall near the ceiling, far above the heads of the others. He pressed his palms together, lacing his fingers, then stretching them stiffly. His hands flexed and clenched, clenched and flexed. They moved compulsively in a handwringing ritual not unlike that of Pontius Pilate. He spoke in a firm but gentle voice: "It is Easter. I am going to preach."

A gasp then rose from the staff as Police Officer Royce Massingill shoved a police-issue bulletproof vest at him. The consensus was that a madman stalked the church, a madman bent on destroying Walker Railey. What place, what day in the Christian calendar could be more fiendishly appropriate than Easter?

Gordon Casad said he would walk through the church and see if he could spot someone or something suspicious. The administrative pastor, next only to Walker in authority, was a tall, powerfully built man in his early sixties with square shoulders and a bald head fringed by straight black hair that he kept carefully trimmed and neatly combed. In an earlier century he could easily have slipped into the brown robe of a monk. In this century, wearing his well-cut, dark blue suit, Casad looked as much like a bank president as a minister.

For the next half hour he paced through the basement and the upper three floors, looking in on people having coffee, people meeting in the recreation room, people gathered in the Sunday School classes, people bringing children to the nursery, people studying paintings in the Goodrich Gallery. They were all people who, if he did not recognize them by name, seemed to belong. Casad covered every area of the church; but, as he wryly thought, he really wasn't quite sure what he was looking for, just something suspicious.

While he had found nothing unusual in the church, when he returned to the offices, he felt the tense and apprehensive mood. Other ministers and members of the staff crowded in the central office pleading with Walker not to preach. Was one Easter sermon worth risking his life? All agreed, definitely not. At least one of the ministers visualized the service with all of them sitting on the dais, like a row of black white-collared ducks in a shooting gallery.

Officer Torres, speaking in a low, deliberate voice, said

that Walker was not to walk in the processional. He would enter unobtrusively from a door to the right during the last verse of the processional hymn and sit on the front row to the far right, between Officers Torres and Massingill. He would wear, under his robe, the bulletproof vest.

It was time now for all of them to don their robes. Casad remembered a former associate pastor telling of the Sunday service when a woman dressed in a nun's habit and carrying a Bible and a butcher's knife, suddenly joined the procession, whispering to the startled ministers that everything was all right. She believed herself to be the Virgin Mary and she intended to preach the sermon. It took two ministers and four laymen to subdue her and take away the knife. There was certainly nothing in the Methodist Book of Rules to cover that situation nor the one they now confronted.

The wall clock in the office read thirty seconds to eleven. A flurry of trumpets announced the processional. In the wide corridor between the sanctuary and the administrative offices the assembled choir began the long march through the main entry hall and down the three center aisles of the sanctuary. According to their rank, seven ministers followed the choir. Casad, the last one in the processional, moved forward when Walker caught him by the arm.

"Gordon, if I'm not there within the next five minutes, you'll have to preach the sermon."

Gordon was startled. For the past hour Walker had insisted upon preaching. If there was a possibility that he might not, why hadn't he said so earlier? If, indeed, he had to preach now, he would have to fall back upon his sermon "The Greatest Story Ever Told," a collection of biblical quotations appropriate for almost any occasion.

The triumphal hymn had begun. The congregation rose. The choir, robed in white with red yokes decorated with the Methodist emblem of the flame and the cross, marched down the red-carpeted center aisle, their red hymnals held in front of them as they sang.

Jesus Christ is risen today, Alleluia!

The sanctuary had filled to its capacity of two thousand people. Two young acolytes with white surplices over their red cassocks preceded the choir, followed by a bearer with a white standard holding a colorful butterfly emblem, which later would be remembered with irony. A slender brass cross about three feet high between two heavy brass candlesticks ornamented the altar in simple old-fashioned Methodist style. An arrangement of lilies and white chrysanthemums stood between the cross and the pulpit. In front of the communion rail two rows of lily plants were bunched tightly together. The heavy scent of the flowers was intoxicating.

It is a beautiful church. The walls are a soft, soothing cream color. The crimson carpets descend gently toward the modest central altar; behind the hundred-member choir, the huge organ pipes of zinc and copper rise majestically, covering the back wall in a show of Gothic splendor.

Hymns of praise then let us sing, Alleluia!
Unto Christ, our heavenly King, Alleluia!
Who endured the cross and grave, Alleluia!
Sinners to redeem and save, Alleluia!

The choir took its place facing the congregation at the front of the church, above the chancel. The drum rolled as the final alleluia echoed and faded. The seven ministers in their black gowns with white-fringed stoles over their shoulders and reaching to the hems of their gowns now sat in heavy leather chairs.

Gordon Casad noticed that Walker had slipped in the side door when the congregation stood. He now sat between the two policemen at the end of the front row. Relieved, Gordon looked at the congregation. Did somebody out there have a gun? He saw a dozen or more men standing in the far aisles, their backs to the walls. Wearing dark suits and short haircuts, they looked like F.B.I. agents or plainclothes detectives.

An assistant minister read the litany; the congregation sang the hymn "I Know That My Redeemer Liveth." Music Minister John Yarrington, Walker's closest friend, led the choir in "Shout the Glad Tidings." The ministers and the congregation read together from the New Testament John 20:1–10, beginning with: "The first day of the week cometh Mary Magdalene early, when it was yet dark, unto the sepulchre, and seeth the stone taken away from the sepulchre . . ." As the young Reverend Hugh Clark said the pastoral prayer, someone in the balcony dropped a hymnal, and inwardly Gordon jumped, certain a gun had been fired. But the prayer ended without further incident, and then Gordon himself stood at the pulpit making the announcements. His thick, rimless glasses reflected the bright lights from the medieval-style chandeliers and the modern television spots. He surprised himself by how calm he felt, welcoming a West German Methodist Youth Choir visiting from Berlin, announcing an Easter buffet in the Church dining room and encouraging the congregation to meet Dr. Walker Railey in the Crossroads Center where coffee and light refreshments would be available immediately after the service.

"Let us pray," Gordon said.

Not all heads bowed in prayer, and not all of those who bowed attended to the words spoken. An air of nervous expectation rippled through the Church. Many in the congregation felt the tension, but only a few understood.

The ushers came forward for the collection. The choir, accompanied by a brass ensemble, sang "Christ Be Thine the Glory." While the collection plates moved along the pews, Gordon again looked over the congregation. People in congregations seldom realize how clearly they are seen by the ministers on the dais. A brightly lit sanctuary is quite different from a darkened theater.

Not a seat in the sanctuary remained empty. Additional folding metal chairs crowded the balcony, and people stood against the back wall. Two large rooms with television sets accommodated the overflow. This diverse congregation came not only because it was Easter, they came because of Walker Railey.

"When Walker preaches, it hits you in the head and the heart and the gut," says Lynn Menges, an attractive, young,

9

professional woman who had moved to Dallas from the East. Walker's hypnotic eyes, glazed like majolica, mesmerized both sexes. "Hearing Walker's sermon on Sunday morning, I become a better man to start the week," says sixty-year-old Ernie Martin.

But this Sunday morning was different. At least it seemed so to those who attended more regularly than Christmas Eve and Easter morning. A ripple of uneasiness swept through the crowd as the regulars realized that Walker was not on the dais. Their uneasiness turned to puzzlement as some in the closest pews saw him seated in the front row. To the far right they passed back the news to the others. A few sat up straight and craned their necks to verify his presence. Why wasn't he where he should be? Certain rituals, like the Easter service, are comforting because of the sameness, their reassuring repetition.

"The Order of Worship says that Walker is going to preach," Mary Ruth Leavell whispered to her sister-in-law as she rolled the paper in her hand like a scroll. "I'll be so disappointed if someone else does."

Betty and Bobby Eubank and Will and Charlotte Lieber, two handsome couples in their mid-fifties who had joined the Church thirty years ago, were typical of the crowd that attends only on Christmas Eve and Easter.

Betty had telephoned Charlotte the day before saying, "Let's go to First Church tomorrow and hear a really good sermon."

At first Charlotte wasn't certain she wanted to go. First Church brought back too many memories of her mother whose death she still mourned. All of her childhood Easters had been spent in First Church, then the Easters of her own children when they were young and then finally the past five years when she and Will had accompanied her frail, widowed mother.

"Charlotte, you said Walker Railey preached the most beautiful funeral for your mother that you've ever heard preached by anybody for anyone."

"He did. It's just that I haven't been there since Mother's death, and I'm afraid I'll start crying."

"That's all right."

"Will and I haven't been regular churchgoers anywhere recently. We transferred our membership to Highland Park United Methodist because of the children and grandchildren, but we don't go all that often."

"You go as much as Bobby and I do. Bobby's kind of lost his faith. He says most ministers are hypocrites."

"Walker Railey is no hypocrite!"

"Then, let's go."

"All right."

They had found spaces in the pews in the balcony, but not together; it was too crowded. The Liebers squeezed into a row behind the Eubanks. Tears came to Charlotte's eyes as she listened to the choir and stared at the chancel, wondering where Walker was. Something about this Easter morning was different, something unsettling, not like the other Easters she remembered.

Gordon saw his wife Dede in the middle of a pew on the far left, stared at her until he caught her attention and then smiled reassuringly. They had been married for thirty-eight years. Next he saw Walker's wife Peggy in the center of the congregation with Policewoman Elizabeth Jasmine on her left and a tall, broad shouldered woman whom Gordon didn't know on her right. Just the sight of her staring straight ahead, her face and eyes expressionless, chilled him. For an instant she seemed to him the focal point of the sanctuary, surrounded by a white light with all else blurred around her. Gordon had the uncomfortable intuition that she, not Walker, was the central figure in this present Easter drama.

Peggy appeared in a trance, distanced and almost hostile. Detractors would say that this behavior typically reflected her naturally cold personality; defenders would say that she was simply composed, appropriately concealing her feelings. A frail looking woman with a strong and determined character, she wore a lavender hat and a lavender and white dress, which she herself had made a few weeks earlier. Not one lock of her short, wavy brown hair poked out of place. Pretty, in an unsophisticated fashion, she seemed on the surface an unlikely source of conflict although her quirky sense of humor and quick sarcasm could put anybody in his place, even Walker. Peggy exercised strict self-discipline, dieting and swimming to keep her weight at one-hundred-and-six pounds, exactly the same as when she had married in 1971. Some said she was anorexic. To those such as Gordon, who liked her, she fulfilled her duties as a minister's wife by singing in the choir, sewing banners and stoles to be used in the services, attending board meetings and playing the piano for the children's choir—at least until the past year.

To her detractors she lacked the charm and poise of her husband. She neglected to attend baptisms, weddings and funerals; she did not seem interested in the lives of the Church members, some of whom she passed in the halls without even speaking.

She is an enigma, Gordon thought. *How can any woman be so detached when she knows that at any moment she may witness her husband's assassination?*

In her own introverted way, Peggy was as extraordinary as Walker, and, like him, she had created herself, a distanced, controlled person with a destiny that only she knew.

Praise God from whom all blessings flow . . .

Gordon suddenly became aware that everyone was standing and singing the Doxology. The ushers stood at the communion rail as the chief steward collected the brass offering plates, which, as always on Easter, were piled high with more five and ten dollar bills and sealed pledge envelopes than on any other Sunday.

Praise Father, Son and Holy Ghost. Amen.

The congregation then joined the choir in the Hymn of Preparation, "All Hail the Power of Jesus' Name." In the mass movement of the congregation rising and singing, the ushers advancing and handing over the brass plates, then returning to their pews, Walker Railey had walked up the steps inside the chancel and now stood at the pulpit. Policemen Torres and Massingill moved behind the communion rail and faced the congregation.

When the hymn ended and the congregation seated itself once again, a hush fell over the packed sanctuary. Walker seized the drama of the moment and looked out over the congregation, directly meeting the eye of worshiper after worshiper. Some were transfixed, others embarrassed, as if this man of God were seeing into their souls.

His voice was controlled, resonant and powerful as he repeated that the Lesson came from the New Testament; John XX, particularly Verse 2. *"So she . . . said to them, 'They have taken the Lord out of the tomb, and we do not know where they have laid him.'"*

Walker took a drink from the glass of water always beside the pulpit when he preached. He then spoke of the book *The Passover Plot,* which presented the theory that Jesus had orchestrated an artificial Crucifixion and Resurrection. He smiled as if sharing a joke with the congregation. Then he told them that the author of *The Passover Plot* had hypothesized that Jesus had worked a deal with Lazarus, to have a young ass tied up and available for what became the triumphant entry into Jerusalem on Palm Sunday. In that way the prophesy of Zechariah would be fulfilled. Furthermore the author claimed that Jesus had manipulated His own arrest and then tried to insure that He would be crucified late on Friday afternoon and not be left up on the cross on the Sabbath.

Walker took another drink of water.

Every time he paused, the seven ministers behind him braced themselves for violence. Instinctively they sensed that a pause, a break in the sermon would be the perfect moment for a gun to be fired.

Walker put down the glass. His hands gripped the edges of the pulpit as he went on to explain that the book speculated that the words Jesus spoke from the cross, "I thirst," could have been a prearranged signal for a co-conspirator to give Him a drug in a wine-soaked sponge in order to simulate death. Thus Jesus was unconscious, but not dead, when He was removed from the cross and taken to the tomb for safe-keeping. During the night He was smuggled out for His wounds to be treated. The man whom Mary saw at the tomb on Sunday was not Jesus, but the co-conspirator who had taken Him away during the night. This was the "Passover Plot." The author then speculates that all of the post-Resurrection appearances of Jesus to His disciples were simply instances of mistaken identity.

Walker stepped back and paused, again singling out various members in the congregation for a few of his penetrating stares. He always spoke without notes, which awed the more naive worshipers into believing his words were inspired instead of carefully written and memorized.

"Easter Sunday, my dear sisters and brothers in Christ, is not an occasion to speculate on Jesus' 'Passover Plot,' but it is a morning to celebrate God's conspiracy of hope."

He paused, waiting for the full impact of his words to strike the worshipers.

"Easter is nothing more and nothing less than a conspiracy unlike any other in heaven or on earth."

Although the silence loomed like the collective holding of two thousand breaths, most of the listeners didn't know of his personal danger. He had the attention of every adult believer or nonbeliever in the sanctuary. He spoke of the despair hovering over the lives of the early Christians and that intelligent people today know the same kind of despair that slowly but surely eats away at life. With a little half-smile he said, *"That is why children do not drink Maalox, but adults do. Christ's empty tomb does not protect us from trying moments or terrifying dilemmas. It gives us strength to endure them because we know God's presence within us is stronger than the world's problems before us."*

He took another drink of water.

"If you have ever known a moment when it felt as if you were at your rope's end, or your wit's end, or God forbid, your life's end—if you have ever reached the point when it felt as if the hope inside your soul was dead and ready to blow away,

then Easter Sunday is for you," Walker told the congregation. He said that Easter was *not* a day to declare what despair was doing to your mortal life, but rather a morning to declare what immortal life was doing to your despair. He pounded his fist on the podium as he declared that God refuses to accept your gloom and doom. Jesus came to raise the dead. *"The only qualification for the gift of the Gospel is to be dead. You don't have to be good. You don't have to be wise. You don't have to be wonderful. You don't have to be anything . . . you just have to be dead."*

Taking out a clean white handkerchief, he stepped back from the protection of the pulpit, tempting fate or God or death. He seemed to be addressing each person individually when he asked if they felt *"more dead than alive this morning, closer to defeat than victory, immersed more in sadness than joy, more acquainted with failure than success."* He was almost pleading with each one when he asked that they allow the angels of Resurrection to roll away the stone of despair from their hearts and free their souls once again to live with exuberance and abundance. *"This is Easter Sunday, a morning to rejoice that eternal life is eating away at your despair. Today celebrates the conspiracy of hope, and the only appropriate response to it is ALLELUIA!"*

Gordon felt relief, an inward Alleluia. This sermon had bothered him at the earlier service. He found it a strange sermon for Easter. How could Easter be a conspiracy? Surely this was inappropriate and difficult to follow. But, how could any of them on the dais or those few in the congregation who knew of the threat concentrate on a sermon when at any moment the pastor might be assassinated?

"All of us attend too many funerals to doubt that Christians die just like everyone else," Walker was saying in a calm, almost conversational voice. *"There is nothing about this morning that spares us from the grave. You will die someday."* He paused. His piercing green eyes passed over the congregation, searching out certain faces. He raised his voice and lifted his arm, pointing with his index finger to

certain individuals. *"You will die someday,"* he repeated slowly. *"You and you—and you."* He pointed to a man on the right side of the Church, to a middle-aged couple in the balcony, and to a strikingly fashionable woman with frosted blond hair who sat beside her mother on the third row of the center section. *"And someday I will die as well,"* he continued. *"Everybody dies, and sometimes the ending of life on this earth is the most redemptive experience available."* He blotted the sweat from his forehead with his handkerchief. The bright lights that accompanied the television cameras made his complexion and his stole and the flowers in front of him seem whiter than they really were. He took another swallow of water and the plain glass caught a beam of light and sparkled like a precious jewel.

"Resurrection does not take away the inevitability of death at the end of life; Resurrection promises the reality of life at the end of death."

Walker told them that their calendars were the stories of their lives and that we all lived one square at a time with each square containing an invisible door leading to the next square. He had a way of personalizing his views by using the first person plural and including himself among the confused and suffering masses. He told them that year in and year out, the doors open and we walk out of one episode of life and into another. But then one day, he cautioned, each of us will enter a particular square that has no door to exit. *"There will be no opening to a new episode in life, no leaving that square for another. That will be the last square in our life. It could be today. It might be tomorrow. Nobody knows . . ."*

Gordon felt a tightening in his throat that he recognized as cold fear. Walker was almost tempting fate when he said that now we must acknowledge that the last square is on its way and that the angels of Resurrection have knocked down all the walls and taken away all the doors. He repeated that Easter Sunday was a morning to rejoice that eternal life was cutting away at death. *"Today celebrates the conspiracy of hope, and the only appropriate response to it is ALLELUIA!"*

Alleluia and Alleluia again, it's over, Gordon thought, as

the organ thundered behind him. Choir Director John Yarrington stood up facing the choir; the ministers and congregation all rose at once. Walker swept past Gordon and down the steps on the left. Gordon became conscious of the black robe crossing the red carpet and the whiteness of the page in the red hymnal as his voice blended with the voices of the choir behind him and of the congregation before him.

Bring forth the royal di-a-dem.

Walker moved down to the center aisle of the sanctuary but remained inside the chancel. The two policemen now stood on either side of him, close enough to touch him. If violence were to occur, it had to be now. Walker extended his arms. Was he asking to be martyred?

And crown Him Lord of all!

After the benediction Gordon sensed more than heard the familiar swish of the swinging oak doors leading out of the sanctuary. He let out his breath slowly. Nothing criminal and evil would happen here now in this holy room that held the presence of God and the hope of Resurrection.

Dark, balding, John Yarrington, Walker's closet friend, led the choir and the congregation in the final uplifting choral response.

Rise, Shine, give God glory, Children of the Lord.

Inside Karen's office the ministers gathered in a huddle, hugging, laughing and slapping each other on the back. They appeared more like an athletic team congratulating each other than a group of ministers after a Christian service. Then, as a victorious team, they walked through the wide hall to the Crossroads Center, a large reception room with Oriental carpets. Already members of the congregation had formed a line beginning at the entrance of the Crossroads Center, through one set of double doors facing a crowded stairway leading down to the dining room, and almost through the open doors of the sanctuary.

The ministers arranged themselves in their usual positions: Walker, Gordon and Susan in a receiving line just inside the room, two ministers at the entrance to move the people forward in an orderly fashion, and the other ministers to mingle among the crowd, welcoming people and directing them to the long tables with glass bowls of icy pink punch and stainless steel dispensers of steaming hot coffee. The smiling hostesses, members of a hospitality committee from one of the Sunday School classes, served them all.

Not everyone in the congregation attended the Church reception. Rodger Meier, a local Cadillac dealer who had met Walker through a civic fund raising association, accompanied his younger daughter Stacy out the main entrance of the Church and down the front steps. Twenty-seven-year-old Stacy had been telling her parents what a wonderful minister Railey was, and, pleased that she had found a church she wanted to attend, Rodger had accompanied her to First Church while his wife Joyce went to their usual church, Lovers Lane United Methodist. Stacy told her father that Walker spoke about problems relevant today and in a manner meaningful to her generation. Rodger, too, liked the way Walker preached. Even more he liked Walker's style of doing business. When Rodger, as a promoter of building a new interfaith chapel at Dallas–Fort Worth Airport, took Walker to lunch to ask for a contribution, Walker said that he was in favor of what they were doing and would recommend it to his board. Shortly thereafter Meier received a check for ten thousand dollars. He admired Walker's gentle but firm control of his business, if, indeed, a church could be considered a business. Rodger noticed the guards with Walker this morning, wondering if they were F.B.I. or plain-clothes policemen or what. He had pointed them out to Stacy, who hadn't seemed particularly interested, and Rodger hadn't wanted to upset her. Unlike most members of the congregation, he knew of the threatening letters, but he didn't tell Stacy until after the service.

Another young woman, Olive Talley, followed them down the front steps. She had recently joined First Church because of the power and relevance of Railey's preaching. A new reporter for *The Dallas Morning News,* Olive was also skipping the reception. She wanted to get back to the office. Like Stacy, she hadn't paid much attention to the guards around Railey.

The Eubanks and the Liebers were walking rapidly toward Will's new white Cadillac Seville. Charlotte was crying and Betty was attempting to comfort her.

"I thought it was a stimulating service," Betty said. "Different. Not the same old Easter sermon we've heard for fifty years."

"Oh, it was different all right," Charlotte sniffled. "Just emphasizing we're all going to die and it doesn't matter whether we're Christians or heathens. You are going to die," she said sarcastically, pointing at Betty. "And you," she told Bobby, "and you!" She pointed her index finger at Will's chest.

"Well, he's probably right about that," Will said unlocking the doors to the car. "Now let's all get a move on it. We have reservations at the club at twelve-thirty. It's really going to be crowded there today."

"I'd just as soon go home now," Charlotte said peevishly.

"I don't see what's the problem," Bobby looked from one to the other in bewilderment. "I thought it was a good sermon. Walker really can hold everybody's attention."

Dede Casad stood near the door of the Crossroads Center, drinking a cup of coffee. She is a striking woman with dark, sparkling eyes and short white hair that had once been black. There is an air of casual elegance about her, a *Town and Country* look. She wears two piece suits and real gold jewelry. Her posture is straight and confident, her hands frequently in her jacket pockets. She disdains carrying a handbag. Smiling graciously with her alert brown eyes absorbing the surroundings, she looks as if she were a golf champion more at home in an expensive country club than at a church social. But, appearances to the contrary, she is excellent in her chosen role of minister's wife without in the least resigning her intellectual interests or her individuality. This morning in her black linen skirt and canary yellow jacket, she observes Walker and members of the congregation discussing the service.

She hadn't especially liked Walker's sermon this morning, but unquestionably she thought him one of the best preachers she had ever heard; and, being a minister's wife, she had heard plenty of preaching over the past four decades. She watched the seemingly endless line of people shake his hand and speak to him. Clearly they adored him. It was important to them to touch him and to talk to him. For young or old, he was never at a loss for words, his incredible memory recalling the names of grandchildren, of boyfriends and girlfriends, of businesses and professions, of graduations and retirements. For some his remembering was the high moment of the week.

"He has the sweetest family," eighty-year-old Roberta Crowe said to Gladys Jarratt, who, like herself, had belonged to this Church for over sixty-five years. Glady's fifty-year-old daughter Judie had flown to Dallas from Brownsville, to take her mother to church on Easter. Roberta had a printed copy of every sermon Walker had preached as senior minister of First Church. She had in fact paid for the first year's printing because she had recognized their theological and literary value long before the Pastor-Parish Committee had. "You can tell Walker just adores his children," Roberta continued, "especially five-year-old Ryan who's the cutest and smartest little boy you ever saw. He's going to grow up to be just like his daddy. Why, already you can tell that he has inherited his daddy's brains. And Peggy's smart, too. If she hadn't married Walker, she could have had a brilliant career in music—but smart as she is, Peggy is delicate," Roberta went on. "For ten years she didn't think she could have children, but then she had an operation that made her able to conceive. And now you've never seen such a sweet little mother. Believe you me, she and Walker have had problems with poor health and lack of money, but you won't find a finer, more devoted young couple anywhere in the country. They deserve all the success he has now."

"Judie, Peggy sews and embroiders beautifully," Gladys said. "She and a friend of hers make all the banners and the ministers' stoles."

"Walker's going to be the youngest bishop in the Methodist Church," Roberta added.

Judie had heard all this a dozen times or more, yet this didn't keep her from admiring Walker, too. She'd grown up in this Church, and, as an adult, she had lived and attended churches all over the world. She had never heard a minister of any denomination anywhere who preached a better sermon than Walker. He was magnetic, even attractive, despite not being handsome.

They now moved closer to Walker, who was flanked by Susan and Gordon. Walker bent over, calling a child Baby Sister Heather and telling her how pretty she was in her Easter dress. Then he asked her father if the construction business was improving. The young man shook his head no and Walker touched his arm in sympathy. Next an old man in a plaid, polyester sport coat pumped Walker's hand vigorously, asking what it took to preach a wonderful sermon without ever looking at any notes.

Walker told him that it took about thirty hours of hard work, and the man hollered and clapped him on the shoulder, as if this were the funniest remark he had ever heard. Next, the minister embraced a young couple whom he had recently married and then told the man's brother that he was proud of his graduating from the University of Texas at Austin next month. He even remembered that the young man had studied engineering.

"An inspiring service," the brothers told Walker.

Then Walker hugged Roberta and asked about her blood pressure and her arthritis and whether she was taking good care of herself.

Whoever the person and whatever the occasion, Walker

would speak the right words. He brought to others his strength, comfort, joy—whatever was needed.

Dede Casad watched the scene in admiration as she overheard two designer-clothed yuppie couples telling each other what a memorable service it had been.

"Awesome," one of the young men commented, nodding his head thoughtfully.

Later there would be almost as many versions of that service as there were those who attended it. No one, including Walker Railey himself, could then foresee that this was the last sermon he would preach at First United Methodist Church in Dallas.

2

ON NORTHWEST HIGHWAY BORDERING INSIDE THE lush green, exclusive suburb of Preston Hollow, the congregation from Northwest Bible Church leaves the church and the large white Sunday School building beside it. As at First United Methodist, the sanctuary here has been filled to capacity with nearly two-thousand worshipers. Most of them are young or middle-aged, well dressed, and affluent. Unlike the membership at First Church, almost all of the congregation here live within five miles of the church.

Typical of the suburban church membership are Bill and Carol Arnold, a handsome couple in their mid-thirties. They have been married seven years and have two young children. She is small with clear blue eyes, a fair Irish complexion and straight shoulder-length, black hair. She wears little make-up and possesses a confident yet reserved take-me-as-I-am attitude. Before her marriage she worked in petroleum land management for her family oil company. Given her "druthers" she would prefer to live on a ranch.

Bill is a native Houstonian who formerly was with the Dallas District Attorney's Office and is now a civil lawyer with a law firm in downtown Dallas. He is over six feet tall, has brown hair and blue eyes with dark eyelashes. His spectacles and three-piece suit add an intellectual edge to his conservative appearance. Both Bill and Carol take their religion seriously. His being a Baptist and her being an Episcopalian resulted in their joining Northwest Bible Church, a nondenominational Christian church with emphasis on biblical study.

As they left their church on that clear, bright Easter morning of 1987, they could never have imagined how intertwined their lives would soon become with the lives of Peggy and Walker Railey.

Ninety-eight miles east of Dallas and five miles beyond Tyler, a town with a population of seventy thousand and the home of the annual Rose Festival, a red dirt farm road leads to a large lake on the edge of the dark piney woods. Several dozen frame cottages with screened porches sit at the edge of the lake on the side closest to Tyler. They constitute Flint, Texas, with a population of considerably less than two hundred. Off the sandy road away from the lake and farther south, horse pastures give away to deer crossings. A small, wooden country church with a shiny gold cross on top of a tall, white steeple points toward the sky; a couple of log cabins, even a gray-white, antebellum mansion in need of repairs stands columned and proud. Real East Texas.

In a rambling yellow frame cottage on the lake live Peggy Railey's parents, Bill and Billie Jo Nicolai and Peggy's eighty-six-year-old grandmother Ella Renfro.

Billie Jo looks younger than sixty-seven. She has a scrubbed, round, almost cherubic face surrounded by short, curly, gray hair, cut like a man's. Her body is short and plump; she wears a pants suit and sensible, flat-heeled shoes, even on Easter afternoon. Life in Flint is casual. She and her husband Bill leisurely read the large Sunday editions of *The Dallas Morning News, The Dallas Times Herald* and the *Tyler Courier-Times*.

Peggy most resembles her father who is two years older than Billie Jo. His thin, muscular and tanned body crowned with thick, wavy white hair looks neat in a short-sleeved sports shirt, a tan cardigan sweater and khaki pants. Retirement and the warm Texas climate have been good for him.

Bill and Billie Jo met during World War II when both served in the Navy. Bill was an electrician from Milwaukee and Billie Jo a gunnery instructor from East Texas. Her ambition had been to marry and raise a family, but first she wanted to go to college. Billie Jo attended Southwestern and Texas Wesleyan where she majored in Speech with a minor in English. She had hoped to attend graduate school at SMU, but even in the depression years of the 1930s, SMU was an expensive, private school. Billie Jo could not afford this luxury. Later, Peggy's attending SMU's graduate school and receiving a master's degree in Sacred Music seemed a fulfillment of Billie Jo's own ambitions. God had truly blessed her with Peggy.

Like her daughter, Billie Jo reads voraciously, but on this Easter, she couldn't concentrate. At three o'clock in the afternoon, she knew that Walker and Peggy and the children had come home from the Church and had finished their Sunday dinner. Soon they would go over to the Oakleys, Walker's adopted parents. Anxious about how the Easter service went, Billie Jo contemplated telephoning them. But she had telephoned Peggy the evening of Good Friday to make certain she and the children had returned safely from Tyler. She didn't want either Peggy or Walker to think that she was interfering or becoming a nuisance, yet the threatening letters troubled her.

Bill seemed unconcerned. He told her that if anything serious or unexpected had occurred during the service, the most likely time for the threats to be carried out, they would have been telephoned by now. More than likely some crazy person envious of Walker had sent those notes just to upset him. If it were the Ku Klux Klan, which Bill didn't think it was, then the threat already would have become a reality.

Billie Jo said she couldn't imagine those threats actually happening today in a sophisticated place like Dallas. And to a minister, a man of God devoting his life to the service of others, it was unbelievable.

Billie Jo was as proud of Walker as of Peggy. She considered him the best preacher she had ever heard. How fortunate they were to have a son-in-law like Walker—yet, Walker, too, was fortunate to have married Peggy. Their interests and talents meshed perfectly, and Peggy was just as smart (or smarter) than he. Everything had worked out so well—two children, a boy first and then a girl; a lovely new home with a swimming pool. If they had little disagreements, they amounted to nothing more than any young couple had. He and Peggy had the whole world before them.

Seven years ago, when he became senior minister at First United Methodist, Walker had made a giant leap in his career. He was both ambitious and mature. It was Peggy who, at thirty-one, had been too young, too shy and too critical to adapt to the position of *senior* minister's wife in a large church in a large city. Yet, over the past two years she, too, had matured and changed. Now Dallas was the ideal place for both Peggy and Walker to be.

3

DALLAS—BIG D—THE METROPLEX; DALLAS, THE myth and the reality. The hustling, high-tech, urban expanse is far more ordinary than the legends surrounding it. Human energy pulsates everywhere, even during bad economic times, such as in 1987. Off the freeways, the air smells cleaner than in most big cities, and the sun shines brighter.

Air conditioning is everywhere, so that office buildings, theaters and churches sometime seem colder in August than in January. In the summer, for weeks at a time, the temperature outside hovers around a hundred degrees Fahrenheit. In winter, within a few hours, the temperature may drop forty degrees or more. In autumn, even sometimes in the sunshine, hail stones the size of Ping-Pong balls bounce from the sky. And, in the deceptively pleasant spring, dust storms, blue northers and tornadoes frequently descend for no more than an hour, leaving behind deadly destruction.

Sprouting up from nowhere, the flat land around Dallas hardens black and dry in the ever-present sun. Underneath the stubborn, arid surface no oil nor gas nor sulphur exist, nor, for that matter, much water. To call the Trinity a river offers a sample of Texas overstatement. Trickling down from nothing, it alternates between a muddy, walk-over driblet and a raging flood. For over a century now the citizens of Dallas have talked about making the Trinity into a commercial waterway to Houston and to the Gulf of Mexico. But it's just talk. If it really were important, it would have been done long ago, like the railroad.

A century and a half ago, when Dallas came into existence no railroad ran within hundreds of miles. Railroads meant growth. So, in the 1870s when the Texas & Pacific asked the state legislature to approve a right of way bill, a few members from Dallas attached a small, seemingly insignificant codicil. Thus, the bill passed with the specification that all trains had to stop within a mile of a watering spot named Browder Springs. Browder Springs was in Dallas, and so, to its astonishment, was the Texas & Pacific.

Even during the bad economy of the late 1980s, the image Dallas had of itself was unabashed success. Winning is all. The winners—rich, powerful and socially prominent—live in the old north suburb of Preston Hollow or in the secure isolation of the enclave cities of Highland Park and University Park with their own police forces, fire departments and public schools. Park Cities people joke about living in the "bubble."

A newspaper columnist in Houston once said of Highland Park, "There is Highland Park and there is heaven, although occasionally the locals get the two mixed up."

Highland Park allows no bars or liquor stores, though a few exist in University Park. Nor are there any churches in Highland Park, although there are a number of churches *named* Highland Park—Methodist or Presbyterian or Baptist or Lutheran. These, too, exist in neighboring University Park. The founding fathers of Highland Park wanted to keep their area exclusive yet convenient to sinful drinking. Churches, if they were going to be open to all, ought to be downtown with the other businesses. Steeples spoiled an elegant residential skyline.

Dallas has one of the highest crime rates in the nation. With heat rising, tempers and crimes climb in proportion to thermometer readings, yet, there are more churches per capita in Dallas than in any other city in America. One thousand, five hundred and eighty-one of them are listed in the yellow pages of the Dallas telephone directory. For the citizens in the Park Cities, or in affluent North Dallas, Methodism is the dominant denomination. With its philosophy of "earn as much as you can, save as much as you can, and give as much as you can," Methodism is compatible with the Dallas outlook; yet, on the whole, Methodism, like other mainstream Protestant churches with their nineteenth-century hymns and creeds, has been declining in membership for years.

There is, in Dallas, however, genuine religious feeling in church attendance, in intuitive, conservative orthodoxy, in study groups and prayer circles. Going to church is good business, too, whether you are a believer, an atheist or an agnostic. In Dallas, church is a good place to meet the important people.

If you are Protestant, you can make the right connections at Highland Park Methodist, or St. Michael and All Angels

Episcopal, or Highland Park Presbyterian. If you are Catholic, Christ the King; if Jewish, Temple Emanu-El. Some who continue to search spiritually find themselves at odds with the old dogma of their childhood churches and have broken away, forming new churches called bible churches. Most are fundamentalist. Northwest Bible Church began forty years ago with a dissatisfied group of five hundred people who left Highland Park Presbyterian Church; now five thousand members attend services. Mainly they are college educated and conduct their own study groups. For the most part, like the Arnolds, they are young, affluent and native Dallasites.

New money, and newcomers, eager to praise the Lord, find their way out to the suburban Pentecostal Church on the Rock, where devotions are spiced with faith healings, exorcisms, and speaking in tongues. Old money, steadfast in faith and social status, still flows downtown to First Baptist, where octogenarian fundamentalist W.A. Criswell preaches, as he has for nearly half a century, heaven for born-again Baptists and hellfire and damnation for unrepentant sinners.

Just two blocks west of the Baptists, at the corner of Ross and Harwood Streets, rests First United Methodist Church. As the Methodist Conference's "mother church," it is also called "the cradle of bishops." And for many years its pulpit has served as the logical steppingstone for those called to that higher office.

Of the nine million, seven hundred thousand Methodists in the United States, over a million live in Texas. First United Methodist Church of Dallas is the tenth largest Methodist Church in America and the third largest in Dallas. This Church, like many downtown churches in large cities, had fallen on hard times, at least until Walker Railey became the senior pastor.

Dallas and Walker Railey had seemed destined for each other in this lingering spirit of the southwest that admires self-made men. At a time when religion appeared to offer little ground between the flashy commercialism of the electronic evangelists and the dull dogma of the mainstream, Walker Railey offered a fresh style. He has wit and a fervor reminiscent of the old-time revivalists.

Frequently he uses the phrase "my dear brothers and sisters in Christ," and, for ensuring attention, he speaks loudly: "Someone present today needs to hear this."

In a sermon at First Church in April of 1983, he told the congregation:

"Ours is not a journey that offers us life when we arrive, ours is a journey that enables us to live as we go ... You do not need to be older or younger, richer or poorer, over here or out there. You have only to live fully right where you are ... If you are seventy-seven, you do not need to spend your day remembering how you lived when you were thirty-seven. You cannot remember that far back anyway. Live now. Be seventy-seven to the glory of God."

Before he became senior minister at First United Methodist, the membership had fallen to less than five thousand with half of them out of town, inactive or going to church somewhere else. For nearly a decade, pleading insufficient funds, First United Methodist had neglected to pay its North Texas Conference dues. Six years after Railey came, the membership was updated and reorganized with nearly six thousand members, most of whom considered themselves active; over fifteen hundred included new members who either transferred from other churches or joined by profession of faith. They comprised the baby boomers, many of whom were young, upwardly mobile newcomers to Dallas. The Church budget increased. The back conference dues got paid in full; financially the Church was up to date with its obligations, and a new outreach program as well.

Railey had succeeded Dr. Ben Oliphint who was elevated to the office of bishop in 1980. For the first three years after he had left Perkins School of Theology at Southern Methodist University, Railey had been with Dr. Oliphint as an associate pastor at First United Methodist. The congregation had come to love and to admire him, except, as one long-time member put it, "his prayers were too long." Those prayers, though, held importance to Walker, and he collected them into a book that the Church privately published.

Walker's next appointment was for four years as senior pastor at Christ Methodist Church in Farmer's Branch, a small community within the Dallas–Fort Worth Metroplex. When the senior position at First United Methodist unexpectedly became available, the Pastor-Parish Committee, headed by Ernie Martin, recommended that presiding Bishop W. McFerrin Stowe appoint Walker Railey.

At the time some older clergymen felt Walker was too young for such a large and difficult church, yet the vast majority were as pleased as if a new messiah had arrived. The aura he created suggested such vitality that he could not be ignored. He had enthusiasm and boundless energy, and he quickly surrounded himself with a bright young staff as full of energy, and new ideas as himself.

Some members of the Church staff affected the new Railey image. Associate Minister Larry Ravert and Choir Director John Yarrington, both friends of Walker's, were balding in the same manner and, like clones, they wore their hair in exactly the same tidied-up 1960s style.

Yarrington said that he and Walker had a wonderful working relationship. "Walker expected perfection from all of us—but he leaves me responsible for everything concerning the choir. Not only what we sing and when we rehearse —but such details as ordering new robes or new music—I just go ahead and do it and send him a memo of what I've done."

Walker's rise in the political and service organizations within the Dallas–Fort Worth Metroplex as well as within the Methodist hierarchy, was as meteoric as his success within First United Methodist Church. The board of directors of the nationally syndicated "American Protestant Hour," a weekly radio broadcast carried in several hundred American markets, selected him to give the sermons for the fall program. He had recorded them this past February of 1987.

He was President of the Greater Dallas Community of

Churches, yet he found time for scholarly pursuits as well, working on two books, including a commentary on the sermons of the late Harry Emerson Fosdick, the first pastor of Riverside Church in New York City and one of Railey's heroes. Another hero was an earlier pastor of First United Methodist in Dallas, recently deceased Bishop Robert E. Goodrich, Jr.

Some clerics spoke of Railey's becoming a bishop in 1988; even among those who thought that at forty he would be too young, there was unanimity that he made a good prospect for 1992. After all there had been a few skeptics who had thought that at thirty-three he was too young to be senior minister at a large, inner city church. They had been proven wrong. Church elders regarded him as a phenomenal man with incredible charm and presence. To his congregation, to the City of Dallas and to the surrounding Metroplex, Walker Railey had everything; fame, respect, a devoted wife, two delightful children, a generous expense account and an almost guaranteed, successful career ahead of him.

His first sermon as senior pastor at First United Methodist on August 24, 1980, he entitled "From Dust to Dreams." Although it was not an especially brilliant sermon the congregation sat spellbound by Walker's persona in the pulpit. Only a few in the congregation later remembered the last words of that first sermon that blatantly expressed his ambition.

> "I do not come here to paddle around with fat ducks in a stagnant pond but to soar with the eagles in search of the riches of Jesus Christ. God fashioned my life and yours from dust; but God created all of us for dreams. And to those who dream, all of life is a journey from despair to hope, from darkness to light, from intimidation to triumph, from dust to dreams. And it is a journey that leads to life!!!"

"From dust to dreams" aptly described Walker's storybook life. The eldest of three children, he was born on June 25, 1947, in Owensboro, Kentucky, a coal mining and manufacturing town, which then had a population of about thirty thousand. His brother Gary was three years younger, his sister Marlene five years younger. Owensboro was a blue-collar town, and Walker's was a blue-collar family. His father Chester labored as a sheet-metal worker, and his mother Virginia was a housewife. Both were alcoholics.

If Chester and Virginia occasionally came to blows with each other during their bouts of drinking, they never struck the children in anger. And, if home life was less than happy, it had seemed to strengthen rather than harm young Walker, who was considered exemplary among the youth of Owensboro. Though neither an accomplished athlete nor school leader, he was a good student who often studied into the late hours of the night while his brother Gary dozed peacefully nearby. In high school he didn't smoke or drink or use bad language the way most boys of his age did. But his classmates liked him anyway and nicknamed him Preacher.

They never teased him. Something about him said: *Don't laugh at me. I'm going to be somebody some day.*

He was not much moved by the style and attitudes of his generation, but neither were most of the boys in Owensboro in the early 1960s. Rock and roll blared from the radio; social protest, shoulder-length hair and untrimmed beards were the national fashion. In Owensboro, the boys wore short haircuts, played football and baseball and, after school, worked at check-out stands and gas pumps.

Like most of the Owensboro boys, Walker had a steady girl, Judy Bassinger, to whom he reluctantly gave his senior ring. First he told her he wanted to wear it himself for a month, which he did. Walker and Judy went to movies or school plays or dances or high school football games together. When he hung around with the boys, he played billiards, went to the drive-in restaurant and then cruised for a while. The only things that separated him from other Owensboro boys of that time and age were his superior intelligence, his interest in religion and his ambition.

When he was sixteen, he asked his mother to telephone Reverend Spaulding at the Woodlawn Methodist Church. Walker wanted to preach a sermon. Reverend Spaulding was taken aback. The pulpit of the Methodist Church was not to be filled lightly by a young man with no experience. But he knew Walker's reputation for seriousness, and he was moved by the mother's request on her son's behalf. One Sunday night not long after, Walker preached his first sermon.

Judy was there, and all of his family and friends. The subject was prayer. From that night on, there was no doubt that Walker would become a preacher. He graduated in the spring of 1965 in the top ten percent of his high school class.

For financial reasons he chose to attend college at nearby Western Kentucky University, at Bowling Green, just seventy miles from Owensboro. He majored in history, took odd jobs to pay tuition and began preaching at rural and small-town Methodist churches, sometimes walking the several miles out to the church. He never stuck out his thumb to hitch-hike, but if rides were offered, he accepted.

After a year at Bowling Green, he broke up with Judy. Both their mothers cried. Walker was growing away from Owensboro, and he made no attempt to hide his determination to find his place in the world elsewhere.

When he graduated from Western Kentucky, he headed south to Vanderbilt University to theology school. After a year there, he transferred to Perkins School of Theology at Southern Methodist University in Dallas where he wanted to study homiletics, the art of preaching, with the renowned Professor Ronald Sleeth.

Professor Sleeth, who taught Walker in both the Bachelor of Ministry and Master of Divinity programs said: "I've had three really brilliant students during my career—and two of them were Walker Railey."

Walker was acknowledging his ambitions, finding by himself his place in life. That place did not include Owensboro, Kentucky. Nor did it include his parents, his brother and sister, or his former friends. He drove to Dallas from Kentucky in an old yellow Volkswagen, which his small rural congregations had helped him to buy. One of the churches had given him new tires as a farewell present.

The rosy, golden sky and the tall sparkling skyline like so

many rising church towers beckoned from the west. He was on his way, from dust to dreams.

Joyce Murray, the wife of SMU Theology Professor Dick Murray, gave an annual welcoming party for new and transferring theology students, and she remembers well that September evening in 1970 when she first met Walker Railey. Unlike most of the students eagerly asking which courses to take and where various buildings and classrooms were, Walker seemed totally absorbed by his surroundings. The Murray home was a large two-story house with reception rooms suitable for entertaining.

After dinner Joyce saw Walker standing alone beside a huge live oak tree. As Joyce approached him, he said he liked Dallas and would like to live in a nice area such as this. She had thought then that Walker was a decisive, ambitious young man who not only knew what he wanted but was smart enough to figure out how to get it.

Long before their lives crossed and joined, similarities existed in the personalities, backgrounds and ambitions of Walker Railey and Peggy Nicolai. Both were the eldest in families with three children, and both were instinctively drawn to metaphysics. Each was academically clever, and each was, in special ways, different from the others around them.

In the fall of 1966, when Peggy Nicolai entered Alverno College, a Catholic women's school in Milwaukee, most girls arrived carrying typewriters. Peggy brought a tool box. She could hang pictures and repair malfunctions, such as broken door knobs or leaky faucets. She was the sort of girl adults recognize as gifted and other children call "a brain."

The first people to realize how special she was had been her parents who had settled in Bill's home town of Milwaukee in a cream-colored bungalow with a long porch in front. There the children played and Bill relaxed on summer afternoons after coming home from his office job at the Schlitz brewery.

The high school was just two blocks away, the Presbyterian Church they attended not much farther. Billie Jo liked the neighborhood and the church enough to endure good-natured teasing from Texas kin about raising her children to be Yankees and Presbyterians.

Peggy was three when she first displayed an independent spirit. Billie Jo had baked some fudge brownies and set them on the kitchen table to cool, and young Peggy announced that she would have one.

"Not until after your dinner," her mother said.

"No. Now," Peggy insisted.

Billie Jo explained to the child that if she ate a brownie now, she would get a spanking. If she chose to wait until after dinner, she would have two stories read to her that evening instead of one.

Peggy frowned, sat down in her little rocking chair and rocked and thought. After about two minutes, she returned to her mother and announced, "I don't care if I get a spanking."

Little Peggy also had a meditative streak. Once, when about five, she simply disappeared inside the house. At supper time neither Bill nor Billie Jo could find her. They searched from the basement to the attic until finally Billie Jo saw an open window and realized the child was sitting on the roof.

"Everything looks so pretty up here," Peggy said.

Unlike most American girls growing up in the 1950s and 1960s, Peggy didn't have a special group of girlfriends, and she didn't have a special boyfriend.

She had inherited her mother's determination and perse-verance and her father's talent for music. Bill couldn't read music. He played the piano by ear—and always in the key of C, Peggy teased.

For her part, Peggy learned to play the piano by the age of seven, and was soon a favorite pupil of Mrs. Audrey Wood, a serious woman and a disciplinarian. Peggy and her younger sister Katie managed to avoid appearing in Mrs. Wood's annual recital for two years, until the teacher finally gave an ultimatum: either play in the recital or quit piano lessons.

Katie decided *not* to play in the recital. Like enduring the spanking in order to eat the brownie, Peggy reluctantly played in the recital because she wanted to continue her lessons.

From her father, Peggy also inherited a love of mathematics and mechanics. Early in her schooling, she scored near genius on an I.Q. test and was classified as a superior ability pupil, or SAP, as the less gifted called them. The SAPs were a small group of students permitted to take special subjects and to study whatever interested them. In high school Peggy's favorite subjects were algebra, geometry and physics. She learned how to work on cars, and could not only change a tire, but she could rebuild an engine, as she once proved to her father.

While her plump and friendly younger sister Katie scattered her clothes on the floor and ate junk food in the attic room that she and Peggy shared, Peggy was neat, ate health foods and exercised regularly. Eventually she became so annoyed by Katie's messy habits that the big attic room had to be divided into two rooms.

Practically the only indulgence Peggy permitted herself was reading mystery novels, using them as a mental exercise to try to solve the crime before the end of the book. She was not only an insatiable reader and a skilled musician, but she became a talented painter, sculptor and seamstress.

By the time she had reached the ninth grade, she wanted organ lessons, displaying her devotion and determination by turning pages for the organist at the Presbyterian Church. Then she took lessons from Sister Theophane at Alverno College and showed as much talent for the organ as she had for the piano. On the same nights that young Walker Railey sat up late studying in Owensboro, Peggy practiced late at various churches in Milwaukee, learning music for weddings and church services and funerals. The money she earned she set aside for a new piano to replace the old upright her father had inherited. But, first of all, she bought contact lenses to replace the thick glasses she had worn since childhood.

When she was a senior in high school and in the top five percent of her graduating class of over five hundred, she overcame her shyness and invited some of the other SAPs to her house after school to drink Cokes and watch *Batman* on television. Most of the time, however, she remained serious and shy instead of flirtatious and social, though both Billie Jo and Sister Theophane knew that what she longed for most was a boyfriend.

After high school, boys practically disappeared from Peggy's life for four years. The summer after high school graduation, she went to Europe with an all female choir from Alverno College; then on a music scholarship, she settled into undergraduate studies at the Catholic women's college.

All through Peggy's growing years, the Nicolais took their vacations in East Texas. The youngest of the three Nicolai children, Ted, felt more at home there than he did in Milwaukee and usually stretched his stay to include the whole summer.

Because of their ties with Texas, the family, and especially Billie Jo, was pleased when Peggy decided to go to Southern Methodist University in Dallas for graduate studies with the famous organ teacher Robert Anderson. For Peggy, moving to Texas seemed almost like moving home. She found a circle of friends among other graduate students in the music school and next door at the theology school. These friends included Walker Railey whom Peggy intuitively knew was destined for success. Their friendship quickly turned into a touchingly old-fashioned romance.

They went to Sunday School together. They held hands while walking on the tree-lined sidewalk that connected the music school and the theology school. On weekends she accompanied him to the small churches in Oklahoma where he preached. Walker stayed at one parishioner's house, Peggy at another's. He translated love poems in Hebrew for her and developed an interest in classical music, attending recitals wherever she performed.

Already Walker was a success; everyone in theology

school believed he would someday be an outstanding preacher. He was smart, but he was more than just a SAP; he was a winner. To Peggy, Walker was perfect in every aspect but one. She confided to friends that she wished she were more physically attracted to him. Still, as they all told her, Walker Railey was "a good catch." And, Sunday after Sunday, when she listened to him preach, she gained a zest for life that she had seldom experienced. She did not question why Walker had chosen her.

Billie Jo and Bill, Katie and Ted drove down from Milwaukee one weekend in 1971 to meet this man whose name had begun turning up in Peggy's letters and phone conversations. That Sunday they all went to Oklahoma to hear Walker preach. The only blight on the otherwise happy family occasion was that teen-aged Ted immediately disliked Walker. Maybe it was only a brother's jealousy, his parents reasoned, or maybe a little rebellion against all the churchly goodness everyone else displayed.

Not long afterward, back in Milwaukee, Billie Jo answered the phone on a Sunday afternoon.

"Mom, it's Peggy," the familiar voice on the other end said. "I'm in Oklahoma with Walker. Guess what? We're going to get married!"

Billie Jo was thrilled. In the background she heard Walker saying with a laugh, "Peggy's happy and I'm broke!"

After they settled that they would be married at Trinity Presbyterian in Milwaukee, Walker made a special request, not so different from one he had made a few years earlier in Owensboro.

"I've always wanted to preach on Sunday morning and get married on Sunday afternoon," he explained to Billie Jo. "Do you think you could find me a church in Milwaukee where I could preach on the day of the wedding?"

Just as his own mother had done for him seven years earlier, Billie Jo telephoned the Presbyterian minister who graciously offered his own pulpit.

Old friends from Kentucky, parishioners from Oklahoma and relatives from all over converged on Milwaukee that

Sunday. Walker's mother Virginia rode the bus from Owensboro, while Gary Railey flew in from Indiana in a small private plane. Walker's father Chester stayed home. Ted Nicolai, still unhappy and opposed to Walker, was consoled by the chance to sit in Gary's plane after the wedding.

On Sunday morning, August 23, 1971, Walker preached at Trinity Presbyterian Church in Milwaukee. Peggy played the organ. Later that afternoon, in the same church, they promised to love, honor and cherish each other, till death did them part.

Weddings became a particular Railey pastoral specialty. As far as anyone knew no bride or mother of the bride (or groom) had ever been less than ecstatic over the ceremony and the way Walker had conducted it. Usurping the duties of the professional bridal consultants, Walker frequently choreographed the entire service—how far apart and how slowly the bridesmaids should walk, how they should carry their flowers, how the groom should lift the bride's veil and kiss his new wife, and so on. A wedding was a beginning, he told the young couples, and the first performance in a new life should be perfect.

Prominent, lifetime members at First Church, active on the Pastor-Parish Committee and in the Aldersgate Sunday School class, Dale and Clare Cunningham praised Walker's performance at their daughter's wedding, which they thought was just about as near perfection as a wedding could be. For weeks afterward they attended Sunday services, describing at Fellowship gatherings in the Crossroads Center what a special service it had been and how wonderful Walker was.

"What he said to the bride and groom," Claire told an old friend who had missed the event, "was just beautiful. He told them that marriage was truly holy and that it could be the most rewarding experience in life's journey, but that every day each of them must give to the other. In a holy marriage there was no taking, just giving and accepting with grace, learning to place oneself second to the other."

"A divorced fraternity brother of mine came to the wedding," Dale added, "and at the end of the service there were tears in his eyes. He said he believed that if he had been married by Walker Railey his marriage would have lasted."

Until 1987 there had been only one shadow on Walker Railey's rise within the Methodist Church. Three years earlier Bishop Finis Crutchfield, former president of the one hundred member National Council of Bishops, and then about to retire as bishop of the South Texas Conference, recommended Railey for pastor of the prestigious and wealthy St. Luke's Church in Houston. Railey flew to Houston, was interviewed by the Pastor-Parish Committee, but not offered the position. The following Sunday back in Dallas, he told his congregation that he *had* been offered the pastorship at St. Luke's but had turned it down because he wanted to remain in Dallas as pastor of First United Methodist. While the Dallas congregation was flattered, the Houston bishop was insulted. There was an acrimonious falling out between the two men that did not heal until 1986, the year before both men, in their separate ways, rocked the very foundations of the Methodist Church.

4

ON JANUARY 25, 1987, ONLY THREE MONTHS BEFORE the fateful night that would change his life forever, Walker had preached a sermon titled "The State of the Church," which pleased most of the congregation but which alarmed several members of the Pastor-Parish Committee as being a more accurate summation of the state of Walker Railey. Johnnie Marie Grimes, wife of retired Theology Professor

Howard Grimes, told Ralph Shannon, then head of the Pastor-Parish Relations Committee, the Church's steering committee on policy and personnel, that the sermon was a cry for help, which, in retrospect, also seemed true to many less active members of the Church. Even Betty Eubank had remarked to her husband that Walker must be under a lot of stress, for he spoke of himself in the third person.

"No one looks forward to Sunday mornings more than Walker. Sunday is my day of celebration. But it is not my day of rest. I must find my Sabbath elsewhere."

He cautioned his congregation not to confuse Sunday with the Sabbath, explaining that Sunday is the celebration of Christ's Resurrection from the grave, whereas the Sabbath commemorates the time God rested after the six days He had spent creating the world, and the Hebrews rested their fields on the seventh year to do the same. He reminded the congregation that he was now in his seventh year as their pastor and that he was willing to confess publicly that he was in need of a Sabbath.

"In 1987 my soul must be allowed to catch up with my body . . . Without a proper amount of Sabbath time, I will end up doing much but being little.

"I have the same concern for all of you. Given your tight schedules, your crammed calendars, your overburdened hearts and your overextended lives, I feel strongly that First United Methodist Church of Dallas is in need of a spiritually rejuvenating year for you and for me."

A week later, before a meeting of the nine member Pastor-Parish Committee, Ralph Shannon met with Walker in the pastor's study, a large comfortable inside room with a mahogany desk and book shelves at one end and lounge chairs and a circular couch at the other.

Shannon is a heavy-set man in his seventies with white hair, a thin white mustache and a military bearing. Formerly he had been an executive with the Red Cross. His presence commands respect.

"Walker, I think you ought to take some time away from the Church," Ralph said. "You mentioned in a recent sermon that everyone needs a sabbatical during a seventh year. And you also said that both you and the Church membership needed sabbatical time."

Walker said that he meant brief sabbaticals, times away on retreats, even some holidays. He didn't want a sabbatical in terms of being away for a year.

"You yourself said quite clearly that you *needed* a sabbatical."

Walker replied that he had said that he needed more *Sabbath time.* As for a sabbatical in the usual sense of a year away, he intended to take that when he reached his tenth year here.

"Walker, there are a number of people in this Church who care about you very much, and they are concerned about your health. They *want* you to have a sabbatical now and return refreshed."

Walker told Ralph that he appreciated the concern but that he had his own agenda. Right now he was just overcommitted. He needed to take more time for himself before he got burned out.

"Burned out" and "stressed out" had become fashionable phrases and fashionable maladies. Walker had both. He had so dedicated himself to his calling that even in this large Church he personally had to take part in every aspect of the pastoral role—preaching, counseling, fund raising, Church and community activities.

"You haven't exactly been noted for delegating authority," Ralph commented mildly. Walker had that inscrutable smile on his face, which sometimes seemed compassionate, sometimes condescending.

"I hear what you're saying, Ralph, and I'm going to do better at that."

Ralph leaned forward, his arm almost touching the arm of Walker's chair. "Walker, you have often said that you feel that I am like a father to you, and certainly I want to do everything I can to help you succeed in your mission."

"I know that, and you have no idea what comfort that gives me."

"Is something troubling you?"

Walker suddenly swivelled in his chair; his eyes both widened and seemed to knife straight through Ralph's solid form. "In my position there are bound to be some people who don't like me, you know, people who are jealous of me and who want my job."

Ralph didn't answer, partly because the famous Railey stare could ferret out the truth and partly because some of what he said could indeed be true. How could any young minister, or, for that matter, any ambitious young man, not admire, or envy, Walker's success?

The desire for self-improvement contributed to Walker's boyish appeal and to his success. His sincerity in wanting to become the very best he could be charmed many of the older clerics. Fifty-five-year-old Reverend Horace Hanley, a Methodist district superintendent in Mississippi, had visited Texas eighteen months earlier and had spent an evening in the Railey home. "It was one of the most pleasant evenings I've had in years," he told a group of Methodist ministers. "With very little notice Peggy prepared a marvelous dinner. The little ones were delightful and so well behaved. We three adults talked about Church matters, and Walker kept asking me to tell him what he could do to improve himself. How could he become a better minister? I can't remember when I've been so impressed with a young minister or been in such a happy home, a home that radiated warmth and caring and Christian love."

Parishioner Mary Ruth Leavell also spoke of warmth and caring and Christian love. A homemaker with two grown children, she and her teacher husband Bill had been devoted members of First Church since childhood. Through over forty years of attendance, neither had been so impressed with a minister. "He was there for me when I needed him most," Mary Ruth said. "I was at a Sunday School luncheon at somebody's house when I sensed that something was wrong and that it had to do with me. The hostess had received a telephone call, and I was in the kitchen helping with the dishes when suddenly Walker rushed through the swinging door. There were tears in his eyes and he hugged me. There was an anguished look on his face. 'It's Bill,' he whispered. 'Your Bill is with the Lord now.' And then he told me that Bill had had a massive heart attack while driving his car. Walker truly grieved for Bill, and he was suffering for me. None of the women at the party had wanted to tell me. They just waited for Walker to tell me that Bill was dead, and—busy a man as he is—Walker just stopped what he was doing and came. Just the way he put his arms around my shoulders and comforted me—I'll never forget that caring and Christian love as long as I live."

Ryan's birthday was on March 12, so Walker and Peggy invited Peggy's parents to spend the weekend with them. For the birthday supper, they also invited Retired Bishop Slater and his wife, and Walker's adoptive parents Knox and Adeline Oakley. The Slaters and the Oakleys had been together with the Raileys and the Nicolais on special occasions. They were an extended family that Walker had created.

When the Oakleys arrived, Walker opened the front door and took Ad by the arm. He said softly, "Say hello to Peggy and then come into the bedroom. There's something I want to tell you."

A candid, strong-willed woman in her seventies, Ad could tell immediately that Walker was upset. She knew him well enough to know that something was seriously wrong.

Calling out "hello" to Peggy, who was in the kitchen, Ad followed Walker into the bedroom while her husband joined the Nicolais and the Slaters and the children. Walker closed the door, and they sat down on the king-sized bed.

Ad stared at him through her blue-tinted glasses. In appearance she personifies the accepted version of what an elderly Texas woman should be. Her large bosoms contrast with thin, freckled arms, and tight, narrow lips; the skin on her face is thick and tanned, a mask of tiny wrinkles, like a map with many intricate country roads. She has a sharp tongue softened by a generous sense of humor, reflected in her blazing blue eyes. She is a formidable woman.

Walker told her about the letters. With tears in his eyes he confided how vulnerable he felt. "I'm not so afraid for myself but for Peggy and the children. If something happened to them, I'd never forgive myself."

Ad told him to take all precautions and do what the police and the F.B.I. told him to do.

When they left the bedroom, Walker headed for the group around the swimming pool, and Ad went into the kitchen.

"I'll bet Walker told you about those letters," Peggy said.

"He did," Ad acknowledged. "And I'm concerned for all of you. I want you to be careful."

"I'll be careful," Peggy replied. "But I don't intend to be intimidated. No one is going to frighten me."

The week before Easter Peggy and the children had gone to Tyler, in East Texas, to visit Peggy's parents and grandmother. Without telling Peggy, Walker also moved out of the house and checked in at the Doubletree Inn. He telephoned Cadillac dealer Rodger Meier and asked if he might rent a car because the F.B.I. didn't want him driving his own car.

Meier drove an inconspicuous used car to the Doubletree Inn, parked it in the parking lot and joined Railey in the lobby of the hotel where he handed over the keys and told Railey that the car was on loan.

"There's something I need to tell you," Railey said. He then explained about the threatening letters and about his belief that he was being followed.

Railey seemed tense and jittery to Meier. After a brief conversation, Meier, feeling somewhat apprehensive himself, left through the hotel's front door where his secretary waited and drove him back to his office.

On Thursday, Walker left the hotel where he had lived for the past five days and moved back home. Then on the afternoon of Good Friday while he was at the Church, Peggy and the children returned from Tyler.

On the front doorstep stood a tall floral arrangement of Easter lilies, white carnations and white irises. Peggy took the arrangement in the house and opened the florist's delivery card that was addressed to her. It read: "With deepest apologies." No name was signed. She couldn't remember being insulted or offended. Then she wondered if the flowers were associated with the threatening letters. With a growing sense of uneasiness she telephoned her friend Maxie Hardin who had collected the mail and newspapers for her.

Maxie and Tim Hardin, both of whom are lawyers, joined First Church because of Walker. They thought him the most magnetic and thought-provoking preacher either of them had ever heard, and they liked him personally, too. He didn't set himself apart from his contemporaries as *the* minister but instead was one of them, sharing the same interests and concerns as they.

Maxie and Peggy hadn't met until over a year later when both of them brought their 3-year-old boys to Vacation Church School. Maxie, an attractive blond with blue eyes and fair skin, was still practicing real estate law in a downtown law firm, and Peggy was accompanying on the piano the children's choir directed by John Yarrington. The two women took an immediate liking to each other and were delighted to discover that they lived only a few blocks apart. As the boys grew older and became playmates, and with Maxie temporarily retired to full-time homemaker, the friendship strengthened between them.

Peggy and Maxie saw each other daily or else talked on the phone. Young Jim was Ryan's best friend, and Peggy thought it would be good for Ryan if Jim came over and spent the night. Maxie said she would bring over the mail and take Ryan and Jim for hamburgers before returning the boys.

When she arrived at the Raileys, Maxie admired the floral arrangement. She was disturbed, however, by the message on the unsigned card. Like Peggy, she wondered if the arrangement had been ordered by the person sending the threatening letters.

On the drive back to the Raileys, after the boys had eaten hamburgers and played for a couple of hours at the Hardins' house, their conversation turned to death. Maxie recognized that the subject of death resulted from the day being Good Friday, and she listened.

It surprised her to hear her son say, "Nobody dies in our family."

Patiently she explained to the children that everyone dies eventually and that those who love and believe in Jesus Christ live on in a better and happier life.

"I don't want anybody to die in my family," Ryan said petulantly as he kicked the back of the front seat and stuck out his lower lip in a pout. "Never. Not ever."

It was a strange remark for a five-year-old child to make. It was as if some premonition had alerted his subconscious. Maxie glanced in the rear view mirror at the boys on the back seat. Ryan was frowning. For no particular reason that she could name, Maxie shivered.

The next day, Saturday, Peggy told Maxie that this was the first morning in their entire marriage that Walker had *ever* fixed breakfast for the children and let her sleep. Walker had never been the sort of husband to help around the house, but over the past year Maxie had found herself increasingly annoyed with him. Not only did he do nothing about the house or help Peggy with the children, but in his sermons, he told amusing stories about his family and his home life, which Maxie knew were untrue. Even when Peggy wasn't feeling well, he had slept late in the mornings, never dressing or feeding the children. Peggy had complained to Maxie about this. Of course lots of wives had this same complaint, but Peggy only had domestic help one day a week and she had been ill most of the fall and winter. She had eye problems and allergies and was still easily exhausted from the bout of pneumonia she had experienced several months earlier. Her mother had to come to Dallas to care for her and the children.

There was something wrong in the Railey marriage, something that had begun long before the threatening letters appeared. Instead of bringing Peggy and Walker closer, the letters had intensified the conflict. Both husband and wife were experienced actors and, if they chose to do so, could rise to any occasion; yet, when separated from the other, each seemed more relaxed. Of course no outsider ever really knows what goes on between two people in such an intimate relationship as marriage, yet to anyone who was exposed to the couple's public appearances and to the company of each without the other, it was apparent that the marriage was not the happy partnership they pretended it was.

Later on that Saturday before Easter, Walker was seen at Sparkman Hillcrest Cemetery at the graveside service for Bishop Walter Underwood, who had formerly ministered in Dallas at First United Methodist. Gordon Casad and his wife Dede noticed his moving nervously on the edge of the crowd.

After the interment Walker told them about the letter which had arrived in the mail at his home that morning: "You have a beautiful home, a beautiful wife and two beautiful children but not for long." He said he had telephoned both the police and the F.B.I. and told them about the letter and about being followed by someone in a gray car. He repeated again he was not so much afraid for himself as he was for Peggy and the children. Gordon suggested that he go home, rest and be with his family. Tomorrow was Easter—a joyful yet stressful day for any preacher.

5

April 20, 1987

AT NINE O'CLOCK ON THE MONDAY MORNING AFTER
Easter, Professor Dick Murray who walks with a cane, left
his two-bedroom brick cottage on Daniel Street behind
SMU. Ten years earlier he and his wife had left the large
house that Walker had so admired when he first came to
SMU. A smaller house closer to the campus was more suited
to their older lifestyle.

The Murrays' driveway bordered that of his psychologist
neighbor Dr. Lucy Goodrich Papillon. Although Dick had
not seen Lucy in several months, he assumed that she had
attended the Easter service the day before at First Church,
as had he and his wife Joyce. Dick had worked for twenty-
five years in the Department of Christian Education at
Perkins School of Theology at SMU and knew of the
threatening letters.

Lucy, an attractive, frosted blond in her mid-forties, was
also heading toward her car.

Dick called out cheerfully to her. "That was an exciting
Easter service at First Church yesterday!"

"Exciting nothing! I was petrified," Lucy replied. "I've
never been so frightened in all my life."

Dick noticed tears in her eyes.

Lucy was a sultry, naturally seductive woman who many
women thought preferred the company of men. Thus, some
women were suspicious and envious of her. Being the
daughter of Bishop Robert E. Goodrich, Jr., a popular
senior minister at First United Methodist from 1946 until
1972, also contributed to Lucy's being a likely target for
gossip. After two divorces and numerous rumored affairs,

49

she was still searching, some church members believed, for a man to equal the adored image she held of her dead father.

Three and a half miles northeast of SMU and Daniel Street, Peggy Railey spoke on the telephone to Maxie, asking if Jim could come over and play with Ryan. Peggy told Maxie that a man from Safetec was coming that morning to examine the Raileys' security system.

Maxie said that she would bring Jim over around ten o'clock and that she would be happy to run any errands for Peggy.

When Maxie rang the doorbell a half hour later, Peggy hurried to the front door, so Ryan wouldn't open it and set off the security alarm. The man from Safetec had not yet arrived, Peggy said, and she was on the telephone. Maxie replied that she wouldn't come in the house but repeated her offer to run errands. Peggy asked her to bring a package of ice and a pound of hamburger meat when she returned for Jim in the afternoon. The boys had already run to Ryan's room to play, and Maxie said she would be back sometime between two and three.

A pleasant, heavy-set man of about thirty, Greg Martin, the technician from Safetec, rang the doorbell of the Railey house at ten o'clock. He took almost an hour to check the entire security system. Mrs. Railey followed him from room to room. She seemed to him to be a precise and conscientious woman. She told him that the security system was one of the main reasons they had bought the house on Trail Hill Drive. The house had belonged to a former basketball coach at SMU, and the sophisticated security system represented an investment of well over five thousand dollars.

Greg carefully examined the system. Everything worked perfectly. The house was an impenetrable fortress. It was also as neat as the proverbial pin. Safetec's records showed that Mrs. Railey used the system carefully.

He told the minister's wife that there were only two additions that would increase the protection. One was for her to wear an emergency beeper around her neck; the other was to include the garage in the system. In the present situation, someone could enter the garage without tripping the system; however, to enter the house from the garage without knowing the code, which had possible combinations of six thousand, one hundred and fifty-one numbers, stretched the law of probability.

Mrs. Railey sensibly said that such extreme measures were unnecessary. Greg marvelled at finding such a tidy house in which two small children lived. Here was an organized woman, the kind of cautious woman who certainly seemed unlikely to become the victim of a crime.

At four o'clock in the afternoon, about an hour after Maxie had delivered the hamburger and ice and collected Jim, the Reverend Howard Grimes received a call from Peggy Railey. A retired professor from Perkins School of Theology, Howard had been appointed four years ago by Walker to be Communications Director of First United Methodist. He supervised sound, lighting, television cameras and Walker's television appearances. Having a recurrence of lung cancer, he had resigned several weeks earlier, but had returned the day before to help with the broadcasting and recording of the Easter service.

Howard and his wife Johnnie Marie had not been close to Peggy, so he was surprised when she telephoned him for help. Later he decided that Peggy had called him instead of the Church because she did not know who at the Church might be Walker's enemy or who might even be her enemy.

Peggy told Howard that she was home alone with the children and that she had seen a brown Toyota driven by an Hispanic man circle the block several times, on each occasion driving more slowly in front of her house. Howard asked if the car was still circling and if she could tell him the license number. In just a few moments she said yes and repeated the first three numbers. He then asked her if she wanted him to call the police. She replied yes. This, too, surprised him. Peggy was an independent woman, a private person who kept her distance. After he had given the police the information with a request to send a squad car to the

Railey house, he decided that Peggy probably had not wanted the children to hear her telephoning the police. That seemed the most logical explanation.

In another sense it wasn't logical at all. If she were worried about the children's fears if they heard her telephoning the police, surely she would have been more concerned over their responses to the sudden arrival of a squad car. Perhaps the police had not informed her of their presence, or perhaps the car had disappeared and couldn't be traced by the first three numbers on the plate. Even more likely she might have felt she had overreacted and subsequently told the police *not* to come, thereby reassuring both the children and herself.

That Monday evening after Easter, Walker did not come home for dinner. He worked late at the church with Elizabeth Jasmine, Ralph Shannon and members of the Pastor-Parish Committee.

The euphoria with which the service had ended yesterday had carried over so that the noise sounded more like a cocktail party than a committee meeting. A general feeling pervaded that whatever danger there had been had passed and that the letters were more likely malicious pranks than actual threats. Still, the first item on the agenda concerned Walker's safety.

While experiencing relief that the final threat had failed to occur, all of the members felt it prudent to continue Walker's protection. Threat or prank, there was someone out there with a hatred not to be underestimated.

One person proposed that a second guard be put at the back entrance near the Church offices. Everyone agreed. Someone else suggested that a steel frame be placed around the door to Walker's office and that the door be strengthened. Again, everyone agreed.

Committee Member John White, a vice president of Texas Industries, offered to have a telephone installed in Walker's car. The offer pleased Walker who said he could give White his car and continue to drive the borrowed car from Rodger Meier. Next he joked that Rodger had given him a nondescript Buick instead of an impressive trophy Cadillac. Elizabeth Jasmine volunteered to order a bullet-proof vest that was the right size for Walker.

While reluctantly agreeing to continue wearing a bullet-proof vest, Walker insisted that he wanted the police protection removed.

"What about Peggy and the children?" Shannon asked.

"I'm not worried about them any more," Walker said. "The security system was checked this morning. They're all right."

He did, however, agree with Shannon's previous idea of taking some time off for a vacation with Peggy and the children. They would take a week's holiday and drive to San Antonio.

It wasn't a sabbatical, but Ralph thought that at least there would be a breathing space during which they would probably learn whether the threats would continue or if the Easter scare had been the end of the harrassment.

That the end of the harassment was *not* the Easter service had become clear when Peggy telephoned Howard Grimes and agreed to his informing the police. Yet, apparently Walker didn't know about the suspicious car circling the house or about the call to the police. If Peggy hadn't telephoned the Church, then she had not spoken with Walker who was "not worried about them any more." Why wasn't he worried? And why, if Peggy was truly frightened, hadn't she asked Howard or some other friend to come to the house and stay with her and the children until the police arrived? Had the police even answered the call? If so, were the children scared? Still, most puzzling of all, was: Why hadn't Peggy immediately told Walker?

6

April 21, 1987

∽∾ AT TEN MINUTES TO NINE ON TUESDAY MORNING,
Maxie Hardin and blond five-year-old Jim walked across the
lawn of the Christian Childhood Development Center at
Lake Highlands United Methodist Church. Waiting for her
on the sidewalk in front of the building was Peggy with Ryan
and two-year-old Megan, whose bottle thick glasses had
been removed to keep her from being conspicuous. On
Tuesdays and Thursdays, which were called Mother's Day
Out, Maxie and Peggy put the children in day care from nine
until two-thirty. They usually met and talked for a while
both in the mornings and in the afternoons. On Mondays,
Wednesdays and Fridays they spoke on the telephone at
least once a day, and often had coffee or lunch together
while the little boys played.

Their conversations the day before had been so hurried
and child-centered that Maxie was glad for the opportunity
to talk to Peggy about the Easter Service and to ask her
about the threatening letters. After they had delivered the
children to their classrooms, they stood alone in the school
hall.

Peggy said she had left early that morning and taken the
children to McDonald's for breakfast. Following police
suggestions, she was leaving the house at irregular times and
varying the routes she took to school. The police instruc-
tions to the whole family now were "to get lost."

"Is Walker being careful?"

Peggy said that Walker had come in late the night before
and was sleeping late that morning.

"I guess you are still concerned."

"I don't want Walker to stop what he is doing. I'm not that nervous. But Walker is." She went on to tell about how Walker had been sure that he was being followed yesterday and had driven to a police station. Then she told her that the Pastor-Parish Committee had voted to order him a bullet-proof vest, and a car telephone, both of which he would get today.

"Do the police have any more information?" Maxie asked.

"Nothing at all," Peggy said casually. "It's still a mystery."

Maxie admired Peggy's attitude, but, being a lawyer, though her specialty was real estate, she wondered how this mystery would be resolved or, more likely, if it would simply disappear.

At five minutes to twelve, Rabbi Sheldon Zimmerman pulled into the staff parking lot behind First United Methodist Church. Standing in the sunshine on the steps of the back entrance to the church, Walker, dressed in a navy blue blazer, tan trousers and an executive's yellow power tie, was waiting for him. Every couple of months the two religious leaders, who had become friends through the Conference of Christians and Jews, lunched together.

Only a few years older than Walker, Sheldon was also balding. He had a fringe of graying brown hair, a dark, heavy, neatly trimmed beard and expressive brown eyes.

They embraced as usual, and Sheldon felt the bulk of the bullet-proof vest around Walker's chest. He was startled; Walker made light of it, joking that Sheldon had to be brave to go to lunch with a hunted man.

It was a pleasant five-minute walk to the 2001 Club at the top of the Bryan building where First Methodist kept a membership. Sheldon liked walking in downtown Dallas among the tall glass, bronze and steel buildings. It reminded him of New York where he had been a rabbi for fifteen years. He had been appointed to Temple Emanu-El, the largest, most prestigious temple in Dallas eighteen months ago. It was located in the suburbs, just north of the Park Cities, and had several acres of ground around it. For the most part the congregation was rich, well educated and casual in its lifestyle.

Sheldon missed the diversity of backgrounds that were a part of daily life in Manhattan. Downtown Dallas, like most of the downtown areas of large cities in the South and Midwest, was in a state of decline; many businesses and the services that catered to them were moving to the suburbs.

Walker told Sheldon about the latest threat that had come on Easter morning and about the Easter service. Acknowledging that at some time or other every priest or rabbi receives hate mail that is distressing. Sheldon said he applauded Walker's attitude.

Walker replied that his attitude really didn't effect what would or wouldn't happen, and that there were worse places to die than in the pulpit.

Over lunch Sheldon noticed how frequently Walker changed the subject and how rapidly he spoke. He talked of delivering the baccalaureate address at Southern Methodist University, and of the sermons he was writing for "The Protestant Hour," and of the Boswell Lectures at First Church, a series of three speeches given by theologians or religious leaders. Sheldon had delivered a Boswell lecture last year, and Walker had spoken at an Interfaith Meeting at Temple Emanu-El.

Every time Walker brought the topic of conversation back to the letters he repeated that he wasn't alarmed by threats to himself but that threats to Peggy and the children worried and upset him. He could never forgive himself if harm came to his family because of something he had done or said.

Sheldon said that with all the stress ministers and priests and rabbis were under today, there needed to be more that they could laugh about together. Walker spoke of "burn out" which Sheldon understood because most of the people he counseled suffered from it.

When Sheldon suggested that Walker take off for a while, be alone with his family and get away from the problems of the Church and the congregation, Walker said that he planned to take Peggy and the children to San Antonio and then, maybe, on to Houston. Sheldon remarked skeptically that cities were not always the best places to relax, and Walker replied that maybe later they would take a longer vacation to some place more peaceful, such as the mountains in Colorado.

"Forget these crazy letters," Sheldon said, as they parted in the church parking lot. "Shalom. We will be together again next month." He could not then have anticipated that he would be beside his friend again in less than twenty-four hours.

Shortly before two-thirty in the afternoon, Maxie walked toward the side entrance of the Christian Childhood Development Center. Leaving the building was Peggy with Ryan and Megan. Seeing Maxie, Ryan tugged at his mother's arm and called out. Maxie smiled and waved at him. Although they were less than thirty yards away, Peggy halted abruptly, frowned and looked at Maxie as if she didn't know her. Then turning curtly, she took the children by their hands and walked across the grass away from Maxie.

Maxie stopped and stared after her. She was stunned. There was no doubt that Peggy had seen her. If she had not recognized her, Ryan had called out Maxie's name. Peggy was deliberately avoiding her. Maxie could not imagine what had happened during the past five hours that could have changed Peggy's attitude toward her. They had parted friends, and Maxie was even thinking of stopping by the Raileys and having coffee and more talk. She knew she had not done anything to offend Peggy, yet in contrast to her earlier mood, Peggy was frowning and preoccupied.

In the two years they had been friends, Maxie could recall only one other time when Peggy had behaved oddly, focused on her own thoughts. Three weeks ago Peggy and Ryan had arrived shortly before noon at Northlake Elementary School to register Ryan in kindergarten. Maxie and Jim were already there and waiting for them.

"Did you save a place for Ryan?" Peggy had asked.

Maxie told her that they weren't too late to register and that there were places still available.

Peggy seemed annoyed. After Ryan was registered, she told Maxie that Walker had caused them to be late because he refused to deal with the garage door repairman. "I could have 'guilted' him into it," Peggy said irritably, "but I didn't."

Peggy had wanted their garage door checked immediately. The night before she and Walker had been awakened by the noise of their garage door rising and then falling with a loud crash. They were both alarmed. No one but the two of them possessed an automatic door opener. Peggy had telephoned the installation company, but Walker didn't want his morning disturbed. He wanted to sleep late and then work on his sermon.

Maxie suggested to Peggy that there had been robberies in the neighborhood and that someone might have been driving through the alleys with a door opener just to see which garages were on the same frequency. Peggy was more angry at Walker than worried by the event. Maxie was more concerned than she that the episode of the garage door might be connected with the threatening letters.

Now, as she thought about it, Peggy's using the phrase, "guilted him into it" bothered her most of all.

All the rest of the afternoon Maxie worried about Peggy. Twice she sat down to telephone her, and then couldn't figure out what to say. If Peggy didn't telephone her tomorrow, Maxie would see her at school on Thursday and confront her. Still, as she was preparing dinner, she thought that as soon as her husband Tim came home, she would tell him. Maybe he would telephone Peggy just to see if she and the kids were all right.

It was after five in the afternoon, and eighty-year-old business manager emeritus Laaden Smith, who two years earlier had suffered a crippling stroke, thought he was alone in the Church offices. Then he heard the jingling of keys, which sounded near the front office. Someone coughed.

Laaden was silent. Since the threatening letters had started coming, he had been more than a little afraid for Walker. Unable to walk without the aid of a steel frame that was waist high, Laaden moved slowly. His left arm was paralyzed. Getting up from his desk chair and reaching for his steel walker, Laaden stepped as quietly as he could. When he reached the door of his office and cautiously looked down the hall, he saw Walker turning the key in the lock of the front office.

"Walker, I thought you were going on vacation," Laaden said, shuffling slowly and painfully along the hall.

Walker said that they were going on vacation at the end of the week.

"Where are Peggy and the children now?"

Walker replied that they were at home.

"They shouldn't be left by themselves!" Laaden was shocked and annoyed.

Walker said he had only returned to the church briefly to pick up some papers he needed to take with him on vacation.

"This is the time to be with your family," Laaden insisted. "We don't want anything bad to happen to any of you."

Walker told Laaden that Peggy was at home now, that the security system had been checked yesterday and that their house was the safest place they could be.

"All the more reason *you* should be at home now," Laaden argued. "If you think your house is the safest place you can be, then surely you must realize that the empty church here is *not* a mighty fortress."

Walker again assured Laaden that he had only come to collect some papers.

An hour later, Laaden finished his work and noticed as he left the building that the door leading into Karen Spencer's office was again locked. An ominous emptiness filled the building. Walker had seemed not in the least concerned for his own safety, the bravado of youth disbelieving his own mortality. What was more puzzling was Walker's lack of fear for his family. It almost seemed as if he knew that his wife and children were out of harm's way. But, clearly, that was impossible.

At a little after eight that same Tuesday evening, Adeline Oakley telephoned the Railey household.

"Peg, it's Ad. How are you all?"

Peggy said that they were fine. Ad asked about Walker, and Peggy told her that he had come home around six and had left soon after, saying that he wasn't hungry and that he needed to do some research at the SMU library. Peggy didn't know when he would be home.

"Peggy, if you're scared being there alone with the children, Knox and I can come over."

Peggy replied that the children were already in bed and that she was going to bed early, too.

"Are you sure you feel all right with Walker not being there?" Ad persisted.

Peggy said that the security system had been checked thoroughly and that she and the children were perfectly safe. Nobody could enter the house without setting off the alarm. As long as none of them left the house or went into the garage, they were protected.

A half an hour later the telephone rang at the Nicolai home in Flint. Billie Jo was anxious to hear from Peggy about the Easter service and how the children were. Peggy told her mother about the letter that had been slipped under Gordon Casad's door on Easter morning and about all the fuss over the bullet-proof vest, the high drama and the anticlimax of nothing happening.

"I'm concerned for your safety and for the safety of the children," Billie Jo said. "Where is Walker?"

"He's at the SMU library finishing some research for a paper he has to complete by the end of the week."

Billie Jo was surprised that Walker had left his family alone at nine o'clock in the evening, but there was nothing apprehensive in Peggy's voice, so she changed the subject. "We loved having you here at the lake last week. It was a wonderful week for us, hiking through the park and doing things with the children."

"The children loved it, too. Playing with the chickens and the cats."

"Oh yes, tell Ryan that the mother cat 'laid her kittens.'"

Peggy laughed and Billie Jo relaxed. Her daughter wasn't frightened. Then she wondered if Walker was safe driving around at night alone. Peggy reassured her that Walker was wearing the bullet-proof vest and now had a telephone in his car.

"Is there any news about the threatening letters?"

"The letters were all typed on one typewriter. And that typewriter is at the church."

"At the church!"

"Yes. At the church."

"How did you find out about it?"

"Walker told me."

Billie Jo knew that Walker was not as uniformly loved by his staff as by his congregation. Someone with inside knowledge about the Church, the rambling layout of the building and the routine of activities, was a far more disturbing prospect than some outside fanatical group like the Ku Klux Klan. "What typewriter?" she asked. "Whose typewriter was it?"

"The typewriter belongs to Jim Reaves," Peggy said.

The Reverend James Reaves was a retired Navy Chaplain who had been on the staff at First Church for the past ten years. Since Walker had been appointed senior pastor, the Nicholais had become friends with Jim and his wife Katherine. They were all approximately of the same age and had shared Navy experiences during World War II.

"They ought not to give out keys to just anyone, and they ought to be sure that the keys are returned," Billie Jo said sternly.

"Mom, we're not going to let anybody frighten us off. We're going to lead a normal life."

Billie Jo understood that this was Peggy's way of changing the topic of conversation.

They talked another fifteen minutes about Megan having

her picture taken for her second birthday and having her hair cut by Peggy's hairdresser, Ernie of the Hair Chateau.

Billie Jo then told Peggy that her sister Katie had telephoned from Milwaukee on Easter. Peggy's brother Ted and his wife Linda lived in Arlington, which was nearer to Peggy and Walker than to the Nicolais, but brother and sister seldom saw each other. Ted still held an almost pathological dislike of Walker and refused to be around him. Ted was big and tough and macho; he thought that Walker was an intellectual, in the pejorative sense, and a sissy. Billie Jo had long since given up attempting to bring them together. That was simply the way things were and would continue to be.

It was nine twenty-seven when Billie Jo told Peggy she loved her and then hung up the telephone.

At about ten thirty P.M. that same Tuesday evening, a loud noise awakened Mary Lou and Daryl Schlashuber, a handsome, blond couple, who, with their two college-aged children, live on Trail Hill Drive four houses west of the Raileys. It was a great thud that sounded as if a block of cement had been dropped in the alley or possibly a garage door had crashed down on a driveway. Daryl sat bolt upright in bed. Three times in the past ten years their house had been burglarized. Only two weeks earlier a large round rock had shattered their living room window.

Now Mary Lou and Daryl listened intently. No other sound followed. Still, the noise had been so loud and had seemed so close that Daryl got out of bed and walked through the house. Then he remembered an old wood-panelled truck parked in front of the other white house a few doors down on the same side of the street. It was the only other white house nearby and looked almost like a replica of the Schlashuber house. Daryl did not know who lived there, although he knew most of his other neighbors. Had he known the residents, he would have telephoned to make sure everything was all right, since the truck had remained in front of the house most of yesterday. Its presence annoyed Daryl. It was the type of old-fashioned, poorly maintained vehicle that was out of place in a high-class neighborhood like Lake Highlands. It would be more appropriate in the large, inexpensive apartment development across the railroad track a half mile away. These rented apartments were let mostly to young, blue-collar people whom the Schlashubers had heard bought and sold and used hard drugs.

Daryl pushed the buttons of his security system and opened the front door. He stepped outside. The street seemed peaceful. There was an eerie stillness, and the full moon cast a spectral glow over the houses and shrubs. There was no wood-panelled truck down the street. The neighborhood revealed nothing amiss, yet Daryl had an uncanny feeling of foreboding around him. Despite the warm air, he shivered.

Then he went back into the house, pushed the security buttons again, and told Mary Lou that everything was all right. There was no sense in making her uneasy when he had found nothing concrete to call for uneasiness. Soon both of them were asleep again.

7

April 22, 1987

AT 12:43 A.M. ON WEDNESDAY, A WOMAN DISpatcher at Central Emergencies, answered a 911 call.

"Dallas Emergency—"

"This is Walker Railey. I'm at 9328 Trail Hill Drive . . ."

"What is the problem, sir?"

"I've just come into the house, and my wife is in the ki— . . . garage—and . . . and somebody has done something to her. Send the paramedics and send the police—please, please . . ."

"Stay on the line with me. What street crosses Trail Hill on the corner?" the dispatcher asked.

"Uh, it's, uh . . . uh; it's between Audelia and, uh, White Rock Trail."

"Is it a house or an apartment?"

"It's a house. It's about four blocks north of Lake Highlands High School."

"Okay. What's your name, sir?"

"Walker Railey. R-A-I-L-E-Y."

"Okay. We'll get them out there."

"Please hurry. Please."

A few seconds later the telephone rang at the Yarrington home. John was in the den watching a late movie. His wife Diane had gone to bed but was not yet asleep. She answered before the second ring.

"Diane, something terrible has happened to Peggy!" Walker cried into the telephone. "Come quickly."

"Is she all right?"

"I don't know. Just come. Please. Come quickly and bring John. Please. Please come right away."

"We'll be there," Diane said. "We're coming now."

She was already out of bed and starting to dress. John had overheard most of the conversation. Within minutes they were ready to leave, Diane stopping in her older daughter's bedroom to tell her that they were going to the Raileys'. As soon as she was in the car, John told her, "Get ready. I'm not stopping for lights."

The call that the 911 dispatcher placed to Fire Station #37 was taken by paramedic Blair Berry, an attractive young woman of twenty-five with short, curly brown hair and brown eyes. Since she was not told that the Trail Hill Drive emergency involved a violent attack, to which police paramedics were usually called, Blair took only the trauma kit. Had she known the nature of the injury, she would have taken more medical supplies. Her partner, a blond young man named Mark, was responsible for driving and for filling out the run sheet; Blair was responsible for patient care.

As Blair and Mark left the station, Charles Massoud and his wife were awakened by their doorbell and by loud pounding on their front door at 9324 Trail Hill Drive. Massoud opened the door and was confronted by his next door neighbor whom he barely knew.

"They have hurt my family," Railey told the Massouds, and he asked Charles to come and stay with him until the police arrived.

A calm, perceptive man in his mid-fifties, Massoud accompanied Railey back to his house, following him through the wide-open front door, through the house and into the attached garage. There was no light except from the headlights of Railey's car. Peggy Railey lay unattended on the concrete floor of the garage.

She was fully dressed, her green knit shirt tucked neatly into her green slacks, her glasses correctly placed on her nose and over her ears, her soft brown hair neatly combed. Had she not been convulsing, foaming at the mouth and gasping for air, she might have been laid out for burial. Her face and neck were swollen, her skin the color of faded blue jeans. The red marks around her throat indicated that she had been strangled. To Massoud she appeared near death.

He looked around the scene. There were no signs of a scuffle. The only item out of place was one of Peggy's pink house slippers, which apparently had slipped off her foot. He observed that the Reverend Railey was behaving strangely, pacing between the garage and the living room where his children were sprawled on the sofa staring at a silent television screen. There was the unmistakable odor of liquor on the minister's breath, yet he seemed under control, far less upset at seeing his wife in such a condition than most men would have been. It bothered Massoud that Railey had not covered his wife with a blanket. Occasionally he knelt beside her but he did not speak to her. He did not caress her or even touch her. He simply observed her. While he stood guard over the body, Massoud studied the minister with increasing suspicion.

Over and over again Railey paced from the garage to the living room and then returned to look down upon his wife.

Why wasn't the minister holding his wife's hand? Why wasn't he speaking to her? Massoud observed that the only light in the garage came through the open back door of the house and from the headlights on Railey's car. Eerie shadows blurred on the garage walls like heavy blocks of modern sculpture. Looking up at the white, finished ceiling, Massoud wondered why there were no bulbs in the lighting fixture. There was a surreal cast to the scene. Something was frighteningly wrong. Even the Reverend Railey himself was a totally different person from the caring Christian minister Massoud remembered. Massoud felt uneasy with this new person.

The paramedics covered the distance between the Greenville Avenue station and Trail Hill Drive in less than five minutes. Just as they arrived at the house, they received a call over Channel Two telling them that the police were involved.

Blair Berry and her partner Mark hurried through the gaping light of the open front door. There was no evidence here of a struggle. The house was incredibly tidy, as if it had just experienced a thorough spring cleaning. Blair saw that two young children were on the sofa in the living room. She noticed that the man had on tan pants, a white shirt, yellow tie and yellow suspenders. He was not wearing a jacket.

When they reached the garage, oddly enough, there were no lights. The victim, a women in her mid-thirties, was lying in front of a Chrysler sedan, close to the back wall between an old refrigerator and a tricycle and stacks of boxes. The instant Blair saw her she believed that there had been a murder attempt. Although there were no outward signs of violence, the woman was in a decerebrate position, which indicates brain stem damage. She had been hanged or strangled, yet with either of those possibilities, she would have vomited. The victim and the area immediately around her were mysteriously unsoiled, too clean to be believed. While there were broken blood vessels in her cheeks, her face looked as if makeup had been freshly applied. Her hair was neatly combed and, incredibly, she was wearing her eye glasses. There were no visible scratches or other marks on her body, except for her elbows, which were scraped and bleeding from her gasping attempts to raise her chest from the concrete floor, then falling back.

Instinctively Blair looked around for a hook or a beam or a rope. There was none. An anxious neighbor stood beside the woman while the man who was presumably her husband stayed in the house.

As she knelt beside the woman, Blair heard the police arrive. It was difficult to examine the victim because she was hemmed in between the wall and the refrigerator. It was a dark, impossible place to work. With a pen light between her teeth, Blair checked the vital signs. Having brought only the trauma kit, she did not have an endotrachial tube to open the airway. The woman had a gag reflex. Blair lifted her jaw, and the victim hyperventilated.

Police officers DeSpain and Jeeter were talking with Mark who had brought in the orange cot with the white sheet and blanket. The husband peered over Blair's shoulder. She smelled alcohol on his breath. To her he seemed excited but unaffected by his wife's condition. *He is too cool,* she thought. *And he won't touch her. He didn't even cover her with a blanket.* The husband was also in the way as the two paramedics lifted the woman on to the cot. Blair is six feet, two inches and built like an athlete with strong shoulders; still it was difficult to get the victim out of the garage. To make a path the policemen and the neighbor moved a tricycle and some of the boxes out of the way.

As they passed through the living room carrying the victim on the cot, Blair again glanced at the children, half-asleep and mesmerized by the television. Or, were they traumatized? Blair couldn't be sure.

In the ambulance she put in an IV tube. Mark went back in the house to question the husband for the medical report. When he returned, he told Blair that the man wouldn't or couldn't answer any questions except to give the victim's name. As they left for Presbyterian Hospital, lights flashing and siren shrieking, Mark said to Blair: "I think he tried to kill her."

Barbara Wedgwood

"I know," Blair replied softly as she touched the victim's forehead. "I know."

The Yarringtons arrived as Peggy was in the ambulance. Two police cars, their red and blue lights swivelling, sparkling and dazzling, were parked in front of the ambulance. At least a dozen neighbors, some in their robes and pajamas, stood on the sidewalk, at the edge of the front lawn and across the street.

Something terrible had happened at the Railey home. Mrs. Massoud said that Mrs. Railey had been attacked by an intruder. No one had heard any screams or alarms. They had the best protection system on the block. That made it more frightening. Not many of the neighbors knew the Raileys personally, but they recognized Peggy and the children and Peggy's blue Chrysler sedan. Everyone in the neighborhood smiled and waved, but Peggy seldom had time to chat. She seemed always in a hurry. One neighbor across the street had met Peggy and Walker on the day they had decided to buy the house. The real estate agent brought them over to use the telephone. She remembered Dr. Railey more clearly than his wife. He had the kind of penetrating eyes that mentally undressed a woman, although she didn't like to say such things about a minister, even if they were true.

"I've never set eyes on him," another woman remarked. "Wouldn't even recognize him in the grocery store."

"You've seen his picture in the newspaper," her husband replied.

"They keep their lawn nice and tidy," another man said. "Seemed like an ideal family to me. Just the sort of people you'd want in the neighborhood."

"I think their white house is the prettiest house on the block," his wife said.

"My sister goes to his church," another woman volunteered. "The Raileys are good people. I hope nothing truly bad has happened."

Another car sped to a screeching halt a few feet behind the ambulance.

68

Diane and John jumped out of their car and ran across the Railey front lawn where they were stopped by Police Officer DeSpain. When they explained that they were friends of the Raileys and had been telephoned by the minister, they were led into the house. Walker sat on a foot stool hugging Megan. Ryan was on the couch, half-covered by a rain coat. A policeman with notebook and pen in hand, stood in the open doorway to the garage.

Diane embraced and kissed both Walker and Megan.

"Take my babies," Walker said, rising.

Diane first hugged Ryan and then took Megan from Walker. She noticed that Walker was sweating profusely.

"Don't leave me, John." Walker put his arms around John's shoulders. "Please don't leave me."

Diane wore her thick, brown hair shoulder length and tightly permed in the casual crunch style. Not wearing any make-up, her skin appeared chalk white. Thin and dressed in a checked shirt and jeans, she still had an adolescent look about her, although she was as serious and completely in charge as a drill sergeant. Seeing that Ryan had on only the top to his pajamas, she went into his bedroom and hastily grabbed another pajama bottom from a drawer and then pulled it on him. The child seemed bewildered and disoriented. Why wasn't he crying? She hurried into Megan's room, grabbing some diapers and a stuffed animal. When she returned to Ryan's room, she saw he was still standing beside his bed, just as she had left him. She snatched the pillow off his bed and grasped him by his hand that was icy cold and trembling. Neither of the children cried.

Charles Massoud wondered why Walker did not insist on accompanying his wife to the hospital. He could not imagine separating himself from his wife if she were in a similar condition.

"I don't know. I don't know. I was just coming home. I drove down the alley to my garage and the garage door was raised about three feet off the concrete floor. I got out of my car and raised the garage door. It was dark inside, but from the headlights on my car I could see her laying [sic] there.

And I knew something awful had happened. She wasn't moving except that she kept heaving her chest and then falling back on her elbows, like some sort of exercise and she was foaming at the mouth and burbling . . . and I don't know what else. How could anyone do this? And why Peggy? Who would want to harm Peggy?"

"That's what we want to find out, Reverend," Officer DeSpain said. "Would you mind if we took a look through the garage?"

Walker said that he didn't mind if it would help find who had attacked Peggy.

Officer Jeeter then asked him if he had been drinking and the minister said no. Railey wiped his eyes and blew his nose; his nose was red and his skin blotchy.

The friend John telephoned his house and then confirmed that his wife Diane and the Railey children had arrived safely. The minister appeared not to take in this bit of information as the police continued to interrogate him.

"How many drinks have you had?"

"I haven't been drinking."

"When was the last drink you had this evening?"

"I haven't been drinking."

"What was the subject that caused the quarrel between you and your wife?"

"There was no quarrel."

"What time was it when you and your wife began to argue?"

Massoud was about to ask the officer if he might leave when John Yarrington introduced himself and asked if he might telephone his wife again, this time from Massoud's house. Massoud and John walked next door. His own house was so quiet that Massoud couldn't help overhearing John's telephone conversation.

"Diane, are you all right?"

"Yes. Are you at the hospital?"

"No. I'm telephoning from the neighbors' house next door."

"Why aren't you at the hospital?"

"Diane, the police are bullying Walker. They haven't

stopped asking him questions, the same questions over and over again. They are brutal. It's not fair. I can't stand by and watch it without becoming angry."

"Do you know what actually happened to Peggy?"

"No, I haven't got any details."

"Try and calm down and call me when you go to the hospital. I'm afraid that whoever attacked Peggy will be after Walker, too."

Massoud's wife begged her husband not to become any more involved. He reassured her that there was no longer any danger at this time. He would ask a neighbor to stay with her. Then he and John returned to the Railey house.

The questioning continued for another hour. Then one of the policemen asked Massoud if he would drive Walker and John to Presbyterian Hospital. The police did not want the Raileys' cars moved.

Because they hadn't completed their run sheet, paramedics Blair and Mark hung around the emergency room hoping to get information. A nurse asked Blair if she had smelled WD-40 or seen a can of it in the garage or on the victim's body. Blair said she hadn't. The only odor she recalled was liquor on the husband's breath. The nurse then said that an empty can of WD-40 had been found at the foot of the cot near the victim's right foot. Neither she nor Mark had noticed it when they put her on the cot and carried her out. Mark was driving, and Blair had been working at the head of the cot. How could an empty can of WD-40 be put on the cot without their noticing? And why? That was bizarre. Another nurse showed Blair Peggy's X-rays, which confirmed her initial feelings. The injuries were to the vertebrae behind the medulla oblongata, a condition known as "the hangman's fracture." Then Blair learned that the victim was the wife of the senior minister at First United Methodist Church.

After Massoud had left Walker and John at the emergency entrance, John again telephoned Diane and told her that Peggy had been choked. A neurosurgeon had explained to them that he didn't know yet if her spine had been broken.

71

Nor could he be certain of the extent of brain damage. She was in critical condition.

Before Diane could ask any more questions, John told her he had to get off the telephone. Walker wanted to make some calls.

8

BILLIE JO AND BILL NICOLAI WERE AWAKENED AT three-thirty A.M. by the ringing of their telephone. Billie Jo answered.

"Billie Jo," Walker's voice quavered. "Something terrible has happened to Peggy. She's been taken to Presbyterian Hospital and I . . . I can't talk anymore."

John Yarrington was on the line. "Billie Jo, I think you and Bill should come here right away. It's bad, real bad, as bad as it can be."

Billie Jo asked if her daughter was dead.

"No," John said. "But she's hurt bad. She may not make it."

"What happened?"

"Someone broke into the garage and choked her."

Bill Nicolai took the phone from his wife's shaking hand and asked for directions to the hospital.

"Stay on Central Expressway and exit at Walnut Hill Lane. Drive east for two blocks. You can't miss it. It's on the south side of the street. Three huge tan brick buildings. There are signs to the emergency entrance."

Before they left their yellow lakeside cottage, Billie Jo awakened her eighty-six-year-old mother and told her that they were leaving for Dallas and would telephone her from the hospital when they had more information about Peggy.

"We should call Ted before we leave," Bill said. "He can be at the hospital in forty-five minutes."

"Yes, we should call Ted," Billie Jo agreed. "Ted thinks on his feet. He's good in a crisis."

At five A.M. John spoke with Walker's secretary, Karen Spencer, who said that she would telephone some of the Church staff. Walker himself telephoned his adoptive parents Adeline and Knox Oakley. Ad assured him they would be at the hospital as soon as they could get there. When Walker was depressed or had a personal problem, he turned to Ad. From the time they first met, fifteen years ago, when Walker was in Seminary and Ad had invited him to teach a Sunday School Class at Highland Park Methodist Church, their relationship had been like mother and son.

Karen telephoned Gordon Casad, who reached across the bedside table before the second ring and picked up the receiver. His wife Dede was a light sleeper and already awake.

"What?" Karen's words stunned him, yet, at the same time jarred him fully awake. "When?" he asked. "Where is she now?" Pause. "I'll be there." Seconds later he hung up the receiver.

"Who was it?" Dede asked. "What has happened?"

Gordon was already out of bed and starting to dress. He told her what Karen had said. Someone had attempted to strangle Peggy Railey. She was now in Presbyterian Hospital. "I guess none of us took those threatening letters seriously enough," Gordon said.

"What else could you have done?" Dede asked. "Walker himself contacted the police and the F.B.I."

"I don't know," Gordon mumbled. "I just don't know."

Suddenly Dede's dark brown eyes sparked. "I think I know who did it."

Gordon stared at her in open-mouthed amazement.

"Janet Marshall," Dede said. "She's in love with Walker, and she loves those kids, too."

"That doesn't make her a murderer!"

"It gives her a motive, and besides, she's just crazy enough to do something like that." A pretty young divorcée with incurable lupus, Janet had attached herself to Walker like a limpet on a rock.

"Dede, don't say such things. Don't even *think* such things."

"It *is* only a thought."

"Well, don't tell it to anyone," Gordon said. "Don't discuss this with anyone." He bent over and kissed her on the cheek. "I'm going to the hospital now." For once he was glad that she was leaving for a monthly board meeting in New York. "I'll call you tonight."

At eight A.M. Officer Jeeter telephoned Inspector Christopher Lawlor of the F.B.I. Earlier Walker had spoken with Lawlor about the threatening letters. Lawlor's card was in Walker's billfold. Jeeter asked him to come to the police station.

Two hours earlier Officer DeSpain had telephoned Homicide Detective Lt. Ron Waldrop, who wasn't called at home unless there was something special about a case. Walker Railey was a prominent man, a well-known figure throughout Dallas civic and Church communities. His wife wasn't expected to live; therefore, Crimes Against Persons was turning the case over to Homicide.

Lt. Waldrop, a large, well-built man with a round face and thick reddish blond hair, has been on the force sixteen years. For the past five years he has been in charge of Homicide. Hard-working and dedicated, Lt. Waldrop has the image of an ex–All-American football player or an All-American crime stopper.

In Dallas tensions between the police and local minorities has increased dramatically. The press is investigating more and more cases in which minorities claim the police have used unnecessary force and, in several instances, shot and killed Blacks and Hispanics without provocation. The media also successfully conducted a campaign to release two prisoners who, the press claimed, were used as scapegoats and wrongfully imprisoned.

An unsolved high profile case was the last thing Lt. Ron

Waldrop needed. He would have to take charge of the case himself and put his top men on it, Lt. Stan McNear and Lt. Rick Silva.

Lt. Waldrop told DeSpain that he would be in the office within an hour and review the information the officers and Lawlor had. Then he would have a planning meeting with Captain John Holt and Chief of Police Billy Prince. They would review the police reports and prepare a statement for the press.

The Nicolais entered the emergency area of the hospital where they were met by Ted, who appeared angry but composed, and by Dr. Lisa Clark, the wife of one of the young ministers at First Church and now Peggy's physician. Walker was crying, and John was trying to comfort him. When he saw Bill and Billie Jo, Walker stood up and opened his arms. There was pain and bewilderment in his eyes as he hugged Billie Jo and stammered: "Peggy. They got Peggy."

The shock of seeing Peggy, bruised and swollen with so many tubes and bandages that they could hardly recognize her coupled with the unfamiliar fluorescent lighting seemed to Billie Jo more like a dream than reality. *Peggy had to live. She couldn't die like this. It was unthinkable.*

Stunned, the Nicolais came out of Peggy's room. Two well-groomed young men introduced themselves as police officers and asked if they might have a brief word with them. The four of them stepped into a small office with a desk and sofa and door that they closed. The room might have been the Chaplain's office.

The questions and the conversation were brief. What startled the Nicolais most was the query: *Would you be surprised to learn that your son-in-law was having an affair with another woman?* Their expressions clearly answered for them, though Billie Jo managed to reply that as their son-in-law was a minister they would be very surprised indeed.

In fact she was more surprised by their asking the question than by the possibility of an affair itself. *How would the police know of an affair and what connection could*

*this have with the threatening letters or with the attack on
Peggy?*

Bill took his wife by the arm and guided her out of the
room and toward the waiting room where their son Ted was
standing, impatiently rocking back and forth on the heels of
his boots. Billie Jo was too absorbed in her own thoughts to
wonder what Ted was thinking, but she was glad that he
hadn't been asked the question about Walker's infidelity.
Sometimes Ted overreacted.

When Gordon Casad walked into the Emergency Room
he saw policemen, various hospital staff and two clusters of
people on either side of the corridor. Bill and Billie Jo
Nicolai and their son Ted were huddled together. Gordon
had never met Ted, who was wearing jeans, a plaid shirt and
boots. A heavy-set man who weighed well over two hundred
pounds, Ted chain-smoked and appeared suspicious of both
the clergy and the hospital staff.

Walker, John Yarrington, the Oakleys and Janet Marshall,
whom more people than Dede Casad suspected was in love
with Walker, were on the opposite side of the corridor.
Walker was flexing his hands and striding back and forth in
measured steps on the green vinyl floor.

Gordon moved from Walker to the Nicolais, to John
Yarrington and Janet Marshall murmuring comforting
words usually reserved for the friends and family of someone deceased.

A young intern told them that Peggy would soon be
transferred to an Intensive Care Unit. Then, with Walker
and John, Gordon went into an emergency examining room
where Peggy lay with a tube in her mouth. It looked like the
bottom of a gas mask and was connected to a breathing
machine. There was an IV tube in her arm, a machine
monitoring her heart and more tubes and machines that
Gordon couldn't immediately identify. Her swollen neck
was bruised a purplish blue with two parallel red lines like
tire tracks sunk in a soft road.

Seeing Peggy disfigured was a greater shock to Gordon
than first hearing of the attack. Her condition was as

horrifying as the suffering he had seen in the destruction of Vienna in World War II. Once again he thought how tenuous all values were in the face of death. He gently clasped her cold, pasty hand and said a silent prayer that God would soon release her from her suffering.

At the foot of the gurney, Walker stood without moving, his face ashen, his eyes focused wide in disbelief. Beside him, like his shadow, was John Yarrington, weary with puffy brown circles under his eyes. When Gordon turned away, Walker and John followed him.

"I'll never forgive myself," Walker said, shaking his head. "They got Peggy instead of me. It should have been me."

Gordon averted his eyes. "You and Peggy will both be in my prayers."

After leaving the hospital, Gordon stopped by the University Park Methodist Church where he met with a weekly Wednesday Morning Breakfast Club of a dozen Methodist ministers. They were astounded, then appalled by his story.

"It's those right-wing extremists," a minister new to the Conference said.

Another minister disagreed. "The Ku Klux Klan is convenient to blame, but they aren't that well organized here." Someone else said that while Walker's views were liberal, they were hardly inflammatory. "It must be some crazy individual who has a personal grudge against Walker," an older minister said.

Gordon shrugged. One guess was as good as another. When he reached his office, he telephoned Conference Bishop John Russell who expressed dismay and then assurance that he would stand behind First Church.

Since Gordon was executive minister in charge of staff, and Susan Monts, who recently had been promoted, headed program coordination, it seemed logical that Gordon remain at the church and Susan stay at the hospital in the unofficial position of gate keeper to protect Walker from so many well meaning but emotionally exhausting people who would come to the hospital to see him. Because Susan lived by herself, Ralph Shannon suggested that she not return to her apartment alone but instead either spend the night at the hospital or stay with other members of the staff and their families. No one knew if the person who attacked Peggy would attack again. All of the staff were fearful, suspecting that if there were a second victim, that victim would most likely be another woman.

While Gordon and Susan met to develop a plan for handling the media and talking with Church members, who naturally would gravitate either to the hospital or to the church, Adeline Oakley telephoned Thelma Goodrich, her close friend and college roommate of more than fifty years ago.

Karen Spencer continued to call family and friends of Walker who were not necessarily part of the First Church community. She spoke with retired Bishop O. Eugene Slater, retired Bishop Ben Oliphint, Walker's psychiatrist Dr. Dwight Holden, Walker's brother Gary, and Rabbi Zimmerman's secretary.

Accompanied by Detectives Stan McNear and Rick Silva and a police photographer, Lt. Waldrop arrived at Presbyterian Hospital around ten A.M. The police photographer went into the Intensive Care Unit to photograph Peggy's injuries.

Waldrop had ordered an examination by a police doctor of the marks on Peggy's neck to rule out attempted suicide. This was standard procedure. But he didn't for a minute think she had attempted to hang herself. There was no rope or cord. It was also difficult to know if the attempted murder was the work of a hired killer. No incriminating evidence such as a cord or garrote had been left behind. Nothing in the garage or house seemed out of place. Apparently there had been no struggle. The victim had no broken fingernails, nor were there scratch marks on her neck as if she had tried to tear off the ligature that was strangling her. Strangest of all, there were no bits of skin or fabric under her fingernails, which probably meant that she had not tried to fight off her attacker. Or perhaps there had been two people, one holding her hands down? Most ghoulish of all was the thought that someone might have taken the time to clean her fingernails. This last was unlikely because if the attacker was a professional assassin, he had certainly bungled it. To wrap the cord around the neck twice was the work of an amateur.

Lt. Waldrop introduced himself to Walker and to Bill and Billie Jo. Then he asked Walker to come downtown and talk about the assault on his wife.

Although the minister appeared emotionally exhausted and his speech slurred, he was not reluctant to leave with the detectives or to talk with them. He was anxious to tell his story, to help the police find the group or the disturbed person who had attacked his wife.

In Waldrop's office Railey told the detectives that shortly before six o'clock on the previous evening, April 21, he had telephoned Peggy on his new car phone that had been installed for his protection at Church expense just that afternoon. He drove into the garage about a half hour later where he said he found Peggy working on the garage latch with a bar of soap. She was trying to lubricate the spring on the latch that had been sticking. Since she and the children had already eaten, and, after his heavy lunch at the 2001 club, he decided to skip dinner. He sat on the hood of Peggy's Chrysler, and the two of them shared a glass of wine and talked for about ten minutes. He said that he told her before they left town on Friday, he needed to go to Bridwell and Fondren Libraries at SMU.

The research at the libraries took longer than he had anticipated. After three hours of checking and cross checking, he was still missing one necessary footnote. Twice he telephoned his wife and left a message on the answering machine saying that if she wanted to go ahead and lock the garage door, he would park his car in front of the house. He used the answering machine because he thought Peggy would be asleep, and she sometimes awakened during the night and checked the machine if he wasn't home. He made a final call to the answering machine, saying that the time was 12:29 and he was on his way home. Instead of parking out front, as he had said he would, he drove into his driveway that was off the back alley. The garage door was partly open, but the garage itself was dark. Bulbs had been removed from the overhead lights in the garage. Leaving the headlights of his own car on, Railey ducked under the garage door and found his wife lying at the back of the garage, writhing in convulsions.

He said he had no idea who would want to harm his wife except the unknown author of the threatening letters. The Raileys now had an unlisted number and the listed phone was always attached to an answering machine. Walker told Waldrop that he wanted to cooperate in every way possible.

And for over three hours the minister *had* been cooperative and polite, yet Waldrop felt that some of his statements were in conflict with what DeSpain had told him.

In the first place, why had Railey left his family alone at night and gone to the SMU libraries? Couldn't he have assigned one of the staff at First Church to do the research for him? Even if he preferred to pursue his own research, why had he chosen to visit the libraries late at night? And why had he driven to the back of the house when he had left the message on the answering machine that he would park in the front of the house? Who had removed the light bulbs from the fixture in the garage? Surely not Peggy Railey. Nor would Peggy step into the garage in the dark. Strangest of all, why on the tape in the answering machine had Railey told his wife to go into the garage when he knew that the garage was the only part of the house that was not safe? The situation was like a jigsaw puzzle in which the pieces in the box didn't match the picture on the cover.

9

AT TEN O'CLOCK ON WEDNESDAY MORNING APRIL
22, Mary Lou Schlashuber was talking on the telephone to a
friend. She was propped up in bed, still in her nightgown
and robe, drinking her third cup of coffee. Daryl and their
two children had left hours ago. Mary Lou had decided to
have a relaxing morning. She would go late in the afternoon
to the catering business that she and Daryl owned.

While still talking she adjusted her position in the bed
and glanced out the glass doors to the patio. She gasped.
Three men in dark business suits were walking around her
swimming pool.

"There are some strange men walking around my swimming pool," she told her friend. "If I don't call you back in
five minutes, call the police!"

She slammed down the receiver and slid open one of the
patio doors. Her hand held on to the door handle, so she
could close it quickly if she were threatened.

"Hey!" she shouted. "What are you doing on this property? This is a private residence. If you don't get off my
property right this minute, I'm going to call the police!"

The three men looked at her in surprise. "We *are* the
police," said a dark-haired young man who was closest to
her. He reached in his pocket and pulled out an identification wallet and badge that he held up in front of him. Mary
Lou stared at it. She didn't have on her glasses. The badge
was silver looking or maybe tin. How was she supposed to
know what a police badge looked like?

"Is this 9328 Trail Hill?" the man asked still holding the
badge for her inspection.

"No," she said. "That's down the street."

"This isn't the Railey residence?"

"No. This is the Schlashuber residence. What's happened? Is something wrong?"

"There was a break-in at the Railey house last night," one of the other men said. "We are sorry to have disturbed you."

"We'll leave through the back gate," said the man with the identification.

"The numbers of the houses are posted on the fences," Mary Lou told them. Then with an unexpected shiver down her spine, she asked: "Are the Raileys all right?"

"We don't know, ma'am. Mrs. Railey is at Presbyterian Hospital."

Mary Lou locked the patio door after the policemen had left through the back gate into the concrete alley that was used as a communal driveway to the garages attached to the houses. Then she called her friend and told her not to call the police because the men in her backyard *were* the police and that something awful must have happened to a Mrs. Railey who lived on her block.

They talked for fifteen minutes about what the world was coming to, with crimes taking place in a respectable neighborhood such as Lake Highlands. If it happened only four houses away it could happen to any of them. Mary Lou wondered if she ought to have told the policemen about the noise she and Daryl had heard around ten-thirty last night. Maybe they would come back and question her.

But they never did.

Rabbi Sheldon Zimmerman was at his home Wednesday morning when John Yarrington phoned with the news of the attack on Peggy. Within half an hour, he was at the Intensive Care Unit at Presbyterian Hospital. Walker was standing alone at the end of the hall.

The first thing Sheldon noticed about him was that he was wearing the same shirt and tie and sport coat that he had worn yesterday at lunch. Except for discarding the bulletproof vest, he hadn't changed clothes or shaved. Sheldon felt pity and compassion as he embraced his friend. How ironic that less than twenty-four hours ago, Walker had said what he feared most was an attack on his family.

John Yarrington joined them, telling them he was going home to rest now. Walker reminded him that George Monroe, the children's pediatrician, was scheduled to examine the children at the Yarrington's home that morning.

Dr. Monroe and his wife Lou Ann were waiting for Walker. Lou Ann hugged Walker, then Sheldon, and stood between them holding each of them by the hand.

"Walker, I have some bad news for you," George began. Lou Ann squeezed Sheldon's hand so tightly that his wedding ring cut into his finger as George explained that Ryan must have seen the attack. The assailant apparently had shoved him away, his hand around the child's neck, leaving choke marks of thumb and fingers, and broken blood vessels in his cheeks. Probably the boy had been choked unconscious.

"Oh, my God," Sheldon said.

Walker's eyes widened in a glazed, blank look, but he said nothing.

On Wednesday afternoon, *The Dallas Morning News* Religion Editor, Helen Parmley, was staring at her computer screen, looking at copy she had put together from the police report and a conversation with Howard Grimes. A handsome woman in her mid-fifties with dark brown eyes and long straight white hair pulled back smoothly and held by a black velvet bow, she was wondering when and if Railey would return her call.

Helen had covered the religion beat for over twenty years. Her two main contacts in the Methodist Church were Spurgeon Dunnam, editor of the weekly newspaper *The Methodist Reporter*, and Walker Railey, whom she had first met when he was in the seminary. She knew that many Methodist ministers resented so much publicity being given to Spurgeon and Walker, but they were the ones she could rely on when she needed a good quote.

Helen couldn't get Peggy Railey off her mind. For weeks she had known about the threatening letters but thought that they must have been sent by some group of crazies. Like many cities in the world today, Dallas was spawning its own peculiar cults. To publicize them, favorably or unfavorably, was not something either she or her paper believed in doing.

The telephone on her desk buzzed; she answered it immediately. Her fingers were poised on the computer keyboard.

Walker said, "Well, they got Peggy just like they said they would."

"Walker, I can't tell you how shocked and how sorry I am. I really don't know what to say."

"There's nothing anyone can say." Walker's voice cracked. "Just pray for Peggy and for the children and for me."

"I will." Helen cleared her throat and drew in her breath. "Walker, if you're not feeling up to an interview now, we can make it later."

"No. People expect me to say something. They want to know what I have to say. And I believe they have a right to know."

"Can you tell me how Peggy is now?"

"The doctors don't think she is going to make it. But I'm not giving up hope. Where there's life, there's hope." Mounting tension had raised the pitch of his voice. He paused, then lowered his voice. "Peggy was such a good mother."

Helen's fingers stumbled over the word *was*. Peggy wasn't dead yet.

Walker told her much the same story that he had told Lt. Waldrop at the police station. "Somebody's walking around out there who's hurt Peggy and who wants to hurt me and my children, too. Tell the police to get them."

"Walker, you have the love and support of the entire community."

"I appreciate that, Helen. I really appreciate that."

After the conversation was over, Helen put her head in

her hands. The Raileys were not the kind of people to whom this sort of thing happened.

Listening to Walker's side of the conversation with Helen, Reverend Susan Monts marvelled at his poise. Susan is a tall young woman with brown hair and brown eyes. Six years ago, while she was still at Perkins, she had met First Church new pastor Walker Railey, who persuaded her to come to First Church. Walker referred to her as his little sister, and, to her, he was an idolized older brother.

Now that they were alone with a police guard to keep anyone from just walking into the suite unannounced, Susan removed a ball point pen and a small notebook from her handbag. She had made a list of people, apart from the church staff, whom she'd thought he would most like to see. The list of about twelve names included Dr. Dwight Holden, Sheldon Zimmerman, Howard Grimes and Janet Marshall. "Any one else?"

"Dr. Lucy Papillon," Walker said.

"Lucy Papillon?" Susan was surprised. "I didn't realize you and Lucy Papillon were friends."

"She owes me one," Walker said. "She can pay me back for my support of her after her father died."

10

❧ THE YARRINGTON HOUSE ON BURNEY STREET WAS guarded by three marked squad cars with two uniformed patrolmen in each car. Diane had sent her own children to school but had kept Ryan and Megan locked in the house with her.

Megan was her usual buoyant self, cheerful and talkative

and constantly underfoot, yet if Diane was out of her sight for even a minute, she screamed and cried but did not venture from the spot where she was.

Nothing that Diane did or suggested held Ryan's attention for more than a few seconds. The visit from Dr. George Monroe had left Diane unnerved. Why had she not seen the marks on the boy's face last night? George had said that the marks would have become more noticeable in the morning. On Ryan's throat there was a bruise made by a thumb, and on the other side of his neck, almost behind his ear, were bruise marks from three fingers. She watched the child closely as he retreated into a silent, terrified world of his own.

Shortly after George left a woman from the police department arrived to interview Ryan. She took Ryan into John and Diane's bedroom, telling Diane that she preferred to speak with him alone.

Five minutes later the police woman returned to the family room, saying that Ryan would not talk, so Diane accompanied her back into the bedroom and sat on the bed beside Ryan, holding his hand.

The police woman asked him if he had seen someone hurt his mother. He nodded yes. When she asked him who the person was, he averted his eyes and said it was his friend Jim.

"Who?"

"Jim," the child stammered.

Neither woman could understand him. Diane remarked that he probably couldn't spell it.

"J-I-M!" Ryan said loudly.

Diane explained to the police woman that Jim Hardin was Ryan's best friend.

Looking from one adult to another, Ryan changed his story. "Maybe it was Jim's daddy."

The police woman waited a couple of minutes and then questioned him again. Becoming visibly more distressed, he admitted that it was a friend of his daddy's. And, finally, highly agitated, he whispered: "Maybe it was daddy."

* * *

John came home from the hospital early in the afternoon. He was still disturbed that the police had been so rough in their treatment of Walker, questioning him as if they thought *he* was a *suspect*. John was also disturbed by the grotesque, tortured appearance of Peggy. He told Diane that there was no way he could prepare her for the shock of seeing Peggy. "We've got to help Walker," he kept repeating over and over again. "It's terrible." Exhausted, John slept the rest of the afternoon while Diane attempted to distract the children with games and stories.

All day the telephone rang as news of the tragedy spread. Diane was afraid *not* to answer the phone for fear it might be the hospital with news of Peggy or perhaps Walker or maybe the Church with something that needed to be done.

At noon a telephone call came from Maxie Hardin, whom Diane knew only slightly. Maxie had heard of the attack and wondered if Diane would like her to bring Jim over to be with Ryan. Knowing the boys were best friends, Diane thought this would be good therapy for Ryan. She was explaining to Maxie about the police blockade on the street when John called her from their bedroom.

"You'd better get Walker's permission first."

Diane told Maxie that she would check with Walker at the hospital and then telephone her back. Both John and Diane got on the telephone with Walker.

"How is Peggy now?" John asked.

Walker said that there hadn't been any change.

"We're praying for her," John said.

Diane told him that the children were all right. Megan was taking her nap, and Maxie Hardin had offered to bring Jim over to be with Ryan. Walker hesitated and then said that the police didn't think that Ryan should be with other children right now. He thought that after all Ryan had been through, he should see a private psychologist first, and the sooner the better.

Diane reported to Maxie what Walker had said. She was grateful that Maxie didn't press her with any more questions.

* * *

When Maxie hung up the telephone, she put her head in her hands and cried. Why hadn't she telephoned Peggy last night and asked her why she was in such a hurry yesterday afternoon that she had ignored her? Something bad had happened to Peggy in the five hours between nine-thirty in the morning and two-thirty in the afternoon. Then something much worse had happened later in the evening. Had Peggy been suspicious or frightened? Would she have told Maxie? Peggy's best friend was her mother Billie Jo, but, if for some unknown reason, Peggy needed help and couldn't or didn't want to confide in her mother, she was sure Peggy would have turned to her. Peggy was not the type of woman who had lots of friends. She was a private person with only one or two confidantes.

Maxie rubbed her eyes with the back of her hand, dug into her jeans pocket for a tissue and blew her nose. It was just so bizarre that such a horrible thing could happen to a regular person like Peggy. She had tried to reach her husband Tim at his law office, but he had been at lunch with a client.

When he returned her call, Tim was equally shocked.

"Veta Boswell telephoned me," Maxie said. "She thought I already knew about Peggy. She was talking about how we could help Walker."

"I'll come home early," Tim said. "But maybe you ought to go on over to the hospital and see Walker now."

"Tim," Maxie began and then hesitated.

"Yes?"

"I know that Peggy didn't go into the garage by herself. And certainly not late at night. The garage was the only place in that house that wasn't safe."

"We'll have to wait until we know what the police report says," Tim replied.

Maxie arrived at Presbyterian around four in the afternoon. The first floor lobby looked like the entrance to a political convention. As she signed the book of those who had come to the hospital to show their concern, Maxie noted that at least thirty or forty people had been there before her. The sheer number of good people willing to share trouble and wanting to help brought a lump to her throat. One of the ministers' wives told her that the Nicolais were in the reception area upstairs and would want to see her. Stepping off the elevator on the second floor, Maxie recognized at least fifteen or twenty members of the Church, standing in clusters with solemn faces and speaking in hushed voices.

Across the room, apart from the others and sitting around a small square table, as if they were intending to play cards were the four Nicolais. Maxie hurried to greet them. She had never before seen Billie Jo sad or distressed. On the few times Maxie had been with her, Billie Jo seemed at least ten or twelve years younger than her true age of sixty-seven. Now her liquid brown eyes were so grief-stricken that tears came to Maxie's eyes, too, as they embraced. Billie Jo introduced her husband Bill and her son Ted and Ted's wife Linda, who was blond and soft-spoken and, like her husband, chain-smoked. After they shook hands, Ted pulled over a chair for Maxie that he placed beside Billie Jo's chair.

Even when they were all seated and exchanging information, Billie Jo held on to Maxie's hand. Maxie told them about seeing Peggy twice yesterday. For reasons she couldn't even explain to herself, she did not tell them about Peggy's strange behavior yesterday afternoon. Instead, she quickly asked what the doctors had said.

"The first forty-eight hours are the critical period," Bill stammered.

"She's going to come through this and be all right," Billie Jo said firmly. "I *have* to believe that."

Ted and Linda's expressions showed clearly that they did *not* believe that. So Maxie asked about Walker.

"That bastard's just loving all the attention and sympathy he's getting," Ted said bitterly.

Ted had been upsetting his parents most of his life. In adolescence he was constantly doing whatever his parents didn't want him to do. He drank, smoked, refused to study and did not graduate from high school, though later he got a

G.E.D. When Ted had seemed most incorrigible, a Catholic friend of Billie Jo's had given both Ted and her silver chain necklaces with medals of St. Jude, the patron saint of hopeless causes.

Unlike his sisters, Ted hadn't known what he wanted to do with his life. He married at twenty-one, had two children, divorced and left for Texas where he had been for ten years. During the past year, he had married Linda, who was older than he, a secretary who was divorced with two children.

By the time Maxie left Presbyterian Hospital, the story was on all three local television news reports and had been broadcast on radio stations several hours earlier. The evening newspaper, *The Dallas Times Herald,* carried it in the late edition, which was the one delivered to the residents. Friends, members of the Church and the simply curious congregated at both hospital and Church. What was a family tragedy soon became the fear and concern of the entire community. Was there really some organization that opposed Walker's preaching? Or was there some madman loose who might strike again? Were their children safe in the day care center or in the Sunday School classes? Was anyone safe at the church? Was anyone safe anywhere?

"Maybe it isn't just Walker," one young member said to another. "Someone crazy might have a grudge against the entire Church."

On that evening, they gathered in various little groups within the church, at the Crossroads Center, in the Goodrich Gallery, in the halls outside the administrative offices and in the main foyer. Ralph Shannon went from one small crowd to another telling them to go into the main sanctuary. "Gordon is going to give us the latest update on Peggy and then lead us in prayer."

Gordon was in his office with the door closed. He had just spoken with Walker who told him there was no change in Peggy's condition. What Walker had said chilled Gordon, shoving his thoughts toward a precipice he didn't want to cross.

"If I were a betting man, which you know I'm not," Walker had said, "I'd say the odds of her living through this are one in a million."

Gordon removed his glasses and rubbed his tired eyes.

The doctors were doing all they could do. The Church members should keep a constant vigil—like a death watch, he thought grimly—and pray for Peggy. All day he had spoken with Church members and listened to their conversations among themselves. It seemed to him incredible how frequently they said "Poor Walker" instead of "Poor Peggy." When Dede called from New York, he told her that this had seemed the longest day of his life, and it still wasn't over. She told him she would be back in Dallas the following afternoon.

It was seven o'clock. Gordon stood up behind his desk, ready to go into the sanctuary. Before replacing his glasses he closed his eyes in prayer. He asked the Lord whether he should pray for Peggy's recovery or for her release from suffering.

Inside the sanctuary were seven or eight hundred parishioners. Among them was the editor of *The Methodist Reporter*, the Reverend Spurgeon M. Dunnam, III, a man in his early forties with bushy brown hair, large eyes and thick, caterpillarlike eyebrows that met over the bridge of his nose. He was accompanied by his wife Dottie, their three natural children Daniel, Delilah and Delayna, and their foster child Irene Mugambi. The family had spent six months in Kenya a year earlier.

Spurgeon, too, had heard the theories of satanic cults and lone madmen. He had also heard enough of the "Poor Walker" comments to sicken him. If ever before he had doubted the solidarity of support for Walker, he no longer did. He and Walker had been associates for fifteen years, intellectual colleagues with different temperaments, liberals who often disagreed, ministers and competitors who knew each other well but who were not friends. As he looked at the hundreds of sorrowful, compassionate and naive faces in the congregation, including those of his own family, Spurgeon felt alone. He thought that he was the only person in the sanctuary who believed Walker Railey had attempted to murder his wife.

11

〰️ IN UNIVERSITY PARK, WILL LIEBER MIXED A DOUBLE martini with four pickled onions for himself and poured a glass of white wine for Charlotte who picked up the television remote control and turned on the "Channel Five Evening News."

Announcer Brad Wright said: "Peggy Railey, the wife of the popular Dallas Methodist minister Walker L. Railey, was found in her garage choked nearly to death early this morning. She lies in a coma at Presbyterian Hospital. Police are investigating."

"I don't believe it!" Charlotte screamed at the television.

Will took a swallow of gin. "The person who didn't shoot Walker on Easter choked his wife on Tuesday."

In the first commercial break Charlotte picked up a Princess style telephone on the table between their two matching blue Laz-E-Boy recliners. "I've got to call Betty."

The telephone rang only twice.

"Turn on the television, Betty. Channel five. Peggy Railey's been choked and is in Presbyterian Hospital about to die!"

"I know," Betty answered in a whisper. "We're looking at channel four, and Bobby's reading about it in *The Times Herald.*"

"Isn't it just terrible?"

"Who could have done such a thing?"

"Commercial's over! I'll call you back after the news is finished."

The telephone buzzed in Betty's ear. "Bobby, it was Charlotte."

"I heard her," Bobby replied staring at the television. "She was shouting so loud she didn't need to use the telephone. Just stick her head out the window and they'll hear about it in Oklahoma."

Betty pulled a Kleenex out of her blue jeans and blew her nose. She curled up on the end of the plaid sofa by the telephone. "It's silly, I know, but I feel as if there has been a death in the family."

"She isn't dead yet," Bobby said, "but she's not expected to live."

"And all because her husband spoke out against racists!"

"Maybe," Bobby said. "And then again, maybe there's something we don't know."

Across town in the northeast suburb of Garland, graphoanalyst Jane Buckner was reading *The Dallas Times Herald* before organizing the notes for her Thursday evening class. She had taught graphoanalysis in her apartment for five years now. There was never a shortage of students of all ages and from all backgrounds, but what she enjoyed more than teaching was analyzing the handwriting of criminal suspects and helping the law solve crimes. This study fascinated her and it was in this area that she hoped to establish her reputation and earn her living. She had never worked with the DA's office in Dallas, but she had recently helped to solve a case of fraud in West Texas. The Peggy Railey case interested her enormously. She could not imagine who would harm a minister's wife, yet she wanted to analyze the victim's handwriting, the handwriting of the minister and the handwritings of any suspects the police might have found. If the suspects were all racists, she wondered how similar their handwritings would be.

Thursday, April 23, 1987

REVEREND WALKER RAILEY'S WIFE IS CHOKED—
ATTACK MAY BE LINKED TO THREATS AGAINST PASTOR,
POLICE SAY

Helen Parmley's interview with Railey and a summary of what was known about the attack were front page news with a banner headline. Half of the telephone lines in Dallas were busy, and half of those that were busy were conversations about Peggy Railey.

As word spread that the popular minister's wife had been strangled, so did a sense of public outrage. Outrage such as had not been known in Dallas since that fateful day a quarter of a century earlier when a popular young president of the United States had been gunned down in the street.

Once again, the city turned inward. Why here? The question seemed to echo off the skyscrapers and along the freeways as commuters making their way to work listened to the news on car radios. Housewives watched the news on television and read the story by Helen Parmley in *The Dallas Morning News.*

Parmley reported that for the past eight weeks Railey had been receiving threatening letters. Most people in Dallas were vaguely aware of hate groups lurking on the edge of civilized society. But it had been years since organized hostilities had surfaced here. Now it seemed that a modern-day Ku Klux Klan was at work, actually attacking a woman whose only crime was to be married to a minister who preached racial equality. Perhaps it was a feeling of vulnerability as a group that compelled ministers to speak out first.

"It's the most horrendous thing I've heard since I've been in Dallas," said Reverend Dan Griffin, pastor of Cliff Temple Southern Baptist Church. "Our reputation keeps getting worse, despite all we do."

Walker's friend Rabbi Sheldon Zimmerman of Temple Emanu-El was careful not to incriminate the city itself. "I've received hate mail. I don't know any rabbi, priest or pastor who hasn't received some kind of hate mail."

But one of Railey's fellow Methodist ministers, Bourdon Smith of Northhaven Methodist, was not so kind to Dallas. "It's not the first time that ministers in this town have been threatened, and it won't stop with this one."

Indeed, there was a feeling that the city was somehow to blame for the attack on the minister's wife. *The Dallas Morning News* editorialized that, *"the vicious campaign against Railey and his family has sent alarms through the church community and city as a whole. The idea that someone would threaten to take lives to stifle public viewpoints is twisted, repugnant, chilling."*

The citizens of Dallas were so infuriated by what seemed to be a resurgence of racism and racial violence that the emotional response to the attack was stronger than the rational. Few newspaper readers even took in that Police Lt. Ron Waldrop was quoted as saying that the F.B.I. was examining the threatening letters and that there was no evidence to suggest a white supremacy conspiracy behind the attack.

Friday, April 24, 1987

Although Walker had said Ryan would have to see a psychologist, Diane Yarrington was surprised when a telephone call came around eleven A.M. from Dr. Lucy Papillon whose professional specialty was eating disorders.

Everyone knew that Lucy was the daughter of the late Bishop Robert E. Goodrich, Jr. Some of the older members of the congregation still referred to First Church as "the Church that Bob built."

As was expected of her, Lucy had graduated Phi Beta Kappa from SMU, married a minister and had two children. Nine years later as was *not* expected, she had divorced, earned a Ph.D. in psychology, married, divorced again, moved to California, appeared on television as a more glamorous Dr. Ruth; then she returned to Dallas where she legally changed her name to Dr. Lucy Papillon.

Now she asked if Diane would mind if she came over to the house and saw the Railey children. She said that she knew them and related particularly well to Ryan. Diane assumed that Walker had asked Lucy to come, just as he had asked the pediatrician Dr. George Monroe to come.

Two and a half hours later Lucy arrived. Diane noticed how attractive she was, as if she had just come from modeling in a fashion show. Wearing an expensive silk print two-piece dress with heavy gold jewelry and bone-colored high-heeled pumps, Lucy selected the big sofa with cushions and pillows. She had brought presents for the children—a cuddly rabbit for Megan and a complicated game for Ryan that would have been appropriate for a child twice his age.

Megan climbed into Lucy's lap, hugging both her and the bunny. Ryan kept his distance, glancing at her furtively, as if he didn't know her well. Diane sat on the floor and began reading aloud the directions to the game. No one was interested. Even in her own home Diane felt ill at ease with Lucy. She didn't know why. Lucy was friendly and caring in her actions toward the children, although clearly she did not have the special rapport with Ryan that she had claimed.

Once again the telephone rang, and since John had gone back to the hospital to be with Walker, Diane left to answer it in the kitchen. A few minutes later Megan came in dragging her rabbit by the ear, and hugged Diane around the knees.

When she returned, Diane was startled that Ryan and Lucy were not in the family room. A panicky feeling came over her. Then she heard their voices. Hand in hand the woman and the child walked back into the room.

"Are you going to come again?" Ryan asked Lucy.

"Do you want me to come again?"

"Yes! Yes!" he shouted. "And bring us more presents."

Lucy smiled. "What would you like me to bring you?" she asked Ryan.

"An alligator!" he screamed.

"You will have an alligator," Lucy said; then she asked Diane if she could drop by again. Diane said, "Of course."

* * *

One hour after Lucy had left, John Yarrington returned home. Susan Monts had worked out a flexible schedule where she, and other members of the staff would be with Walker, who was unable to sleep and was physically exhibiting dangerous signs of stress and exhaustion.

As yet Diane had not left the children or been to see Peggy. John had agreed to stay with the children this afternoon while she went to the hospital.

After all the things John had told her about Peggy's condition, she still was unprepared for Peggy's appearance. Peggy was even more bloated and bruised than she had imagined. Walker, who was standing at the foot of the bed, could barely look at her; but Billie Jo held her hand and spoke to her as if she had just closed her eyes and was simply resting for a while. Diane plugged in the recorder, put on a cassette with Peggy playing a Bach cantata. Then she placed the pictures of Ryan and Megan on the night stand beside the bed. Walker stared at his children without emotion as if the plastic frames were objects expected to clutter the nightstand beside a hospital bed. Gordon brought in a chair for Diane. While Billie Jo sat on one side of the bed, Diane sat on the opposite side and touched Peggy's arm. She bent over and whispered into her ear.

"Peggy, please come back. The children love you and need you. Walker loves you and needs you. John and I love you and need you." She was conscious of Gordon's standing close behind her chair, of Billie Jo caressing her daughter's hand and of Walker standing at the foot of the bed and looking down on all of them. "Peggy, you don't have to worry about Ryan and Megan. They are safe. They are staying with John and me. We're taking good care of them. But they miss you so. They want their mother."

"Look," Gordon said.

Tears trickled from the corners of Peggy's closed eyes. Diane, Billie Jo and Gordon bent closer to her, all speaking at once.

"Peg, it's Mom. We all love you and need you."

"Peggy, thousands of people are praying for you and sending you their love," Gordon said.

"Ryan and Megan, Ryan and Megan, Ryan and Megan," Diane whispered, over and over again, like a liturgy.

Suddenly, without moving any other part of her body, Peggy opened her eyes and for nearly five seconds looked directly at her husband standing at the foot of the bed. It was more than a blink. It was a steady, focused stare.

Walker stepped back, his eyes, as Gordon would later describe them, "widened in astonishment." Then Peggy closed her eyelids and could not be coaxed into opening them again or into giving any other response. Walker slowly backed out of the room and then bolted down the hall. Spotting Dede Casad, he ran into her arms. Dede had returned from New York that Thursday afternoon and gone straight to the hospital. She had not yet spoken with Walker and was waiting in the reception area with Howard Grimes and Ad Oakley.

"Dede, I didn't do it!" Walker said. His face was no more than six inches from hers. "If I had done it, I would have succeeded."

Dede was disconcerted. Taken by surprise, she stammered: "Why, Walker, there, there. I know you didn't do it. Why, well—there, there." She was babbling, hardly knowing what she was saying.

This strong man of God, this leader of thousands was trembling and pathetic in his fear. Had he *really* said what she thought she had heard him say? What did he mean that *if* he had done it, he would have succeeded? Never had it crossed her mind that *he* might have done it. He was a brilliant preacher, a man of God, a wonderful, young minister. Ministers don't attempt to murder their wives. That he claimed he would have succeeded was the strangest idea she had ever heard.

She pulled away from his clinging embrace to look at him, but he lowered his eyes and turned away, instinctively moving toward his adoptive mother Ad Oakley who opened her arms to him.

The Interfaith Prayer Service for Peggy Railey, held in Thanksgiving Square in downtown Dallas, was attended by three thousand people. In the large crowd Ralph Shannon could not get to Gordon either before or after the service. Gordon had spoken with eloquence and with hope. He was the new leader to whom people wanted to speak, to touch and to ask questions. In times of tragedy, the Lord always brings forth some person of strength. In this particular tragedy clearly that person was Gordon Casad.

Gordon had telephoned Ralph around six o'clock in the evening, before the prayer service. He told him in detail about the tears on Peggy's cheeks and the sudden opening of her eyes, before she lapsed back into a coma.

"Do you think that there is a chance she might recover and identify her attacker?" Ralph asked.

"The Nicolais and Diane are expecting just that to happen."

"And the doctors?"

"They aren't so optimistic."

"The Lord works in mysterious ways," Ralph said. Then he told Gordon that Walker had already received over a hundred cards and notes of hope and sympathy, as well as numerous telegrams, including one from Billy Graham and one from the Reverend Jesse Jackson.

"Those telegrams must have made him feel better," Gordon replied without the slightest note of sarcasm entering his voice.

As Gordon spoke with Ralph, the telephone rang at Paramedic Blair Berry's apartment. She had just stepped out of the shower after washing her hair. Paramedics work shifts of two days and two nights, and then have off the next two days and nights, or forty-eight hours. Blair had worked with Mark Tuesday and Wednesday. Today she had stayed at home, taking life easy, watching the television news broadcasts and reading the newspaper articles about Peggy Railey. She couldn't get that incident off her mind.

At six-thirty P.M. she threw on her bath robe, wrapped a towel around her wet hair and answered the telephone. A man's voice with an unnatural sounding East Texas accent asked: "Is this Nancy Berry?"

Nancy was Blair's mother's name. Although she was christened Nancy Blair Berry, Blair had always been known by her middle name. Her mother was Nancy.

"No," Blair answered truthfully.

"Are you a paramedic?" The voice sounded like a thug's; the twang was very pronounced.

"Yes."

Then the man said: "I don't know what you did, but she was dead when I left her. When you came into the garage, your being a girl confused me. If you ever get a call to respond to that address again, let the police arrive first."

Blair was more shocked than frightened. Before she could reply, she heard a click in the phone and then the buzz of the dial tone. After thinking the matter over a few minutes while she towel-dried her hair, she concluded that, apart from Mark only four men had seen her in that garage on Trail Hill Drive—two policemen, the next door neighbor and Walker Railey. She wasn't frightened, but she didn't want to be foolish. Someone had threatened her, someone who had taken the trouble to discover her unlisted telephone number, which wasn't an easy thing to do. Someone believed that she knew more about the murder attempt than she did. Whoever had attacked Peggy Railey was dangerous and sadistic.

She called her supervisor at the Fire Department. He telephoned Police Detective Stan McNear who, in turn, telephoned the F.B.I. For the next three weeks Blair's telephone was tapped. She did inside work at the station, not going out on a single call. Nothing more happened.

She was never interviewed by the police.

12

IT WAS AFTER TEN P.M. AND THE REVEREND SUSAN Monts was exhausted. No one was left in the hospitality room at the hospital. Only Howard Grimes was upstairs with Walker in his suite; Susan decided that it would be all right to retire to her room on the tenth floor. It was between the Nicolais' and Walker's rooms. No one else would be coming to see Walker at this late hour, and Howard would stay with him as long as he wanted company.

She walked to the elevators and pushed the up button. When the elevator doors parted directly in front of her, she was startled to find herself face to face with Lucy Papillon. Lucy smiled. In her hand was a glass bud vase, which contained a single red rose.

"Going up?" Lucy asked.

"No. Not just now. I'm going down."

Lucy smiled again as the elevator doors closed. Susan was astonished that Lucy would come to the hospital so late. She was certain that the rose was for Walker, and yet, Lucy had not stopped on the second floor to ask if Walker was able to see her. She had known that he wanted to see her and that she didn't have to ask permission from Susan or any other member of the Church staff. Susan was shocked by the unworthy thought that sprang into her mind—surely she must be wrong.

Howard was also stunned by Lucy's appearance, though Sheldon noted that Walker appeared to have been expecting her. She placed the rose on an end table and then sat demurely on the edge of the sofa.

The two men, who had risen upon her entrance, sat down

101

again, Howard on a straight-back chair and Walker on a lounge chair near Lucy. He took her hand, lacing his fingers through hers. *Like teenagers in love,* Howard thought, appalled at their brazenness.

"Howard, it's late and Johnnie Marie will be worrying about you," Walker said.

"She knows where I am," Howard replied, looking at Walker and Lucy disapprovingly. He was amazed at how natural they seemed as a couple.

Howard had known Lucy most of her life. As Director of Communications for the Church, Howard along with Jo Anne Hill, the executive producer of the show "Faith Focus," had introduced Lucy and Walker. Lucy had appeared on the show with Walker and Howard had thought how well they complemented each other. He had not imagined anything more. "I'm not tired," he told Walker almost belligerently.

The First Church ministers had all agreed that one of the staff should be with Walker at all times until he retired for the night. It was Howard's night tonight, and he was not about to shirk his duty.

"Well, you *look* tired," Walker said. "A man your age and in poor health needs his rest. Go on home now. I'm in better shape than you are."

"I'll leave when I'm ready," Howard answered in an aggrieved voice.

He shifted his frail body on the hard chair and crossed one thin leg over the other. Lucy and Walker were whispering to each other. *Like adolescents, insensitive to everyone but themselves,* he thought.

"I am tired," Walker said. "I would appreciate your leaving now because I need some therapy. I need to talk with Dr. Papillon alone."

Howard had forgotten Lucy was a psychologist. Therapy was what Walker needed. He felt relieved. "Walker, I hope you will get some rest," he said, rising.

"I will," Walker replied, his lips twisted in a sideways smile that seemed to Howard almost a smirk. As always, Walker was an enigma.

13

〰️ CHARLOTTE LIEBER DROVE TO DALLAS–FORT Worth Airport late on Saturday afternoon. It was a clear and cool day for a Texas spring. Last month there had been a rare snowstorm in Dallas, the first snowstorm in March in over fifty years. This afternoon the sky was blue and cloudless, a typical Texas sky. Off the freeway leading to the airport were clusters of wild flowers, bluebonnets that were a deeper blue than the sky, reminding Charlotte of school art exhibits. Everyone in Texas painted bluebonnets until the real thing resembled picture post cards and motel art instead of the other way around. There were also Indian paintbrushes and sunflowers and yellow fields of mustard as well as pink, petunia-type flowers that Charlotte couldn't identify.

At the airport she collected her friends Ann and Charles Nichols who had returned from a month's holiday in Europe. They drove through the exit toll gate from the airport. Ann was talking about the plays they had seen in London and about the antique china they had found in Wales when Charles interrupted and asked Charlotte if anything exciting had happened in Dallas while they were away.

"You are never going to believe what has happened in Dallas."

"What?" Ann and Charles asked in unison. They had known Charlotte for over forty years and understood that she was too pragmatic to be animated about anything that wasn't really sensational.

"Walker Railey's wife Peggy was attacked in their garage. She was strangled, but she didn't die. She's in a coma."

"That's horrible," Ann said.

The Nichols, like the Liebers and the Eubanks, had attended First Church since they were children and left only when their own children chose to go to Highland Park Methodist Church to be with their friends. The Nichols are a civic-minded, socially prominent couple whose families have resided in Dallas for several generations. Married for over thirty years, they are seldom apart and seem more like best friends than husband and wife.

"Poor Walker," Charlotte continued. "Can you imagine anything worse?"

"Is she expected to live?" Charles asked.

"She's on the critical list and—I don't know, of course—but some people say her brain is gone and that if she does live, she'll be nothing but a vegetable."

"Who would *do* a crazy thing like strangle a minister's wife?" Ann asked.

"Somebody or some group who didn't like Walker and what he was preaching."

Ann frowned. "Then why didn't whoever it was strangle *him* instead of *her?*"

"I don't know," Charlotte said, turning her new Cadillac Seville off the freeway and on to Royal Lane. "Will and I and the Eubanks went to hear him on Easter Sunday, and the sermon made me so angry, I said I'd never go back to that church again."

"Why did it make you angry?" Charles asked.

"It was all about death and Christ's Crucifixion being a conspiracy and, I don't know—I couldn't follow it too well—but it was depressing."

"It sounds depressing."

"But that sermon wasn't the reason Peggy got strangled," Charlotte continued. "Betty Eubank found out that Walker had been receiving threatening letters for nearly three months."

"What does Roberta say?" Ann asked.

Ann's and Charlotte's deceased mothers had been close friends with Roberta.

"You'll no doubt have a letter and a copy of the Easter sermon from Roberta in your pile of mail," Charlotte said.

"No doubt," Ann answered grimly.

"There's something about this story that isn't right," Charles said thoughtfully.

Charles Nichols was not the only person in Dallas who felt that something wasn't right about the Railey case. Bill and Carol Arnold were in their den listening to the local news on television.

"I didn't know Peggy Railey well," Carol told Bill during a commercial. "She was the music teacher at Ursuline and I didn't study music, but I do remember seeing her in the halls at school. She was young and friendly—always said hello to everyone."

"There's just something not right about this attack," Bill said. "I'm no longer a prosecuting attorney, but I can't see some organization like the Ku Klux Klan attempting to murder a minister's wife because they don't like the liberal ideas a minister is preaching."

"It would make more sense if they tried to murder him, wouldn't it?"

"Exactly. Murdering the minister's wife isn't going to stop the minister from preaching."

"I can't imagine anyone wanting to murder Peggy Railey. She just wasn't the sort to have that kind of enemies."

"Ministers and their wives aren't usual candidates for murder," Bill replied. "There's something about this case that just isn't logical. We haven't been told all the facts yet. And when we are told, I'll bet a lot of people, including us, are going to be surprised."

The four men went into the Railey house together. The two policemen sat on the sofa in the living room. Walker headed straight for the garage with Sheldon following. He unlocked the trunk of his tan Honda and removed his briefcase, which he quickly opened and checked. Seemingly satisfied, he took the case with him, telling Sheldon that here, in the garage, was where the attack had taken place, near the refrigerator. He pointed to the spot where Peggy had been lying. Sheldon looked around him at what seemed to be a perfectly ordinary, unremarkable garage. The banality of evil. The ordinariness and the quietness. A small bicycle, a tricycle, an old refrigerator and the two cars, dark and strangely ominous in the sunlight. The gasoline heaviness of the air was warm and oppressive.

Inside the house, Walker became more nervous. When they were in the bedroom, he opened the drawers to his dresser and mumbled, "See, see. They've already been through everything."

Sheldon thought that the drawers of socks and underwear and pajamas were extremely tidy. Walker already had told him that he had given the police permission to search the place. Walker looked in his own closet and then went into Ryan's room where he rummaged through drawers and then began throwing clothes from the child's closet.

Sheldon attempted to stop him. "What are you doing?"

Walker said he was looking for Ryan's windbreaker, "A white jacket just like mine."

"What's so important about a coat?" Sheldon asked. "Let the Yarringtons come get his clothes later."

Walker ignored him, and Sheldon suddenly was hypnotized by a nursery rhyme which Peggy had embroidered and framed and hung on Ryan's wall.

> *Peter, Peter Pumpkin Eater*
> *Had a wife and couldn't keep her*
> *Then he put her in a pumpkin shell*
> *And there he kept her very well.*

For some inexplicable reason the familiar verse seemed perversely appropriate. Peggy's helpless, comatose state a kind of closed pumpkin shell. Walker brushed Sheldon aside and headed across the living room toward the kitchen.

He was oblivious to the policemen. "I've got to find that jacket."

Sheldon followed him into the kitchen where he was struck by an uncanny feeling that the answer to the mystery lay here. While the atmosphere of the garage was eerie, the kitchen reeked of lingering terror. Sheldon caught his breath. Whatever terrible encounter had happened had surely happened here. Yet, the room was immaculate. Peggy's blue apron with the duck motif hung on the back of the pantry door. The kitchen counters were clear. The only items that were out of place were Megan's straw hat, which was on the breakfast table, and one of the brown, upholstered breakfast chairs on rollers that appeared to have been shoved about twelve feet across the room, its back against some cupboards.

Walker paced the room, his fists clenched, like a child about to have a temper tantrum.

"Get hold of yourself," Sheldon said, seizing him by the shoulders. "There's no jacket in here."

Walker broke away and headed back toward his bedroom. He sat down on the bed. Rocking back and forth, he cried, "I've got to find Ryan's coat!"

"What does it look like?"

"It's a windbreaker. With a zipper down the front and a drawstring around the waist."

Sheldon sat down beside him. He had never seen Walker behave like this. Why was the child's coat so important?

When Sheldon and Walker and the policemen returned to the hospital, it was early in the afternoon.

Holding Walker's briefcase, Sheldon went up in the elevator with him. The two policemen, who were carrying Walker's suitcase and a stack of books he had selected hurriedly, took the briefcase from him.

There was a reception area in the main lobby where friends and sympathizers could sign their names in a register. On the second floor was another reception area adjacent to the Intensive Care Unit. The second floor was closed to people who were not involved in the Railey case. Uniformed guards were everywhere.

Walker entered the room and headed straight for the telephone, punched some numbers and waited for a reply. Having checked the suite, the two guards left the room. Sheldon moved toward the door after them. Walker smiled and waved a flat-handed "see you later" sign. "Got an urgent call from Helen Parmley at *The Dallas Morning News,*" he said.

Billie Jo Nicolai had never been so tired in her life. The hospital held a dreamlike quality for her. The schedule was so precise, the routine so regulated that she was able to get through the day without even thinking about what she was doing. This was a saving grace, this and her belief that some morning Peggy would wake up and be all right and tell the police who had attacked her. The doctors explained to Billie Jo and Bill that all cases of this sort were different; sometimes a patient came out of a coma in five days or five weeks or even as long as five years. Some functioned quite well with only partial brain damage, others remained in what they called a persistent vegetative state, which meant that they were helpless both mentally and physically. Still others never came out of the coma, yet remained alive when the life supports were disconnected. Billie Jo could not imagine disconnecting a life system no matter what condition her child was in. As long as there was life, there was hope. She and Bill just had to keep on hoping and praying for a miracle.

The Nicolais' only respite from the hospital was occasionally visiting Billie Jo's nephew who lived in a nearby suburb or spending an afternoon with their grandchildren at the Yarringtons. John Yarrington stayed at least a part of every day with Walker, more time than anyone else, except Ad Oakley. When the Nicolais stayed with Ryan and Megan and the Yarringtons' adopted seven-year-old daughter Barbara, Diane had time to run her errands and to be with Peggy.

Billie Jo thought she was glad that Ryan and Megan were with the Yarringtons who were such good parents to their four children, two of whom were adopted and to over thirty foster children who had been in their care over the past twelve years. She could understand why Walker and Peggy had asked them to take the children should anything happen to them. And yet, certain aspects of the arrangement disturbed her. Having been around the hospital for three days among Church staff and members of the Church, she could not help but hear gossip and rumors, particularly about Walker. One of the rumors she had heard whispered shocked her so that she confronted John with it.

"John," she had said in an off-hand manner when Diane was present, "there are rumors that you and Walker are homosexual lovers."

John answered flippantly in an affected, effeminate voice: "He's not my type." Then he left the room.

That was not exactly a straight answer, yet it was not a subject Billie Jo felt comfortable discussing. It did not occur to her to wonder why she felt more at ease asking John than Walker. She never even thought of asking Walker.

And when she did think of talking with Diane, she had lost the initiative. Diane returned to the hospital almost immediately after John had left.

Billie Jo wondered if Peggy had confided to Diane problems that Billie Jo didn't even know Peggy had. Diane confided her problems to Peggy. Of this Billie Jo was certain. One afternoon at the lake, when Diane's name entered the conversation, Peggy had lifted her eyebrows and rolled her eyes. "Mom, let's not talk about it," she had said. "Diane has the worst problems of anyone I know."

Billie Jo wondered what a minister's wife might consider "the worst problems." She knew little of Peggy's and Walker's problems or intimate life. She was still reeling from the police inspector's assertion that Walker was having an extramarital affair. That was the last problem she would have imagined Peggy having. Less than a year after Walker and Peggy were married, they had met the Nicolais for a vacation in Arkansas. Billie Jo would never forget one evening when she and Walker were sitting on the front porch overlooking the lake.

Walker had casually remarked to her that he could easily lead a celibate life. Billie Jo was astonished and even more taken aback that he had told her. It was hardly the sort of spiritual admission a mother-in-law expects from the young husband of her newly wed daughter.

Her mind was muddled. Each day it seemed to her that more and more people came to the hospital, mainly to comfort Walker, of course, but many whom she didn't even know came over to her and Bill, too. Bishop Russell had come with Retired Bishop Stowe, who had appointed Walker to First Church. Every day Bishop Emeritus Eugene Slater had come to pray with Bill and Billie Jo and Ted. In his concern for Peggy and for Walker he had not forgotten them.

To almost everyone, including Billie Jo, Eugene Slater looks and acts the way a bishop should. In his eighties he is a trim, well-dressed man with thick, white hair and gentle brown eyes. His demeanor is modest, which is unusual today for a man who has been chosen by his associates for the Episcopacy. Billie Jo sensed he was not only a godly man but a kindly man. She asked him to be Peggy's pastor now.

Bishop Slater was surprised when Billie Jo asked him to become Peggy's pastor, though not as surprised as he had been seven years ago when Walker Railey, whom he had never met before, stopped by his office at Perkins School of Theology to tell him that he was being appointed senior minister at First Church and wanted Slater to be his personal pastor.

He had told Walker that he was removed from politics in this Church Conference. Retired Bishops maintain their religious affiliations in the Episcopacy. Bishop Slater's wife had her membership at Highland Park Methodist. Walker said that was all right with him. And so, believing it his duty *not* to turn away any of God's children, Eugene Slater had become Walker's pastor.

Every six months or so Walker would come by for lunch or dinner, always alone, never with Peggy. The Slaters were sometimes included in the Railey family gatherings. Frequently they attended early service at Highland Park and then the eleven o'clock service at First Church. It was part of their mission to help Walker and to support him in his career, though the Bishop had noticed a disturbing difference in Walker since the 1984 National Conference in Baltimore. There was a new "swagger in Walker's stride that was obviously egotistical" and he seemed to think of himself as "high and mighty." *This young man needs help,* Bishop Slater thought, *I must pray for him.*

With the attack on Peggy and with the Nicolais wanting him to be Peggy's pastor, too, Bishop Slater felt a deep obligation not only to those involved in the tragedy but to the Church as well. At times like this the Church must appear strong and decisive, a tower of strength to those confused and in danger of losing their faith.

After his conversation with the Nicolais, Bishop Slater telephoned Bishop Russell and offered to be of counsel and to help ease this difficult situation in any way that would assist the family or the Church. Bishop Russell politely thanked him and said that he was in daily counsel with Bishop Stowe.

The organization of the Methodist Church is a democratic, connectional structure with a hierarchy of conferences. There are annual conferences to which both ministers and lay people are delegates. Every four years in July there are also jurisdictional conferences and a general conference in April. Every five years there is a world conference. Bishops possess the power of governing and ordaining; they are elected at jurisdictional conferences and assigned to their conferences by the Episcopal Committee of the Council of Bishops, which is concerned with doctrine, discipline and policy. Each Conference bishop has district superintendents who assist in administration. The philosophies behind the organization of the Methodist Church are government of the Church by the episcopacy (bishops), which was derived from Catholic and Anglican Churches, and preaching the gospel through itinerant preachers who travel from place to place. Like all democratic, power-structured organizations, the Methodist Church is political.

* * *

Ralph Shannon was all too familiar with Church politics and with Walker's moods. He was one of the few lay members of the Church who knew that for the past eighteen months Walker had been seeing a psychiatrist at Timberlawn, the city's oldest and most exclusive private psychiatric hospital. From past experience Ralph knew that Walker's periods of depression were frequently followed by highly active and often extravagant behavior. While the salary for the senior minister at First Church was over eighty thousand dollars a year, there was also a generous expense account. Responsible for discretionary funds and expense accounts, Ralph asked Walker to return to him his American Express card.

A fear permeated not only First Methodist but the entire city, with parishioners of all faiths believing that if it happened once, it could happen again. The general consensus now was that a madman with a grudge against clergymen had attacked Peggy Railey. If that madman was still at large, no minister or his family was safe.

"The letters figure strongly in the course of our investigation, but that's not the only motive we're considering," Police Captain John Holt said in a newspaper interview. *"We're keeping an open mind. We're pursuing some other leads that have come in."* What other leads, he did not specify.

14

Monday, April 27, 1987

SIX DAYS AFTER THE ATTACK ON PEGGY RAILEY, Maxie Hardin telephoned Detective Rick Silva. The more she thought about the attack and the more she discussed it with Tim, the more convinced she became that whatever had upset Peggy that last day had something to do with the attack.

Rick Silva listened and then asked her if she knew of any troubles in the Railey household. Maxie replied that "Peggy had never indicated any serious discord, though she had the same gripes a lot of women have, wishing he would come home more, wishing he would help more with the children. He was completely consumed with the Church, and she was totally devoted to her children. They were moving in opposite directions, but I thought they were content. I thought they had made peace. They were very Christian toward each other."

Silva asked her if she knew anything about Peggy's journal, written on lined yellow legal pads, which Peggy kept hidden in the linen closet and which the police had confiscated. Maxie said she did not.

Silva then questioned her as to *why* Peggy's behavior less than eight hours before the attack made Maxie anticipate violence.

"We've been good friends for over two years, Peggy never before ignored me or avoided me. She wasn't like that," Maxie explained. "She would have confronted me if something were the matter between us. And, I'm sure that never, ever would she have gone into her garage at night when she knew that the garage was the only unsafe part of the house.

Peggy would never expose her children to any unnecessary danger, however slight the danger might be."

A couple of days later Maxie was surprised when Walker dropped by her house and inquired if she knew anything about Peggy's journal. Again she truthfully said that Peggy had never told her about the journal.

On Thursday, April 30, police had interviewed Walker again and then released to the press the information that the threatening letters to Walker Railey had all been written by one person and on one typewriter at First Methodist Church. This news prompted a new round of speculation and gossip. If the letters were all typed by one person on one typewriter in First Methodist Church, did that mean only one person—some crackpot with a grudge against Walker— was responsible for the attack on Peggy? Or could it be that one person had sent the letters on behalf of a particular group who opposed Walker's ideas? And was that person a member of First Church, perhaps even someone on the staff?

Susan Monts read the newspaper early that morning and then telephoned Karen Spencer. They spoke for only a few minutes; then Susan was on her way downtown to the church. Although it was the rush hour, the drive on Central Expressway from the hospital to the church took only fifteen minutes.

Inside the church Susan and Karen walked up the wide, vinyl-covered steps to the third floor where Reverend Jim Reeves, who was semiretired, had an office on the third floor. This area of the church building was an area seldom seen by anyone not at the core of the Church's activities. On the second floor was a seldom used study which Walker had sequestered for his private use when he didn't want to be disturbed by his staff. This area of the church building hadn't been remodeled or decorated in fifty years.

The two women stood in front of Walker's locked door for a moment, drew in their breaths and silently prayed that what he had told them would be true. Only a few days ago he had mentioned to each of them separately that he had been using Jim Reaves's typewriter because the typewriter in his hide-away office was broken.

The two women entered the office cautiously. There it was in the middle of the desk, an old fashioned electric typewriter that looked like a relic from the 1950s. Karen touched the keys. They were locked. It wouldn't work. It *was* broken. She gave a sigh of relief and then began to laugh. Susan laughed, too. They both laughed until there were tears in their eyes. How could they ever have thought Walker would lie to them?

Friday, May 1

On Friday afternoon, the usual crowd of Susan Monts, John Yarrington, Gordon Casad, Howard Grimes, Bishop Slater and a dozen or so other clergymen, some from First Church, some from other Methodist Churches, others from Churches of all denominations, as well as laymen like Ralph Shannon, Janet Marshall, Diane Yarrington, Maxie Hardin, Ad and Knox Oakley and Ken and Lynn Menges visited the hospital and talked. They whispered among themselves. Like a Greek chorus they repeated the same words—inside the Church—typewriter inside the Church—betrayal, betrayal. They attempted to find some logical explanation for what was beyond logic. If someone from the Church had assaulted Peggy, wouldn't that person next attempt to murder Walker or his children? The threatening letters had mentioned all members of the family. Why was Walker now so cavalier, so seemingly unconcerned about his own safety?

On the evening of Friday, May 1, Walker, Bill and Billie Jo made the last of the six daily visits to the Intensive Care Unit where Peggy lay motionless, her eyes closed, her face blue and bloated.

"Hello, Peg," Billie Jo said in a cheerful voice. "We are all here with you. Walker, Bill and me." She touched her daughter's hand and kissed her forehead. "We love you."

Peggy made no response. Her eyes remained closed. There was no change in her appearance. She was the same as she had been when Billie Jo first saw her after the attack eight days ago. Neither Bill nor Walker spoke. The only sound in the pale green, wedge-shaped room was the hissing of the breathing machine.

Billie Jo spoke of Ryan and Megan and how much they missed their mother. She said Diane and John were looking after them well. There was nothing for Peggy to worry about.

"Megan did a funny thing this afternoon," Billie Jo continued. "Walker, would you like to tell Peggy what Megan said to you?"

Walker's expression was blank. He hadn't the faintest notion to what she was referring. With a helpless shrug of his shoulders, he shook his head no.

"Then I'll tell Peggy," Billie Jo said, picking up her daughter's hand and holding it between both of hers. "There were several ministers gathered at the Yarringtons, and Walker was more or less lecturing to them about the issues that would emerge at the forthcoming regional conference. Megan was walking by when Walker changed thought in the middle of a sentence. 'Megan, babykins, come here and give Daddy a hug,' he said. 'Daddy needs all the love he can get now.' Megan stomped right past him, shaking her head from side to side like the pendulum on a clock—'Yak, yak, yak, yak, yak,' she said and marched out of the room."

Walker offered no more response than Peggy. He just stood at the foot of the bed, staring at his wife's bruised eye lids. His stare was intense and piercing. To Billie Jo it seemed as if he were sending thought waves, as powerful as any hypnotist could. The stare made her uneasy.

When the Nicolais and Walker returned to the hospitality room, only Knox and Adeline Oakley were there. It was nine P.M., and everyone else had gone home.

Ad hugged Walker and patted him gently on the back. It was a light, tender caress to which Walker responded by leaning his head against hers. They were truly mother and son in spirit if not in flesh. Billie Jo felt sorry for Chester and Virginia Railey who had not lived up to Walker's expectations of what his parents should be. She still kept in touch with them at Christmas, but she did not know how many years had passed since Walker had returned home to Owensboro. She had ceased to inquire about them because Peggy agreed with Walker. The elder Raileys had not been good parents, mainly because they were drunks—not alcoholics, just drunks.

There are not many women tougher than a former Navy gunnery instructor from World War II, but Billie Jo suspected Ad Oakley might be one of them.

Ad was opinionated and quick to take offense. When angered, her eyes narrowed and her throat reddened. Her voice rose reverberating with sarcasm and hostility. If sufficiently provoked, she shouted. Her anger was personal, not directed at situations, but at individuals. Ad was not a person to have as an adversary. Half a dozen or so years older than Billie Jo, she had been raised in an educated, religious, upper-middle-class family. Her brother had been the senior minister at Highland Park Methodist. Like Walker, Ad expressed her convictions, which were never wishy-washy because she didn't give two slaps about anybody's approval. She had been kind to both Walker and Peggy. Knowing Peggy had skin allergies and could only wear gowns that were washed in Ivory Soap flakes, Ad got permission to take home the hospital sheets each night, wash them and bring them back the next day. She cooked fresh crisp bacon for Walker and brought it to the hospital each morning. Walker didn't like hospital breakfasts.

Bill and Knox had taken two straight chairs a distance away from the comfortable brown tweed chairs where Walker now sat between Ad and Billie Jo. Slumped between the two women, he reached for the hands of his adoptive mother and his mother-in-law. His palms were cold and sweaty, and Billie Jo was aware of his heavy breathing. Each day he had worn a dark suit, a white shirt with a stiff collar and a conservative tie. It was as if he were prepared for his ministerial duties. Bill and Knox wore sport shirts and slacks.

"We have to live each day at a time, Walker," Billie Jo said. "We have to be patient and pray. We have to believe in God's mercy and that Peggy is going to live and be all right."

Walker looked straight ahead, and Ad's eyebrows wrinkled closer, the corners of her mouth twitched tightly downward. She patted Walker's hand in a manner that made Billie Jo feel excluded and told Walker that he looked tired. She reminded him that he had a difficult day tomorrow, another interview early in the morning with the police who wanted to ask him about "inconsistencies in his account of his actions and whereabouts the night his wife was attacked." Then his brother Gary was arriving in Dallas in the early afternoon.

Billie Jo knew that Peggy resented Gary's impositions and intrusions into their lives. Two years ago, Walker checked Gary into Baylor Hospital where it was discovered that he had a brain tumor. Gary had no job and no insurance; Walker paid seven thousand dollars for the operation and the hospital care. Of course, neither Walker nor Peggy believed that Gary would ever reimburse them, whatever he promised. And whenever Gary's name was mentioned, Peggy recalled all the things that they could have bought for themselves and the children with seven thousand dollars. Billie Jo understood the way she felt. Walker either ignored her or flew into a rage.

Now he finally broke the silence. Looking first at Ad and then at Billie Jo, he asked if they thought it would be all right if he went to his suite now.

"Of course," Billie Jo said, as once again Ad embraced him.

He kissed Ad first and then Billie Jo before he rose to shake hands with Knox and Bill. Billie Jo watched the sag of his shoulders and the clenching and flexing of his damp hands as he walked toward the door. He was the doomed protagonist in a Greek tragedy.

When Walker reached the door, he turned back and looked with blood-shot eyes first at Ad and then at Billie Jo. "I love you both very much," he said.

* * *

THE DEMON INSIDE

The following morning Walker did not appear for the eight o'clock visit with Peggy. This was not unusual. He had missed visits before, especially those in the mornings, so Bill and Billie Jo went into the Intensive Care Unit alone. At a quarter of nine, the operator telephoned Walker's suite and received no answer. At five minutes to nine, a security guard knocked on the door to his suite. Lt. Ron Waldrop and Detective Inspector Stan McNear were waiting to interrogate him at police headquarters at nine-thirty. Still there was no answer. The door was locked from the inside with a chain. Alarmed, two security officers broke into the room and found him fully dressed and sprawled across his bed; he was unconscious, but alive. An empty bottle of prescription drugs and a four-page, handwritten letter lay on a desk nearby. An emergency medical team rushed him to Intensive Care on the second floor, the same unit where Peggy was.

Now husband and wife lay within a few yards of each other both unconscious and both in critical condition.

PART II
The Idol Shepherd

"Woe to the idol shepherd that leaveth the flock! The sword shall be upon his arm, and upon his right eye: His arm shall be clean dried up, and his right eye shall be utterly darkened."

Zechariah 11:17

PART II

The Idol Shepherd

"Woe to the idol shepherd that leaveth the flock!
the sword shall be upon his arm, and upon his right eye:
his arm shall be clean dried up, and his right
eye shall be utterly darkened."

—Zechariah 11:17

15

TED NICOLAI SAT ALONE IN THE HOSPITALITY ROOM, drinking coffee, smoking and waiting for his parents to return from their early morning visit to the Intensive Care Unit.

They had been gone longer than usual. He grew weary. There was much more noise than usual, the thud of rubber-soled shoes, the metallic squeak of wheels and the bump of a cart against the plaster walls.

Ted stood up just as a nurse brought his parents out through the swinging doors. The elevator opened in front of him and two young interns in green surgical suits and caps stepped out, hurrying toward the swinging doors.

Ted shouted to them all, "What has happened to my sister?"

The interns did not answer but the nurse accompanying his parents approached him and spoke in a soothing voice.

"Your sister's condition is the same. Dr. Railey has taken an overdose of pills. He, too, is in Intensive Care."

Ted felt as if he had been struck on the back of the head. "Walker tried to kill himself?"

The expression on his parents' faces told him this was true.

123

"That bastard tried to kill my sister!" he screamed, flailing his arms and kicking the leg of a chair.

"Ted, please don't be so loud and angry," his mother said.

"I damn well have a right to be angry!" Ted shouted. "That's my sister lying in there unconscious and about to die!"

Through clenched teeth, Billie Jo answered scathingly in a strong but subdued voice. "She's *not going to die*. She's going to get well, and she's going to tell us what happened."

Ted's rage vanished into pity. "Mom, she may not ever be able to tell us anything," he replied appeasingly. Then resentfully, he added: "The first time I saw that egotistical sissy, I saw straight through him. And then when I heard him preach, I *knew* he was a phony, too. You remember his joking about that little congregation in Oklahoma not minding his swimming in the dangerous lake because they knew he could walk on water."

Ted had never felt such hatred for anyone as he felt for Walker. It was irrational. Just thinking of Walker made him double his fists. He wanted to grab Walker by the collar and punch his hypocritical face. He wanted to beat him until his face was as battered as Peg's. Ted knew he could do it. He outweighed Walker by at least fifty pounds and was seven years younger.

"Walker tried to murder Peggy, but he's such a wimp he made a mess of it. I won't make a mess of choking him."

"Ted, please," Billie Jo said firmly as she sank into a chair. She was only beginning to realize just how upset she was. Ted's words frightened her. Never in a million years would it have occurred to her that Walker would harm Peggy. However strained their marriage was, Walker wasn't a murderer. She couldn't believe that he was capable of murder, even though it was sometimes true that he told lies from the pulpit.

If the people of Dallas were shocked by the attack on Peggy Railey, only eight days later they were stunned and dismayed by Walker Railey's suicide attempt. Within the Church his friends and followers were devastated. There was no acceptable explanation as to why the minister should choose to take his life. This act skewed all their other fears in an entirely new direction. The Reverend David Shawver, pastor of Plymouth Park United Methodist Church told reporters, "I'm praying that it is *not what it looks like*. I'm praying that what the police are suggesting could never be true. I'm praying this will all come out some other way."

Susan Sanders, a lawyer and member of First Church, was not alone among the bewildered congregation in remembering words Railey had spoken from the pulpit six weeks earlier on the tragedy of four teenagers in Bergenfield, New Jersey, two sisters and their boyfriends, who made a suicide pact and then took their own lives. In his usual dramatic manner, Walker had stepped back from the pulpit, paused, looked out over the entire sanctuary from the highest seats in the balcony to the front row. His voice was soft and sad, the words formed in a deliberate manner.

"Somewhere along the way those four budding adults had burned out on life itself. Despite almost thirty calls to friends the night of the fourfold suicide, there seemed to be no clear motive for their action and certainly no person who expected it to happen.

Walker suggested that maybe those four teenagers were just tired of the daily grind, exhausted by the pressures of making it through the day, but with no feeling of having accomplished anything. Possibly those youths no longer expected life to offer them anything more than they had experienced. Perhaps they felt that life was nothing more than a dead-end street, *"that they were trapped in their situations, trapped in their lifestyles, trapped in their souls.*

"They felt burned out and they were burned up. Seeing no other alternative, they turned on the engine of their car and turned off the reality of their lives . . . It is indeed tragic they did not perceive the other option. Instead of opting for life after death, they could have sought birth after life. Had they done so, they would be living today, and with abundance."

Why had Walker Railey, if he felt burned out, not opted for birth after life instead of turning off the reality of his own life? And what indeed *was* that reality that had driven him to such an extreme act? Was he himself trapped in a situation, trapped in a lifestyle, trapped in his soul?

The police immediately searched his rooms at the hospital, confiscating the suicide letter, which they refused to reveal to the media.

Reverend Susan Monts was at the Church at nine-thirty in the morning when she received the signal on her beeper to call the hospital. One of the younger ministers told her what had happened. Stunned with disbelief Susan picked up the telephone and tried to reach Walker's brother Gary in Terre Haute, Indiana. Finally catching him at the Indianapolis Airport, she told him of the suicide attempt and warned him that the press might be at the Dallas airport.

Sheldon Zimmerman was at his North Dallas home when some long-time members of the Temple who knew of the close relationship between Sheldon and Walker came to Sheldon's house to tell him Walker's now being a prime suspect in the attack on Peggy.

Sheldon sat in a chair in his living room and listened. There was a dazed, far-off look in his eyes as he murmured, "So that explains it."

Actually, nothing had been explained, for nothing was logical or rational.

Two hours later as Gordon and Dede Casad stepped off the elevator and into the main lobby of the hospital, they saw City Councilman Craig Holcomb sitting in a chair near the main entrance. His legs were crossed, and one foot jiggled nervously. He is slight and dapper with long, prematurely gray hair worn in a fluffed-up, blow-dried style.

"I want to talk to you," he said directly to Gordon.

"What's it about?" Gordon asked.

"Well," Craig began, "I want to tell all of the staff at one time."

"When?"

"Now."

Gordon was annoyed. Craig spoke in a demanding voice. There was so much to be done now at the Church, and Gordon couldn't imagine that what was so important to Craig would be all that important to the Church staff.

"There are not many of the staff here now."

"Well, however many are here, I want to get them together privately and tell them something they all need to know. They need to know it now. And so do you."

Gordon took Dede by the arm, and the three of them walked back to the elevators, riding in silence to the second floor. There they gathered together Howard Grimes, Susan Monts, Joe Poole, and Hugh Clark leading them toward a room in the East Wing, away from the reception area. Dede elected not to join them.

When the five of them entered an empty room across from the guarded Intensive Care Unit, Craig closed the door behind them. His fists were clenched and his voice was high pitched and shakey. "I think Walker is going to be arrested. I know that this is a real possibility and you need to be prepared. There may be people who will connect him with a gay movement within the Methodist Church."

There was an ominous silence. It was as if a bomb had been dropped and the explosion yet to come.

Holcomb continued. "And I want you all to know that I will not have the homosexual community blamed for Walker's suicide." (Later, Holcomb would deny these were his exact words. He recalled telling the ministers that there were too many outrageous rumors circulating about Walker. When pressed by interviewers as to what specific outrageous rumors, he used the example of Walker being "part of a gay motorcycle gang that was going to ride down the center aisle of the Church." Then he said that he was joking and that the bicycle gang was an extreme example.)

Gordon was disturbed. To his way of thinking Holcomb was making accusations, which, ought not to be made, at least not now. He suggested to Holcomb that he was upset over Walker's action. Like all of them he was mystified and concerned for Walker's life. They should all unite and pray together that Walker and Peggy would survive and be whole again.

The events of the morning had so far overwhelmed the ministers that no one could think of anything else to say. Naively they thought nothing more could happen.

After Dede left the hospital, she went to Northpark Shopping Center. Gordon had told her briefly what had happened. While she was shocked, she was more concerned that if Walker died Gordon would become Acting Senior Minister, at least for a period of time. Ten years ago he had suffered a major coronary and then underwent triple bypass heart surgery. She was afraid that the stress of steering the Church safely through this crisis would endanger his health.

Having suddenly lost interest in the clothes she had anticipated buying, she walked aimlessly through the mall occasionally glimpsing her own shadowy reflection in the wide glass storefront windows.

She did not want her husband to take on this responsibility. She acknowledged that there was no way she could persuade him to turn down the position if the Church asked him. Suddenly it occurred to her to talk with Albert Outler.

One of the most respected Christian scholars in America, Outler was also one of the most influential clergymen in the North Texas Conference. The last time she had seen him was at the 1986 regional Conference in Wichita Falls when Walker had said before the assembled group: "Let this Conference be remembered as the one that Walker Railey debated Albert Outler." Many people thought Walker was intolerably arrogant to place himself on Outler's level. Others thought Walker handled the debate well and that the outcome was a draw.

Outler was in his library and saw Dede immediately. The first thing he said when she entered was: "Walker has created a black hole. We do not know how black or how deep."

Regarding her concern for Gordon, Outler pointed out

that even if Walker lived, he could not return to the pulpit at First Church. Gordon would have to take charge of the Church, until a new younger pastor was found and a new course set.

While Dede was speaking with Dr. Outler, it was almost eleven A.M. Pacific Standard time. Dr. Lucy Papillon was about to address several hundred therapists gathered at the Marriott Hotel in downtown San Francisco for a conference on marriage and family therapy. She was backstage waiting to begin her speech when two F.B.I. agents approached her and showed her their badges.

Lucy was shocked, then alarmed. The F.B.I. men asked her if she knew Dr. Walker L. Railey of Dallas, Texas. When she replied that she did, she was then asked if she had been having sexual relations with Dr. Railey.

Lucy quickly denied that there was anything between them. "There never has been anything in an intimate way," she said. She was simply a member of Dr. Railey's Church.

The agents then told her that some time during the previous night Walker had taken an overdose of tranquilizers and was in critical condition.

Lucy walked on to the stage for her lecture, her hands and knees shaking. Later she wondered how she ever got through that lecture, which she could no longer recall. But before she left California, she placed a call to Rabbi Sheldon Zimmerman who was in Florida at the annual meeting of the Central Conference of American Rabbis where he was to deliver a major address the following morning. When she finally reached him, she asked him to recommend a lawyer. Sheldon replied that he would ask someone in his congregation for a recommendation. A few days later Lucy became a client of criminal lawyer Phil Burleson who had gained notoriety defending Jack Ruby after the murder of Lee Harvey Oswald.

Susan Monts and former executive minister Larry Ravert met Walker's brother Gary at DFW Airport. They told him that although Walker's condition was serious, he was expected to live. Peggy Railey was still in critical condition, her future uncertain.

Gary, who bears a strong resemblance to Walker, stayed in his brother's house and drove his brother's car to the hospital. He went into the Intensive Care Unit to see Walker and Peggy. He spent time with the Nicolais and with Megan and Ryan at the Yarringtons. Ryan asked him if he was a friend of his daddy's. When Gary said yes, Ryan replied: "My daddy's name is Walker." Two-year-old Megan, who was sitting in Gary's lap, said, "My daddy's name is John."

Gary met Dr. Lucy Papillon and spent two evenings with her at the hospital. He also met Hal Brady and visited with Gordon Casad who had always heard that Gary was the black sheep of the Railey family. It struck him that the roles of black sheep and shepherd were now dramatically reversed. When Walker regained consciousness, Gary brought clean clothes to his brother. Before he returned to Indianapolis, he told Susan and Gordon that he had spoken with Walker and that there was no way that he could ever believe his brother had anything to do with the attack on his wife.

Sunday, May 3, 1987

Dr. Gordon Casad walked to the pulpit for the eleven o'clock service. The sanctuary was filled. All eyes were upon him. Knowing that this was one of the challenges of his life, he spoke in a deep, gentle voice.

"Remembering that 'He who dwells in the shelter of the Most High, who abides in the shadow of the Almighty, will say to the Lord, My refuge and my fortress; my God in whom I trust.' Psalm 91:1–2.

"With these words as a preface I want to address each of you this morning in our worship in this sanctuary and our television congregation at home, saying first of all the events and happenings of these past days, which have left us shattered and bewildered.

In our shock, our grief, our pain and our anguish we must recognize THE CHURCH IS OF GOD AND WILL ENDURE UNTIL THE END OF TIME.

"In the midst of all the police and media reports that attempt to discern fact from fiction, and truth from sensation, we must strive to maintain the quality of mercy that befits the followers of Jesus. We must remember our pastor is troubled in mind and spirit, the depth of which only the future will tell.

"We must especially remain strong in the faith that Walker Railey presented so clearly and so eloquently from this pulpit, Sunday after Sunday. We have known few people more articulate in expressing the appropriate word, at the appropriate time, in the appropriate way, than Walker Railey. If there is any basic flaw revealed it will surely be that he tried to do in his own strength, what can only be done in God's Grace and as the burden became heavier than he could bear, his reason, his will, his understanding and his perspective crumbled and he fell under the weight of it. Walker's condition has moved from critical to serious and is now satisfactory. Peggy's condition remains critical.

"We must know that the faith the Church embodies and proclaims, is a word not dependent upon any one of us or any group of us. It is a WORD that has come by those inspired by the Spirit of God and tested by the milleniums of time.

"Through our connectional system our District Superintendent, B. C. Robertson, and Bishop John Russell, have been pastors to the Raileys, the staff and the Church. Bishop Russell today has published a comforting and strengthening statement, that will say to us and the world, the place the Church has and our Church in particular has, in being a witness to truth. They stand ready to aid in whatever decisions are deemed wise as we face the future.

"When the men of Capernaum asked Jesus, 'What must we do to work the works of God,' he gave them an answer that has come thundering down the ages . . . 'Believe in Him whom God has sent.'

"Let us stand as we sing 'Praise to God Who Reigns Above.'"

John Yarrington led the choir and the congregation in the hymn. His gestures and facial expressions were less animated than usual. Not even the joy of the hymn energized him. His round naturally sloping shoulders seemed to slope down even farther. By contrast, Gordon who was standing a few feet from him, looked like a leader, a tall, strong ruler with his broad shoulders thrown back and the hymnal held at chest level. His presence commanded respect. He had met his challenge. The congregation had a shepherd who would keep them together. And there was no doubt that this shepherd perceived Walker Railey as a flawed and fallen figure.

16

"WALKER RAILEY, RIGHT OR WRONG!" ROBERTA Crowe announced defiantly.

"You don't really mean that," Ann Nichols told her over the telephone.

As Charlotte Lieber predicted, Roberta had called Ann to discuss the Railey situation every morning since Ann had returned from Europe. "Ann, you don't know Walker as well as I do," Roberta said. "He's just like a son to me and has been for six years. Why, honey, I helped that young man mature into the position he's holding right now. He's come to me for advice and I am absolutely positive he could not do anything terrible like choke his wife."

"Then why did he try to kill himself?" Ann asked impatiently.

"Honey, I don't know why he tried to kill himself. I guess he is just so upset over the condition Peggy is in that he isn't himself. He just momentarily lost his mind."

"He momentarily lost his mind when he strangled her," Ann said, realizing she was provoking a showdown.

"You have no loyalty to anyone or anything!" Roberta screamed. "Your parents would be turning over in their graves if they knew how you'd deserted the Church and become an atheist!"

"Roberta, please . . ."

"Don't 'Roberta' me! I've been watching you this past twenty-five years, and I've been hoping and praying that some day you'd see the error of your ways. But now I give up on you. You're just a selfish, conceited intellectual. And if you think Walker strangled Peggy, then I don't want to have any more to do with you, no matter how much I loved your mother and daddy!"

"Roberta, I'm sorry. I do think Walker strangled Peggy."

Roberta slammed down the phone so loudly Ann's left ear resounded with a ringing, humming sound. She had hardly replaced the receiver when the telephone rang again. This time it was Charlotte.

"Walker Railey is guilty as sin," Charlotte said.

"Roberta doesn't think so. She's never going to speak to me again."

"Well, that's no bad deal."

"Come on, Charlotte. Roberta is eighty years old. There is no way she can give up her beliefs now."

"Age doesn't have anything to do with it. Some people in their twenties won't change. Look at my children. But anybody with common sense knows an innocent minister doesn't attempt suicide."

"I don't believe you can use common sense in this situation."

"Well, someone in the police department said Walker's guilty as sin," Charlotte said authoritatively.

"Will and I were at this cocktail party and he said Walker

is guilty, but he also said that he would *never* be prosecuted."

"Charlotte, I can hardly believe that."

"It's the gospel," Charlotte said and then laughed at her unintentional joke.

Many practical and intelligent people at First Church fell into a state of denial. Whatever facts emerged, they believed that Walker Railey was innocent. Dale Cunningham told anyone who asked him that he believed "a man is innocent until proven guilty, and that includes Walker Railey." Ernie Martin walked outside from a party where Will Lieber found him with tears in his eyes. Will had always thought that Ernie had been the inspiration for the phrase "straight as an arrow," and his opinion was reinforced. "I'll never believe he did it," Ernie told Will, "unless Walker tells me he's guilty."

"There's no way I'll believe he did it," Diane Yarrington announced. "Whatever else he may have done, he wouldn't do *that* to her."

Mary Lou Schlashuber spoke with a neighbor who was a Presbyterian and he said he believed it.

Carol and Bill Arnold believed it, too. They heard of the suicide attempt on the early evening news on channel five television. Carol was feeding the baby in the kitchen, but she stopped and brought the baby into the den where they could see the news.

"Bill, this is terrible. This is the worst thing I could imagine."

"The first thought I had about this attack was why would the Ku Klux Klan harm Peggy?" Bill said. "A more likely suspect is her husband."

"Of course we don't *know* that he attacked Peggy. We just know that he attempted suicide, and, well, it's not likely, but there might be another reason."

"I can't think of one," Bill said. Then, with a wry little smile, he added: "And there *is* one thing both these episodes have in common."

"What's that?"

"Both the attempts were failures. It's a real coincidence if two *related* crimes were botched by two *different* people."

Ralph Shannon, too, believed that Railey committed both crimes, but he didn't *want* to believe it. He guarded his words, not only from the media and the Pastor-Parish Committee, but from everyone he encountered. Over and over again he repeated that "the police were investigating and that there really was nothing to say until the police completed their investigation. There was no point in speculating."

May 4, 1987

From all the chaos of the past few days, several indisputable facts emerged. Walker was recovering; his suicide attempt, the sincerity of which many now questioned, was another failure. Real or faked, the suicide attempt cast him in an entirely new role. The Church would have to place him on an extended leave of absence. Although he had not been charged with any crime, clearly he needed the advice of an expert criminal lawyer. While the Church itself could not hire a lawyer, prominent members in the Church could *select* a lawyer for him. They contacted former criminal prosecutor Douglas Mulder, who in sixteen years has lost few cases as either a prosecutor or a defense lawyer. Nicknamed Mad Dog Mulder, he had been first assistant to long-time, controversial District Attorney Henry Wade. An assistant district attorney supporting Wade said Wade wouldn't indict "unless there was plenty of hard evidence. That was why his conviction rate was so high."

On the other hand, a former prosecutor critical of Wade said Wade's philosophy was "use any means to obtain a conviction." When Mulder left the DA's office for the more lucrative profession of criminal defense, he stated that his philosophy remained the same as Wade's. Critics claim that with Mulder *and* with John Vance, Mulder's successor in the DA's office, there is no concern for innocence or guilt.

Contrary to Article 2.01 of the Texas Code of Criminal Procedure, which declares that, "It shall be the primary duty of all prosecuting attorneys . . . not to convict, but to see that justice is done," the goal of prosecutors today is to win at any cost.

Mulder agreed to talk with Walker at the hospital; then he decided he would represent him. When Shannon made the announcement that Doug Mulder had been retained to advise Walker, there were those in the congregation and in the media who assumed that this indicated Walker was a suspect, no matter what the police said. There were a number of lawyers in the Church who were friends of Walker's, including Ken Menges and Susan Sanders, whose counsel was not sought in choosing a criminal lawyer for their friend and pastor. They believed that the mere association of the Reverend Walker Railey with Mad Dog Mulder suggested not only suspicion of guilt but *actual* guilt.

In answer to questions by reporters, Mulder coolly replied, "If Railey's worried about his public image, he should hire a PR guy and not a lawyer. It's my job to keep my client out of jail. That's all that matters."

It was not all that mattered to the Methodist Church or to the media. A shadow side to the Reverend Railey alarmed the Church and intrigued the media.

On Friday May 8, Religion Editor Helen Parmley spoke on the telephone with Railey who was still in Presbyterian Hospital, protected against unwanted intruders, including the police. A copyrighted article appeared in *The News* with an unflattering photograph of Railey, which captured the transfixing stare, the straight-lined tension in his mouth and the enlarged vein in his forehead. Beneath the photograph was a far from enlightening Railey quote: *"To be honest with you, I just don't know. I don't know anything."*

Parmley wrote in her article, that Railey said he would like to talk to the police to *"find out what kind of scenario they have worked out."*

He pointed out that everyone was waiting to see how his

family was going to get together and that those were the things that occupied his mind.

"'The Dallas police have been wonderful,' he said. 'The police, the F.B.I., the hospital—there are so many players in this game and everybody is playing it well . . .'

"Railey said he is convinced his wife hears some of what is said to her, and that one day she opened her eyes. Railey anticipated returning to the pulpit, but he doesn't know whether he can ever go back to their home. 'I have gone there twice to get clothes for the children. But I cannot go into the garage.'"

Railey declared that he was "overwhelmed" by the loving response he has received from the community and the Church and that he was praying for strength and hoping for the best.

"'You know the old adage—Where there's life, there's hope?' he asked. 'Well, I would add to that, Where there is hope, there is life. That is my faith.'"

Detectives Rick Silva and Stan McNear, who had been trying unsuccessfully for two weeks to question Railey, were startled to read that Railey would like to talk with them "to find out what kind of scenario they have worked out." Not only the police, but also the F.B.I. and the administrative staff at Presbyterian Hospital, were chagrined to read that Walker viewed them as "players in this game." The doctors in charge of Peggy were amazed to read that Walker believed Peggy could hear and comprehend some of what was going on around her. And Sheldon Zimmerman was surprised to read that Walker was emotionally unable to go into his garage when that was the first place he went when Sheldon had accompanied him to his home. Some of the ministers and members of the Pastor-Parish Committee were disturbed that Walker was anticipating returning to the pulpit.

On May 11, Ralph Shannon, John Yarrington and Dr. Dwight Holden accompanied Walker to Timberlawn in a van. They left Presbyterian Hospital by way of the laundry room, thereby avoiding the media. A police car led the way.

Having Walker admit himself to Timberlawn was Doug Mulder's idea. At Timberlawn he would be protected from the police, the F.B.I., the media and anyone else Mulder didn't want to question him.

On the drive Dr. Holden was silent, disconcerted over Walker's unpredictable behavior. He had visited Presbyterian Hospital almost daily. He was a conscientious man, and Walker had been his patient for nearly two years.

After the episode with Craig Holcomb and the ministers, Shannon had taken Holden aside and asked him if it were possible that Walker was homosexual. Holden lifted his shoulders and stretched his hands. "How would I know?" he sighed. "I didn't even know about Lucy!"

Later both Shannon and Holden would be even more shocked to learn that Walker and Lucy together attended *marriage counseling sessions* with a psychologist at the Pastoral Counseling Building on Lemmon Avenue, just outside the Park Cities.

At Timberlawn Walker became both a celebrity and a curiosity to the other patients. Clearly he was at the hospital to hide. A safe haven was more important than treatment.

Only three days after Railey had transferred to Timberlawn, attorney Doug Mulder, whom Ralph Shannon had explained was hired "not to defend him [Railey] but to protect his rights," arranged a polygraph test for his client. The test was administered by Bill Parker, a former homicide detective, and it indicated that Railey had not attempted to kill his wife. Consequently Mulder approved a police-administered polygraph for the following day. That exercise was described by Mulder as inconclusive. A police statement said that the test was not only "inconclusive" but that Railey had "failed" parts of it.

"The results showed that he didn't have anything to do with the attack, nor did he conspire with anyone," Mulder said. "We had some technical problems with the second test that, I think, can be straightened out. When they are ready to give another test, we are ready to take it. And I am totally convinced that he will be cleared completely." What technical problems Mulder didn't say.

The police repeated their statement that Railey had failed

the test; they wanted to interview him about "inconsistencies" in his explanation of events on April 21 and April 22. Mulder would not agree to his client's being interviewed until he had taken a third lie detector test. The police accused Mulder of being uncooperative. Still Railey refused to discuss the case with investigators. The conflict had reached a stalemate. That polygraphs are inadmissable as evidence in Texas courts seemed not to bother anyone.

The national press picked up the Railey story, and an article by Daniel Pedersen titled "A Cloud Falls on a Dallas Preacher" appeared in *Newsweek* on May 25, 1987. It began with a summary of events; the threatening letter that was slipped under the door on Easter Sunday, the attack on Peggy, Walker's attempted suicide, the revelation that the letters had been typed on a Church typewriter, Walker's checking into Timberlawn and remaining "beyond the reach of frustrated investigators."

Then journalist Pedersen offered a new explanation for the letters and the attack. He reported that some well placed Methodists thought that the answer to the Railey riddle might be related to a failure to match his imperious ambitions to the realities of Church politics.

Pedersen then suggested that the Easter service during which Railey preached about the possibility of Christ faking his Crucifixion during Holy Week to live up to the Hebrews' expectation of Him might have been the same sort of deception Railey was doing to live up to the expectations of the people of Dallas. Some Church insiders observed that the death threats against him came just before Church leaders were to elect the north Texas delegation to the 1988 Methodist General Conference in St. Louis. Railey headed that group in 1984. Since then his support had eroded among liberals and Blacks, the same groups that had rallied to him after he announced that he was receiving Klanlike death threats. Maybe Peggy had discovered the plot and threatened to expose her husband's duplicity. Maybe Railey panicked. *"One parishioner held out hope for a scenario that would entirely clear Railey: 'A lot of people would like to embrace one—if they could think of one.'"*

For the past ten years, editor Spurgeon Dunnam III and Walker Railey had been rivals for power and influence within the Church. Both had made enemies; neither had many close friends.

While Walker was pacing the halls at Timberlawn, Dunnam was attending the North Texas United Methodist Annual Conference where he was elected to be a delegate to the 1988 General Conference. After the Conference was over, he wrote to Walker, enclosing a letter that Presley Hutchins, another delegate at the Conference, had asked him to deliver to Walker.

Spurgeon's letter said that he had missed Walker at the Conference, that he was concerned and perplexed by what had happened but that he was Walker's friend and colleague in the ministry and that Walker remained in his prayers.

A week later Walker replied, thanking Spurgeon for his concern, "however feeble it might have been." He accused him of creating the scenario for Pedersen's story. He told Spurgeon that he always had something to say even when he had nothing to say, which was why so many people considered him "a pompous ass." Walker's letter also stated:

Sometime inside the next year, probably around General or Jurisdictional Conferences, I will respond to that malicious piece of urine-yellow journalism [Pedersen's], and in the process will return to you what you have so generously given to me. You have always acted like such a deserving person, Spurgeon, and I want you to know that within the next twelve months, you are going to get exactly what you deserve . . .

Spurgeon was not afraid of Walker, at least not as long as he was in Timberlawn; however, Spurgeon believed that Walker had never in his life done anything that wasn't calculated. Clearly the letter *was* a threat, and he took it to the police.

There was nothing the police could do except record in their files that here was an example of Railey's hostile, potentially violent temperament, the Mr. Hyde in the gentle minister's personality. The angry tone of the letter suggested to some a familiarity in composing threatening words that were most unlike the preferred sentiments of Methodist ministers.

The spring of 1987 was a bad time for Methodism in Texas. Southern Methodist University, the denomination's leading university violated the rules on football recruitment, even when the team was already on probation for that same offense. The board of trustees of the university, powerful businessmen and church members, knowingly disregarded the NCAA rules and regulations. They set themselves above the law, and they lied. The Chairman of the Board of Trustees denied any participation in the wrongdoings until he was elected governor of the state. Safely in office, he apologized, and the university's football team was suspended from conference play for two years. The president of the university was fired; all trustees resigned and a new board was established.

Next came the attack on Peggy Railey and Walker's suicide attempt. A month to the day after the attack on Peggy, the attention of the Church was directed to Houston where a Methodist scandal of even greater proportion had imploded.

Retired Bishop Finis A. Crutchfield, Jr., died at Methodist Hospital in Houston. The cause of death listed on the death certificate was AIDS. The bishop's wife and only son Charles, also a Methodist minister, found the AIDS diagnosis impossible to accept. Neither had any suspicion of the bishop's homosexuality, which was well known in the gay community and widely rumored, though ignored, among the Methodist clergy. Indeed as the bishop's death became imminent and some public statement was expected, several bishops and retired bishops advised the family to maintain silence, as the Church had done for so many years. Spurgeon, however, told them that if they ignored it, "it would not keep the information from being revealed, it would just eliminate their say in it."

Reverend Charles Crutchfield wrote a statement for *The Methodist Reporter* that described a conversation with his father shortly before his death. The bishop told his son that he had had no homosexual or extramarital sexual contact. "We are left with the conclusion," Charles wrote, that "we simply do not know, and may never know, how he contracted the virus." The statement went on to relate that the bishop, in his retirement years, had ministered to victims of AIDS. "As a compassionate and caring minister of Christ, he responded to the needs of others without thought of possibly harmful consequences for himself."

There were uproars in both the gay community and the Methodist Church. Gays feared reprisals because of the implication that Crutchfield had contracted AIDS through casual contact with homosexuals suffering from the disease. The Methodist Church was confronted with the indisputable fact that a man who had reached the highest position in the hierarchy of the Church, President of the Council of Bishops, had violated the beliefs of his Church. He had denied the truth of his double life, even on his deathbed.

The stonewalling tactics were failing. The silent, solid walls of the Church had begun to crumble.

17

IN A NARROW, GLASSED-OFF OFFICE ON THE METRO-politan floor of *The Dallas Morning News*, Metropolitan Editor Stuart Wilk and Assistant City Editor Don Smith lounged in padded, maroon swivel chairs around a small round plastic-wood table. On the wall behind them is a blown-up photograph capturing opposite reactions from President and Mrs. Bush. She is cutting an anniversary cake at a military base in Texas. Jet fighter planes salute the occasion with a low formation flyover. The president laughs and looks up at the sky while his wife grimaces at the almost deafening noise. It is a prize-winning photograph.

This morning the editors drink coffee and discuss the Railey case. The local television stations and the rival evening paper *The Dallas Times Herald* continue to carry the story daily, even if it was only an update on Peggy Railey's medical condition. Clearly the story was not going to die, and equally clearly, it was not the sort of story appropriate to the religion section of the newspaper. It was sensational, front-page news.

While Helen Parmley might continue to write news stories about the affects and responses within Methodism, it was apparent to the two editors and to Helen that what the paper also needed was an investigative reporter to cover the story.

Olive Talley had only been with the *News* six months when she was called into the meeting in the Metropolitan Editor's office and asked to take on the Railey case.

Although she was certain she could report objectively, she wasn't anxious to pursue an investigation of a man whose ministry had persuaded her to follow him or to examine with a cold, objective eye the "behind the scenes" in the social and spiritual life of the Church she had elected to join.

Olive had been raised in the Methodist faith, witnessed its positive effect in her mother's life, and, with her career advancement, determined to make progress in her own spiritual development as well. Shortly after her arrival in Dallas she had joined First United Methodist Church.

The editors were adamant. Energetic, tough talking and not yet thirty, Olive had a reputation for courage in reporting. Disarming both personally and professionally, she is dedicated to her career. Nominated for a Pulitzer Prize, she is one of the youngest and best investigative reporters in the country.

She agreed to take on the assignment, but expressed her

feelings that probably the most interesting part of the story had already happened.

On June 10, Attorney Mulder, evading police and press, took his client to Salt Lake City for a third polygraph test to be administered by University of Utah Professor David C. Raskin, a nationally recognized expert in the field. Mulder and Railey returned the same day, both refusing to comment on test results. There was speculation among police that the results of the first test had been misinterpreted and that Raskin did not administer a third test. Whatever the true story was, it was never revealed in the press. Members of the Church were bewildered and suspicious.

The day after Railey returned from Salt Lake City, Church officials scheduled a press conference. The purpose of the conference was to announce that the Pastor-Parish Committee had requested the bishop of the North Texas Conference, Bishop John Russell, to appoint a new senior minister to lead First United Methodist Church. Ralph Shannon had met with Walker at Timberlawn on June 5, and the two men discussed the necessity of Railey's departure from the Church.

"Dr. Walker Railey agrees with this action," read a prepared statement by the committee published in *The Methodist Reporter. "In no way should it be considered an indication of guilt or innocence, but it is apparent that any further delay in filling our pulpit will seriously impair the Church in its mission."* The committee praised Railey for his "dynamic leadership" and expressed its love and support for him and his family.

The Reverend Gordon Casad explained that the members of the congregation did not want to take any action that could harm the Railey family, yet they wanted the Church to move forward. "They feel like this is hanging like a cloud with nothing being resolved. That's the real burden they feel."

It was more than a burden, however. An angry group of Church members, led by Attorney Ken Menges and City Councilman Craig Holcomb, vowed to keep the pulpit open until Railey's return. Menges himself told an impromptu press conference that Railey had been "forced" to agree with the committee and that he (Menges) expected "an independent petition to be presented to the bishop to protest this move."

Ralph Shannon assured Menges that no one wanted Railey ousted, but "in view of all the circumstances, we asked if he can come back to this pulpit and be an effective pastor. The consensus, including that of Railey, is that he cannot."

This view was disputed by Menges and Holcomb. A rift was developing in the Church between the "old guard" and what Holcomb described as "the new power structure."

Those who did not agree with Railey's dismissal blamed the police for their continuing campaign to question him, which now, in his supporters' eyes, had become persecution. "If they [the police] have evidence, he ought to be charged," Menges maintained. "If they don't have the evidence, they should remove the cloud. I don't blame his attorney for doing his best to defend his client against a one-track, rabid police department."

The police became the scapegoat. Frustrated by Railey's failure to cooperate and sensitive to public criticism, the police department issued a reply: "We are not one-track and rabid, but we are relentless. We'll do everything in our power to find the person who attacked Peggy Railey and bring that person to justice. We do not have a closed mind as to any possibilities in this case. The lack of cooperation by Walker Railey has proved to be a serious impediment to the progress of our investigation. Railey is a key witness in this case. Without his help, it makes it very difficult to find the person who attacked his wife."

Not only was there an impasse between the leaders of the two factions within the Church, but individuals within Sunday School classes began to quarrel.

"I'm afraid that there is only one plausible excuse why he won't talk with the police," sighed eighty-four-year-old Gladys Jarratt who was talking on the telephone to Roberta Crowe.

"You don't know what you're talking about," replied Roberta. "If you are going to be a Judas like some of these other women in the Susanna Wesley class, then I'm not going to drive you to Church anymore."

Tension mounted within the Church. Meetings were held, accusations made and friendships strained. Spurgeon Dunnam and his wife Dottie no longer spoke of the matter to each other. Spurgeon believed Walker quite capable of strangling his wife; Dottie denied any possibility of Walker behaving in a violent manner. Claire Cunningham sadly conceded that the known facts indicated Walker had a strong motive; her husband, Dale, insisted that whatever the facts seemed to indicate, a man was innocent until proven guilty. Janet Marshall said that Walker was being crucified, like Christ. Ernie Martin said that there was no way he could believe Walker guilty. Johnnie Marie Grimes agreed, while her husband Howard said that the evil was too dark to contemplate. The Eubanks, the Liebers and the Nichols debated the matter weekly over drinks and dinner, often changing points of view. They were the Greek chorus, chanting and repeating the attitudes of the city.

Bishop Russell neither appeared nor made any statements. Menges and Holcomb drew up a petition, and, through meeting after meeting, Shannon and Casad attempted to unite the congregation. Finally the conflict was diffused when Shannon revealed that he had in his possession a letter from Railey asking to be reassigned from First Church because circumstances had turned him into "more of a liability than an asset."

When pressured by Olive Talley as to when he had received the letter and why he had not revealed it sooner, Shannon said that in mid-May Walker had written the letter marked CONFIDENTIAL to Bishop Russell but with a copy to him.

Menges wondered aloud why "if the letter was confidential at the time, I don't know why he has not kept it confidential." Others in both factions of the Church wondered why Bishop Russell had not revealed it himself or indeed, why, since his office was in Dallas at Highland Park

Methodist, he was so conspicuously absent during this time of crisis. Though Russell justified his distance from the scandal by saying that it was an internal matter in First Church, his explanation angered more than soothed. What was the role of a bishop if not to help solve Church problems?

Menges and Holcomb abruptly dropped their campaign. Holcomb said, "We want a public display of support for Walker Railey. We want to make certain that Peggy Railey's medical expenses are covered for the rest of her life and we want there to be a living wage for Walker for the next two years so that he has ample opportunity to get his life back in order."

The compromise reached was that Walker would be kept on the Church payroll through August, that the Church would continue to carry medical insurance on both Peggy and Walker and that a search would begin immediately for Walker's replacement as senior minister. Gordon Casad announced that four trust funds were being set up for the members of the Railey family—one for Peggy, one for Walker and one for each of the children.

These actions were Christian and caring. The ministers all spoke of the Church family becoming closer as a result of the tragedy. Yet, despite pronouncements, actions and surface behavior, the First Church family remained, at least in part, a house divided.

18

OLIVE TALLEY ATTENDED THE OPEN MEETINGS AT First Methodist Church; she interviewed Ken Menges and Susan Sanders as well as Ralph Shannon, Gordon Casad and Susan Monts. She tried Doug Mulder, but he didn't return her calls. She interviewed the Raileys' neighbors on Trail Hill Drive, and Peggy's friends Diane Yarrington and Maxie Hardin. To the degree that they would talk, she spoke with the police and the F.B.I. She telephoned Bishop Russell who refused to return her calls.

Olive did not easily accept evasiveness. In a month she knew more about this case than anyone, except possibly Railey himself, and she believed that the bishop's opinion was something the public had a right to know. So, when Russell was preaching a Sunday service at First Church, Olive slipped in the back of the Church, walked down the aisle after the service and confronted the bishop as he stepped down from the dais.

"I'm Olive Talley, Bishop Russell. If you won't call me back during my working hours, then we'll have to meet during your working hours," she said.

The bishop is not known for either smooth handling of thorny issues or for having a sense of humor. He replied arrogantly that he did not feel it was his responsibility "to feed news to the media," adding that anything he wished the media to know he would issue in a press release.

Members of the Church staff who overheard this exchange groaned inwardly. The last thing that the Church needed now was hostility from the media. On an earlier Sunday when the bishop was leaving First Church, a reporter followed him down the front steps pressuring him to make some statement. "No comment," the bishop said several times, as the reporter bombarded him with questions. Finally he turned to the persistent young man and asked sincerely, "Son, are you deaf?"

To Olive and to many who were not associated with the press, it seemed that the bishop was the one who was deaf to the cries of his flock.

June 20, 1987

Walker Railey left Timberlawn and returned to his home on Trail Hill Drive where a number of his friends and supporters, including the Yarringtons and Janet Marshall, were waiting to welcome him. He told his friends that he did not want to discuss details surrounding the tragedy, that the house held too many memories and that he would be making plans to stay elsewhere.

On the outside of the Railey house was a metal mezuzah containing a parchment inscribed with religious texts. It is customarily attached to the doorposts of orthodox Jewish homes. In the entryway inside the house, Peggy's love of music was reflected by an antique pine harmonium and by the spinet in the sewing room. Framed needlepoints and crewels hung on the walls and a hand-embroidered "Shalom." A blue-duck motif, much in style that year, decorated the immaculately clean kitchen and was repeated on dish towels, pot holders, an apron and other items both useful and decorative.

In the master bedroom a book case crammed with paperback mysteries, including all of the Agatha Christie stories, squeezed against one side of the bed. In the living room on a wooden book stand on a low, round coffee table lay an open copy of the Torah. Also in the living room was a built-in wet bar, something virtually every house in the neighborhood had. Builders in Dallas long ago had learned that a few simple touches of symbolic luxury—a raised ceiling, a chandelier, a skylight or a wet bar—increased the value of a house by thousands of dollars.

The wet bar at the Railey house was not stocked with liquor. It held a record player, and a collection of light classics, Walker's taste. Though Methodist ministers are no longer forbidden to drink socially, an ostentatious display of alcoholic beverages would have been unbecoming. Bottles of white wine and rosé were kept in an old refrigerator in the garage, some red wine was stored in the kitchen pantry, poured into empty bottles of Welch's grape juice. Peggy's brother Ted had driven her to Plano and other suburbs in the Metroplex where she was unlikely to be recognized in a liquor store. He thought she was fooling Walker and all the other Methodist wimps who believed preachers' wives shouldn't drink. He didn't know that when his parents drove from Tyler to Dallas they usually brought several cases of wine for Walker and Peggy. Upstairs in a bathroom off Walker's study five or six cases of wine were stacked in the bathtub.

Just as the downstairs of the house reflected Peggy's tastes and personality, the upstairs study was a profile of Walker. His life, past, present and future, was shown on the walls of this large single upstairs room. Off limits to other members of the family, it was the most expensive and tastefully furnished room in the house. To the right of a mahogany executive desk, hung over built-in filing cabinets, was a large framed watercolor of a white-columned antebellum mansion. The title MY OLD KENTUCKY HOME engraved on a small brass label attached to the frame did not represent Walker's childhood home as it really had been. Instead, the gracious, aristocratic home was what he *wished* it had been. It was his past, not as remembered, but as created.

On the opposite wall were three matching vertical frames, spaced about four inches apart and hung about fifteen inches above a nubby weave sofa. The sequence of pictures had a chilling effect on those who understood their meaning. The first was an ink drawing of First United Methodist Church of Dallas, the second was an ink drawing of Riverside Church in New York City, the most liberal and influential Protestant free pulpit in America. The third picture was a book plate with a crest under which was printed in bold script: BISHOP WALKER L. RAILEY. These were admirable ambitions for a young man whose father was a sheet-metal worker in the blue-collar community of Owensboro, Kentucky.

Few of Walker's associates and acquaintances had been invited to the room upstairs. On the morning of his return from Timberlawn, he remained downstairs with his supporters. Long time members of the Church, Ernie and Lucy Martin, offered him their home for the next two weeks while they were on holiday. There were several other offers of homes that Walker agreed to consider.

"I'm going to find a place to be alone. I haven't been alone since April 21. My spirit is strong; there is a peace within."

If anyone there at the house wondered how he could feel peace within when the attack on his wife remained unsolved, when he himself was considered by the police to be the chief suspect in the crime and when he had been removed from his pulpit, no one commented.

Walker expressed gratitude to his friends for their support and then said he needed to be alone for a while.

An hour after the Oakleys, Janet Marshall and other Church members had gone, Walker left the house in his tan Honda and drove to The Inn on a Gold Mark in Richardson, a Dallas suburb, where a room was booked, and Lucy Papillon was waiting.

When he returned to his house the following morning, he packed a suitcase of casual clothes for his stay at the Martins. Next he telephoned friends in the media. He granted Helen Parmley an interview, and he agreed to appearances on television. As long as he set the parameters, he was willing to talk to almost anyone, except the police.

The article Helen wrote had a string of Walker quotes which, taken together, failed to reassure even his most devoted followers. "I am deeply grieving . . . There is some deranged mind out there that did something to Peggy. That worries me . . . I'm going to spend Father's Day with my babies." Remembering that he would turn forty next week, he commented, "I am at a new crossroads in my life, and I am ready to meet the challenge . . . I received one thousand seventy-five letters while I was in the hospital . . . I'm a little scared about some unanswered questions . . . I feel there is still a sermon within me somewhere."

On television he said: "I didn't attack my wife; I didn't plan to have somebody attack my wife; I didn't orchestrate the plan to attack my wife, and I didn't write the letters. And, as I said to someone else who asked me, having said I didn't write the letters, had I written the letters, I wouldn't have written them on a typewriter in my own Church. That's not even smart."

But as he spoke, and the television camera held a close-up on his face, he didn't seem grief-stricken and *that*, more than what he had said, was what television viewers remembered.

The police were becoming increasingly frustrated. To themselves, as well as to the public at large, they appeared foolish. Their chief suspect was speaking to millions of people on television, but he wasn't speaking to them. Bobby Eubank remarked: "In a way it is comical. The Dallas police look like the Keystone Cops, chasing about in all directions and bumping into each other while Walker, like Charlie Chaplin, deftly moves from one hiding place to another."

Others in the Church failed to see the humor and reacted with anger. "What sort of inept police department couldn't keep up with a prominent man in his own city? Was Railey above the "strong arm of the law?"—Maybe the friend of someone in power? Or was he simply that much smarter than the police? What ever happened to law and order anyway?"

Railey left a thank-you note and a box of chocolates on the kitchen table at Ernie and Lucy Martin's house. Carefully disposing of any trace of Lucy Papillon's presence, he moved out before the Martins returned. He did not leave a new address. Over the next few weeks he occasionally visited the house on Trail Hill Drive to pick up clothes, books, writing material. He never stayed long, just disappeared again to wherever he was staying, which was frequently with Ad and Knox Oakley, who refused to give comments to the media, to the police and to all but a select few from First United Methodist.

The more evasive Walker became, the more farfetched the gossip became.

"Walker is gay."

"Walker is having an affair with a glamorous woman from California."

"Walker is schizophrenic."

"Walker has had a complete mental breakdown, which the Church is trying to conceal."

Gordon Casad and others on the staff said that some things might never be known and that the Church must put behind it the recent tragedy and move forward in its traditional mission. But Gordon knew that this was one scandal that couldn't be swept under the rug. How could the Church expect a story so sensational and so mysterious to slip silently through the system with no media attention? Following the bishop's example, and hence implied instruction, more Church officials became deliberately vague. They didn't want to discuss the Railey case or have it discussed. Leave it alone. No good can come of talking about it. The Church hierarchy will discipline its own, resolve its problems in private. Even attempted murder? Even attempted murder.

For laymen and ordinary citizens this wasn't good enough. With the doors of the inner sanctuary now closed, there remained only the ultimate weapon, the power of the press. Until there was some resolution, the Railey story would continue to fester.

19

❦ FIRST ASSISTANT DISTRICT ATTORNEY NORMAN Kinne was following the Railey case closely. He assumed that sooner or later he would receive a call from the police department; the case would land on his desk in one form or another. When the case first broke, he hadn't expected it to be assigned to him. The victim was still alive; the most serious charge that could be filed was attempted murder. Kinne handled murder cases for which the death penalty could be sought, and, from what he read in the newspapers, it didn't seem that Peggy Railey was likely to die any time soon.

A fifty-two-year-old native of Brownsville in South Texas, Norman Kinne had been in his position only three months when the Railey attack occurred. It would be his first big case as Chief Prosecutor, and it would pit him against his old rival in the D.A.'s office, former Chief Prosecutor Doug Mulder.

"This desk I have used to be Mulder's desk," Kinne said in an interview. "This is the same office Mulder had. It hasn't even been painted."

Kinne is a short, brown-haired man with graying sideburns and a neatly trimmed gray and brown mustache. He is an attractive man with brown eyes that twinkle above the horn-rimmed half-glasses that slip down the bridge of his nose. Unlike many prosecutors, he has a sense of humor not entirely concealed by the usual legal poker face.

Norman Kinne and Douglas Mulder reached their respective positions from opposite directions. Mulder went directly into the District Attorney's office from Southern Methodist University Law School, hand picked by Henry Wade, who had retired only last year, after forty years as District Attorney. "Join the Wade parade," had been the campaign slogan, and Mulder had done just that.

Kinne, on the other hand, had graduated from Texas A&M University with a degree in animal husbandry. After two years in the army, he went to law school at the University of Houston. Two years later he came to Dallas as an insurance adjuster, passed the bar exam, and for the next seven years was a defense attorney.

"For a young lawyer it was very challenging and exciting and everything," he said, "but, boy, I got tired of representing criminals. I got real tired of it. When you're over there representing a guy and doing everything you can to get him off when you know he's guilty—it just rubs me the wrong way."

In 1971 Kinne applied for a job with Henry Wade, presenting references from several of Wade's employees, including Doug Mulder. For ten years Kinne and Mulder worked together in the D.A.'s Office—until Mulder left to become a defense attorney, where there was a lot more money to be made, even if you were defending criminals.

June 29, 1987

The police department received a letter believed to be from a woman who appeared to have some genuinely important information. Apparently she was frightened, for she didn't sign her name. Through the press, the police appealed to the woman to telephone or to write again. But this was just one more frustrating episode in a series of dead-end clues, many of which the police refused to divulge. Meanwhile Walker successfully evaded police attempts to interrogate him.

Instead of leaving the city, as one might have expected, Walker remained in Dallas, moving from one place to another, from one section of town to another. There were still friends and members of First Church willing to protect him. Walker had taken to a variety of nonclerical disguises. He wore dark glasses and jogging suits. Occasionally he exchanged these for vivid, Hawaiian print shirts, casual slacks and an assortment of unusual hats, from wide-brimmed white Panamas to plaid golfing caps. Frequently, like a pack rat in the night, he slipped back into the house on Trail Hill Drive to exchange wardrobes, usually careful to keep his presence concealed from the neighbors.

Beleaguered by criticism and public outrage, Lt. Ron Waldrop finally summoned for sworn statements a number of people who allegedly had seen Walker on the day of the attack. One of those summoned was Dr. Lucy Papillon.

Papillon of course was not Lucy's real name; it was the name she had chosen for herself after she had experienced in California a major spiritual change in her life. Shortly after the death of her father Bishop Robert E. Goodrich, Jr., she had legally changed her name to Papillon, the French word for butterfly. Presumably the name implied a metamorphosis from the ugly, plodding, earthbound caterpillar to the beautiful, free-spirited butterfly. When asked the question by a reporter of why Papillon, a former college friend replied: "Because she didn't know the French word for fruitcake." A kinder explanation was offered by Reverend Howard Grimes: "Lucy is a lovely girl. She just didn't go through adolescence until she was thirty-five."

The second child of Bob and Thelma Goodrich, Lucy has an older sister and two younger brothers. Like most preacher's children, she was the subject of flattering attention. "A nice, sweet, friendly, down-to-earth girl" is the way she is remembered by older members of the Church.

Graduating in 1959 from Hockaday, Dallas's most exclusive and prestigious girl's school, Lucy smiles sweetly and innocently in her graduation photograph in *Corner Stones*, the school's yearbook. Under the photograph is a quote from Wordsworth:

> A spirit still, and bright
> with something of an angel light.

Her nickname was Motormouth, and she is remembered by a former Hockaday classmate as "good at sports, music and academics. She was a cheerleader and she was religious —really the ideal preacher's daughter."

For the yearbook, Lucy herself wrote: "When I think back over my days at Hockaday, I will remember most enjoyably the Dad's Days because I love to see Daddy happy. He enjoys the day so much, especially the year he had to recite in Latin class . . . My major goal in life is to be the best I can and do the best I can in some field of church work, perhaps through music . . ."

She attended Southern Methodist University, majoring in music education. Good at academics and active in her sorority, Lucy was a daddy's girl and, as the popular expression then was, "boy crazy." Following her junior year, she married a young theology student at Perkins, James E. Caswell.

They lived in a dorm at SMU, working as hall directors, and then moved into their first house a year later. After her own graduation in 1963, Lucy supported Caswell's post-graduate studies by teaching music at L. K. Hall Elementary School in Oak Cliff. She resigned in 1966 after the couple's first son was born. In 1969 Lucy returned to SMU and received a master's degree in liberal arts in 1971. Two years later, after the birth of a second son, the ten-year marriage ended in divorce.

Following her sister Thelma Jean, who had earned a Ph.D. in psychology, Lucy attended numerous human potential workshops, while also employed as a model at Handel's, an exclusive women's clothing boutique. In 1976 she entered North Texas State University in Denton to pursue part-time a doctorate in psychology. A year later she married psychotherapist Irwin Gadol and divorced him four years later when she received her degree. Pursuing further studies in California, she left her sons in the custody of their father, assumed the name of Papillon (though not yet legally) and hosted her own television show "Psychologically Speaking." She did not return to Dallas until 1985 when her father became terminally ill with cancer.

On July 3, 1987, accompanied by lawyer Phil Burleson, Lucy went to the police department, was interrogated by Detective Rick Silva, Detective Stan McNear and Lt. Ron Waldrop, and gave a signed statement.

Sensitive to criticism, the police were not cooperative with the press. Determined to track the story one way or another, Olive Talley got access to Railey's telephone records from a confidential source. When the police learned this, they attempted to dissuade senior editors at the *News* from publishing the story by saying that revelation of this information now could hamper their investigation. The editors disagreed.

Olive's article was published. It reported that according to telephone records Dallas psychologist Dr. Lucy Papillon was called twice from a mobile phone in the Reverend Walker Railey's car on the night of the April attack on the minister's wife and that Dr. Papillon, accompanied by her attorney, Phil Burleson, gave a signed statement to the police.

"Mobile telephone records obtained Tuesday by the Dallas Morning News also showed two calls were made from Railey's car phone to his home shortly before he reported finding Margaret 'Peggy' Railey choked nearly to death on the garage floor of their Lake Highland's home.

"Earlier that night, the records show two phone calls were placed to psychologist Lucy Papillon: one to her office at 5:58 P.M. and another to her home at 7:32 P.M. Each call lasted a minute, the records show.

"Norman Kinne, first assistant in the Dallas county district attorney's office said Ms. Papillon is likely to be called as a witness should the case be taken to a grand jury."

The news horrified the membership of First Church. In a peculiar Methodist way, the revelation of another woman was almost as much of an outrage as the attack itself. Attorney Phil Burleson said that there was no personal or intimate relationship between his client and Reverend Railey. Few people believed him.

July 10, 1987

Lt. Ron Waldrop and Detective Rick Silva were downtown in the district attorney's office discussing a grand jury fact-finding investigation when Sheldon Zimmerman received a call at the Temple from Walker. Sheldon had not seen or spoken with Walker since his release from Timberlawn three weeks earlier.

Walker told him that Peggy was being transferred from Presbyterian Hospital to The Clairmont, a nursing home in Tyler near the Nicolais. He wanted to purchase from the Temple gift shop a gold Chai as a gift for Peggy. A Chai is two Hebrew letters which together mean life, a symbol of good luck. If it seemed a strange gift for a Methodist minister to his injured wife, Billie Jo Nicolai understood. When Peggy and Walker married, Peggy had engraved in

Walker's gold wedding band the two Hebrew letters. After he arrived in Milwaukee for the ceremonies and learned what she had done, Walker hurriedly took her wedding band to a jewelry store and had the same symbol engraved in it. The gift of a Chai as Peggy left Dallas was a farewell, just as the symbol inside the rings had been a hopeful beginning.

Sheldon was surprised, though somewhat relieved, when Howard Grimes appeared at the Temple to pick up the gift. Howard said there was going to be a small service at the hospital before Peggy left in an ambulance for Tyler. Sheldon declined to attend the religious service.

At Presbyterian Hospital Walker, Howard, Susan Monts, the Yarringtons, the Oakleys, the Slaters and the Nicolais gathered around Peggy's bed. Bishop Slater said a prayer and then Walker said a prayer, similar to a parting prayer that might have been used at a funeral. It was impossible, as well as unnervingly inappropriate to place a chain around Peggy's neck, so Walker laid it on her pillow. Everyone there was genuinely moved when Billie Jo took the Chai and told Walker that she would have it framed and hung on the wall beside Peggy in the nursing home.

July 14, 1987

Chief Prosecutor Norman Kinne met with Captain John Holt, Lt. Ron Waldrop, Detectives Rick Silva and Stan McNear at the police department. The meeting had already lasted over two hours, and the media, who had been told that an announcement regarding the Railey case would be made, were becoming impatient as they waited in the hall outside Captain Holt's office. There were deadlines to make; it was already too late for the evening's edition of *The Dallas Times Herald*. As usual television would break the story first. Police reporter Lori Stahl and Olive Talley of *The News*, Jerry Needham of *The Dallas Times Herald*, Bud Gillett of station KDFW and several cameramen, sound and lighting crew were eating candy bars, telling jokes and complaining about the heat when the door to Holt's office suddenly opened and Norman Kinne came storming out like a movie sheriff leading a posse. Wearing a snappy gray suit and red tie, he was breathing like a horse. The media surrounded him. Reporters whipped out their note pads, sound booms wobbled over his head, cameras rolled and spotlights illuminated a new media personality. Kinne delivered his lines like a pro, straight to the cameras.

"I'm going to tell Walker Railey I'm tired of you messing with the Dallas Police Department, and you're going to come before a grand jury and clear up these discrepancies, or you're going to leave the country," Kinne said angrily.

"When will the grand jury take place?" several reporters asked.

"I'll subpoena him and have him appear before the grand jury *as soon as I can find him.*"

"Don't the police know where he is?" another reporter asked provocatively.

Kinne evaded the question and again angrily denounced Railey. "I'm tired of this man messing with this investigation. I'm tired of this man fooling with the justice system and with the life of his wife. He says he's concerned about this assault on his wife but won't cooperate, won't talk to the police department. Now he can come downtown and explain it to a grand jury."

"Will you subpoena Lucy Papillon?"

"Others will be subpoenaed, but I'm not prepared at this point to say who." Kinne jabbed his right index finger at the nearest of the four television cameras. "What I'm saying now is 'Walker Railey, you got two choices—talk or walk!'"

He pushed through the media crowd, more gently than his tough, twangy, baritone voice had sounded, and headed for the elevators. "No more questions now. Captain Holt has an official statement."

Captain John Holt came out of his office and explained the steps the police had taken to solve the case.

"How do you feel about your officers not being able to find Reverend Railey for nearly three months?"

"Norm Kinne said everything there was to say about that," Holt replied.

"Wow! He did," one of the camera crew said to another. "He gave quite a performance."

His co-worker winked and whispered: "John Wayne couldn't have done better."

20

THE GRAND JURY SYSTEM, WHICH EVOLVED FROM EARly English law, is the only legal process in America still held in secret—or, *supposedly in secret,* for there are frequent leaks to the media, some with the tacit approval of the prosecution. The system provides that selected members of the public convene and determine if a suspect should be indicted. The judge's role is minimal; he is there only to maintain order. Thus the grand jury system is often attacked as archaic and unfair, a procedure designed to help the prosecution. No defense attorneys, reporters or members of the public, other than those on the jury, are present at the proceedings. Witnesses may, however, request permission to leave the room to consult with lawyers. Only the prosecuting attorney and the witnesses, who have been interviewed, subpoenaed and sworn to secrecy, are allowed in the room. There are twenty-three members on federal grand juries; in Texas there are twelve members.

To arrest a man, to accuse him before a grand jury and then to indict him and bring him to trial, the state prosecutor has to be armed with physical evidence. Norm Kinne had subpoenaed Walker; Lucy Papillon; Stephen Mbutu, an employee at Fondren Library at Southern Methodist University; Reverend Howard Grimes; and Dr. Dwight Holden.

The grand jury hearing for Walker Railey was scheduled for July 24, 1987. What troubled Kinne most was that the evidence the police had given him was all circumstantial. What he needed was physical evidence, such as the cord that had been twisted around Peggy's neck or some microscopic clues that a forensic pathologist could connect with both the attacker and the victim—or, best of all, a witness who actually saw the crime committed.

Ironically, had Peggy Railey been dead when the police and the paramedics arrived, there would have been greater care taken to protect potentially incriminating clues in the house and garage. At the time, however, all energies were directed toward saving her life. Also, had Peggy been dead, the forensic pathologists would have been able to perform tests that are impossible if a person is alive. A psychiatrist had been working with Ryan, but the five-year-old child often confused reality and fantasy, and it would be months, if not years of therapy before he *might* be considered a reliable witness.

Kinne told Olive and other members of the press that he was overcome by anger when he saw pictures of Peggy Railey in her present condition and knew that her minister husband, a supposed moral leader and pillar of the community, was avoiding the police and thereby failing to cooperate in finding his wife's attacker. This anger had brought on his "talk or walk" outburst in front of the television cameras. Kinne didn't really want Railey to walk. He wanted to bring him before a grand jury and *make* him talk.

Naturally he and Mulder spoke about the upcoming grand jury proceeding, and Mulder had told him that his advice to his client would be to take the Fifth Amendment. Kinne wasn't surprised. It was what he had expected Mulder to do and what he would have done had their positions been reversed.

With Railey refusing to answer questions, Kinne's job was reduced to breaking down Railey's resolve to remain silent. How he was going to do this, to make Railey angry enough to defend himself, to enter into an argument with the prosecutor was what was keeping Kinne awake at night. Railey was no fool, no ordinary criminal; he was a shrewd, sophisticated man, accustomed to appearing before an audience, to performing. Kinne well knew that if he didn't break him this time, he probably wouldn't have another chance.

Three days before the scheduled grand jury appearance, a former district attorney from the Career Criminals Division telephoned Kinne with a suggestion. Kinne's former colleague told him about certified graphoanalyst Jane Buckner, who had helped police in criminal detection before and who would be willing to analyze Walker Railey's handwriting and provide a complete personality profile of Railey without charge. The lawyer then explained to Kinne that graphoanalysis is a science, unlike graphology, which is just a form of fortunetelling or party entertainment.

Kinne was skeptical at first, but he was frustrated enough with the investigation to consider anything that might prove helpful. He was grasping at straws and he knew it, though two of Kinne's virtues, which made him a good prosecutor, were a willingness to listen and an unprejudiced mind.

"Have her be in my office at eight-thirty in the morning," Kinne demanded.

The following morning at eight-thirty sharp Jane Buckner arrived at Norm Kinne's office. She is a slender, energetic woman in her fifties with dark hair, dark eyes and a passionate belief in her chosen profession. She has already had a successful career in purchasing management for a hotel company with a thirty-million-dollar budget. For a divorced woman raising two children alone to give up a successful and secure career in mid-life demands dedication and confidence, especially when the new career is one generally misunderstood and ridiculed.

Kinne had already been advised that she needed a two- or three-page sample of Railey's handwriting, preferably something that was written spontaneously. He offered her Walker's suicide note that had been provided by the police.

"What else will you need?"

Jane said all that she required was some small, quiet private space with a bright light, no interruptions, a large jug of water and directions to the ladies' room. She had brought all of her necessary "gear" in her briefcase and a brown bag lunch of cheese and apples. She expected the task to take all day.

Jane liked Kinne from the start. He was polite and considerate, not making any comments as to what he expected of her or whether he anticipated believing her.

After he left, she sat down, opened her briefcase and took out her worksheets and her measuring equipment. Next she unfolded Walker's suicide letter and spread the pages flat on the desk. She placed a thin onion skin tissue over the first page and drew base lines under the letters of the words and the necessary one hundred consecutive upstrokes. Then she measured the slant of the letters above the line and listed them on a worksheet. Jane was so completely focused that she ignored the content of this important unpublished document.

At five minutes to five p.m., she asked Kinne's secretary Judith if she might have a word with Kinne. When she stood before him, briefcase closed, she said, "This is such heavy stuff it sends chills down my spine."

Kinne motioned her to sit down. "Can you give me an insight into whether or not Walker Railey is capable of murdering his wife?"

"I'm not finished," Jane replied, lowering the inflection in her voice. "I'm going to work most of the night to complete this analysis, but tomorrow at noon, I can tell you exactly what to say to make him crack."

"Can you condense it into a few pages and put it into a letter or report form?"

"No problem."

For a moment in silence the two stared straight into each other's dark eyes, neither wanting to be the one to look away first.

"Before I leave," Jane said, "maybe I ought to tell you something about graphoanalysis, so you can see where I'm coming from and know what to expect."

"I'm listening," Kinne replied.

"It's heavy stuff. Graphoanalysis is not looking at overt behavior or the personality mask that people use in everyday relations. We rip off that mask in order to get to the emotional responsiveness level. This is like open heart surgery only it's on the gut."

She paused, but he asked no questions.

"The beauty of graphoanalysis is that it is a complete blending of right and left brain functions. Like medicine, it's a blend of art and science. The measurement is an exact science, the art is in the interpretation. People are walking illusions."

Kinne made no comment. In or out of the courtroom he had seldom encountered such a theatrical woman.

"I'll have in your hands by noon tomorrow a complete assessment of Walker Railey. I will have studied at one hundred and four character traits and how they interface with each other in total complexity, including his childhood."

Kinne looked at her skeptically, as if he wanted to say, "Yeah, sure you can," but was too polite to do it. Then he got to his feet. "I'll see you at noon tomorrow."

Jane also arose from her chair. When she reached the door, she turned back to him, dramatically lowering her voice. "Wouldn't it be fabulous, absolutely fabulous, if I could see Peggy's handwriting?"

Kinne peered over his glasses and said, "Yeah, that really would be."

"Let me tell you something," Jane said, widening her large brown eyes. "I'll go really out on a limb. If I can get hold of that woman's writing, I can tell you exactly what happened in that garage."

Kinne stared at her as if she were a freak in the circus. "Well, yes—I'll tell you *that* would be fabulous. That's the kind of ammunition I need."

"Good night," Jane whispered, softly closing the door behind her.

After she had left, Kinne sat down, leaned back in his chair and closed his eyes. Then he shook his head to clear his thoughts. A few moments later he leaned forward, picked up the telephone and dialed the Federal Bureau of Investigation.

The next day Jane arrived at Kinne's office half an hour early. The door was open. Kinne swung around in his swivel chair and called out to his secretary. "Judith, get Jane her water and hold all my calls and shut the door. I do *not* want to be disturbed."

There was elation in his voice. Jane thought he looked like the Cheshire cat.

"Something has happened since I saw you last," she said.

He reached into a drawer and slapped on top of his desk three yellow legal pads. "Peggy's journal," he said. Then, steadying his chair and looking over his glasses, he asked, "Let me have the report."

Jane handed him the first two pages of the three-page report, keeping a copy for herself. She knew that attorneys could read aloud faster than the Indianapolis speed car races, even upside down and sideways, but Kinne broke all the records.

"The writer [Railey] displays an extreme degree of composure and will register only a minimal level of internal emotional responsiveness. He is, therefore, ruled by his head rather than his heart . . ."

As he read the next part of it silently, his glasses slipped lower and lower on his nose. Then he read parts of it aloud again:

"This man has experienced emotional trauma strong enough to cause him to reject a loved one or a cherished hope or belief. He, himself, likely experienced rejection or disillusionment in his formative years, which caused a retreat from emotions. He simply has sought to anesthetize himself from further pain . . . Little things annoy Walker, and those in his inner circle have heard him lash out sarcastically in retaliation. His temper can be enflamed [sic].

Then she leaned forward, speaking slowly and precisely, the final page held closely in front of her pleated, cherry red silk blouse. "Your parting comment to me last night was that you needed ammunition for the grand jury trial."

She gave him the last page of the report and watched him absorb the first two paragraphs, admiring the quickness of his mind as he grasped the meanings.

He read the final paragraph again, this time aloud:

"In a social setting this man can be diplomatic, making him appear to be concerned about others' feelings. His self-assured, quiet demeanor draws admiration from his extremely few friends. He is only at ease with a very narrow stratum of society with whom he will likely seek to enjoy sensual pleasures . . . The 'demon' within demands to be tamed!"

There was a silence during which she was conscious of the almost audible whirring of his mind. She remarked, "If it feels right, this will come closer to getting what you want than anything you could ever have." Calm in her speech she was shaking so much in her limbs that she thought surely she would levitate.

Kinne removed his glasses, rubbed his eyes between his thumb and forefinger and exhaled in a loud, deep sigh. "God—Jesus—God." He picked up his unlit pipe from a messy glass ashtray and poked the stem between clenched teeth at the back of his mouth, causing his lips to curl in a snarl. He struck a wooden match on the side of a match box and held it in front of him so long that it burned his finger. He shook it vigorously, removed the pipe from his mouth and shoved the yellow legal pads toward Jane.

"Let's take these with us to lunch, and see how much you

can tell me about Peggy Railey in two hours." Jane looked startled. "I know it won't be scientifically measured," he told her, "but maybe you can pick up something."

There aren't many (if any) good restaurants within a block or two of the courthouse. Kinne selected Sam's Cafe, a coffee shop in a cheap hotel across from the old Union Station. The wine-colored table cloths, the yellow sheer curtains and the multicolored Jackson Pollack–looking carpet are all worn thin. There are the stale odors of food spilled and rubbed into fabrics, of coffee heated and reheated and then reheated again, of cooking oil into which more oil has been added as fish are deep-fried three or four times a day. There is a buffet table on one side of the room with fried fish, fried potatoes, chicken salad, canned tuna fish, canned beets, canned chick peas and a make-your-own salad of lettuce, tomatoes, cucumbers and onions. While not a gourmet's paradise, it is a quiet, convenient place for lawyers to meet clients and potential witnesses. Jane wasn't really hungry anyway, so she picked at a small salad, drank water and studied Peggy Railey's handwriting while Kinne filled two plates from the buffet, with an assortment of everything.

"How are you doing?" He placed the plates on the table.

"This isn't going to be absolutely accurate."

"What do you make of the content?"

"Usually I don't notice the content. In graphoanalysis, it doesn't even matter what language it's written in. I've done a character study from a letter written in German, and I don't speak German."

"Just tell me what you think."

Jane drew in her breath. "This woman is to be pitied. She is so unhappy and so frightened."

"Is she afraid of her husband?"

"She's afraid of abandonment."

"It hasn't been a happy marriage," Kinne said dryly. "See, she talks about 'the wilderness of the past five years.'"

"Who is Janet?"

"Janet Marshall. A young woman in the Church who is in love with Walker. Babysits the children sometimes."

"Peggy writes that she asked the Lord for a penance—'You gave me one . . . Janet. Lord, I accept . . . I have turned my heart away from the pain I have inflicted on her. Lord, it is a difficult situation. You handle it.'—What does Peggy mean 'difficult situation?' "

"I don't know."

"Peggy mentions her several times—'hatred, anger, disgust'—is Janet going to testify before the grand jury?"

"No. The police interviewed her because Walker telephoned her the night of the attack. But they didn't think she knew anything."

"Even after they read what Peggy wrote here?"

"There's somebody else more important in Walker's life," Kinne said. "Just give me some insights into Peggy's character."

"She talks about her own faults—and she's honest about them. On the surface she and Walker must have seemed ideal for each other, but, underneath, their relationship is completely destructive."

Kinne looked at her over his glasses, a fork of chick peas held steady a few inches from his mouth. "You're not telling me he had *reason* to strangle her?"

"Nobody *deserves* to be strangled," Jane said indignantly. "I'm telling you that she had a helluva temper. She was argumentative and sarcastic. She baited him, like a squirrel switching its tail at a dog. She played it closer and closer, and it was a heavy, explosive situation—both of them were capable of violence."

"A crime of passion?" Kinne looked skeptical.

"You can't categorize something like this. We need two or three weeks to analyze it from every angle."

"Woman, we haven't even got *twenty-four hours!* I've got to spend the rest of this afternoon and this evening working on the questions I'm going to ask."

"Make Walker wait. From my findings, he will have sweaty palms if you stretch the timing."

Kinne simply looked at her.

"Now, let's choreograph your walk," she said.

His eyes widened in astonishment. "You really are serious about this, aren't you?"

"Yes. And when you walk down that corridor, you will pass him with no eye contact. Then as you get so many paces down the hall, turn with your back at an angle to him, and make a remark that he will only hear as a hiss, hiss and—"

"There isn't time for acting lessons," Kinne said firmly.

Jane wondered if in her enthusiasm she had overstepped the boundary of propriety. "I know the grand jury is closed, of course, but I surely wish I could be a fly on the wall in that courtroom tomorrow morning."

Kinne nodded. There were a lot of people with that same wish.

21

Wednesday, July 29, 1987

NORMAN KINNE ARRIVED AT HIS OFFICE AROUND TEN-thirty A.M., approximately an hour later than usual. He had worked late into the night on his questions for Railey and how he should approach him. He had not slept well.

His secretary stood up from her desk, preventing him from entering his office. Her eyes sparkled with excitement. "You had an important telephone call about twenty minutes ago."

"From whom?"

"Walker Railey."

Kinne grinned. He could take a joke. "Yeah, sure. Well, you tell the Reverend Railey, and President Reagan, too, that I'm busy and won't be able to return their calls until late this afternoon."

"I'm serious," Judith said. "Walker Railey *telephoned* you, no more than twenty minutes ago."

It wasn't a joke. She *was* serious. "Did he leave a number?"

"No. But he said he would call back. He said it was important that he talk to you."

"I hope to God he does call back," Kinne said just as the phone on Judith's desk buzzed, startling them both.

"I'll take it in my office," he said, hurrying through the door and shoving it shut behind him. "God, let it be Railey," he muttered as he picked up the phone.

"Norm Kinne here," he said calmly and clearly.

"Hi Norm. It's Doug," said the voice on the other end of the wire.

"I was hoping it would be your client. I understand that he called me earlier this morning."

"Yeah, he did. I'm glad you weren't in."

"I'm not. What did he want to talk about?"

"Nothing now. He's changed his mind about talking to you. That's why I'm calling. I just wanted you to know that he's not going to be talking. There aren't going to be any surprises, unless, of course, he surprises me."

"I sure hope he does."

"Yeah, well—I don't think he will. I'll see you in front of the grand jury room in half an hour."

"I'm sure as hell glad you can't be *inside* that grand jury room."

Mulder laughed. The two men had usually been on the same side, sometimes working the same case together. They knew each other's tactics. They might have exchanged sides, and the case would still be handled in a similar manner. There was no personal enmity between them. Outside the courtroom, probably over a couple of drinks, they would discuss this case.

At eleven A.M. the hallway leading to the grand jury room in the Dallas County Courthouse was crowded with reporters and photographers, some lawyers, policemen and friends and relatives of the five witnesses who were subpoenaed.

When Railey appeared in a navy blue suit, escorted by Mulder and followed by John Yarrington, the media went wild. Lights brightened the scene, cameras whirred and reporters shouted their questions.

"What's Railey going to say?" a reporter shouted at Mulder, who is a handsome, well-built man in his forties with dark, kinky hair, graying slightly and plastered straight back, as in an old Brylcreem ad.

"I've advised Walker when he goes before the grand jury to assert his Fifth Amendment privilege against self-incrimination and say nothing," Mulder said slowly and distinctly, so that the newspaper reporters would have time to take down his words exactly. "If he follows my advice, that's what he'll do."

"It makes him look guilty by pleading the Fifth Amendment," the television reporter persisted.

"I understand that, but that's just a cross he'll have to bear," Mulder said, unaware of any play upon words.

Late that same afternoon Railey left the grand jury courtroom and, again joined by Mulder and Yarrington, made his way through the media crowd to the bank of elevators. This time he was not as calm as he had been earlier.

"Is there an indictment?" a reporter asked.

"No indictment," Mulder replied for Railey.

"No indictment," several people echoed.

"Walk more slowly, Reverend!" a television cameraman called out.

Startled, Railey slowed his pace, asking, "Is this all right?"

When he reached the bank of elevators, there was no open one waiting. Mulder pushed the down button. To the delight of the press the normally slow elevators took even longer in coming. Railey's jaws clenched, the muscles in his cheeks quivering, his lips narrowed in a slash. Flexing his hands and shifting his weight from one foot to another, he fidgeted waiting for the elevator. The television cameras hummed.

"Did you take the Fifth Amendment?" a reporter asked.

Without answering Railey turned his back on the reporter. Mulder pushed the elevator button again. Yarrington moved closer to Railey.

"The Fifth Amendment!" another reporter repeated. "Did you take the Fifth Amendment?"

"I have followed the advice of my lawyer consistently and will consistently do that," Railey said, as the doors to an elevator parted. Yarrington entered and Mulder shoved Railey into the elevator in front of him. Several reporters crowded in with them.

The big news, however, was not to be gathered in that descending elevator but from several sources who had been inside the grand jury room and who preferred not to be identified but who were willing to talk.

Friday, July 31, 1987

Olive Talley and *Times Herald* reporters Debra Davis and Jerry Needham spent all day Thursday ferreting out information in depth that could not be covered in the television news clips.

Kinne told reporters that his role in the case so far had been that of helping the police gather information by calling witnesses before the grand jury.

"I don't know whether it's clear to the public, but we [the district attorney's office] don't *investigate* criminal offenses. We *prosecute* criminal offenses when the police put the cases together. This is a Dallas Police Department investigation ... There is a big difference between talking to a police officer and going before a grand jury under oath saying 'I refuse to answer on grounds that it may incriminate me.'"

Other sources informed the media that it was true that Railey had answered only his name and then taken the Fifth Amendment forty-three times.

Reporters from *The Dallas Times Herald* spoke with John Holt, Captain of the Crimes Against Persons section, who said he would still like to interview Walker Railey. "But I don't see any hope in it. The concerns and questions we had prior to the grand jury session remain. Those questions may never be resolved, but I'm not prepared to say a case will never be filed."

Lt. Ron Waldrop was somewhat more positive. He told reporters Davis and Needham that the police were reviewing the testimony "to compare it with what we had and see what there is to work on. It will be a week or so before we see if there is anything beneficial to come out of it . . . We still have a lot of discrepancies, but we're not going to discuss them . . . Our concern is with finding the person who strangled Peggy Railey. We intend to do that, and we're going to commit all the manpower and resources we need to that. We don't plan to stop . . . There is no statute of limitations on attempted murder, and that's how long we'll be working on it."

The comments of the district attorney's office and the police department were a necessary part of the reporters' coverage. They were not, however, what caught the attention of the Dallas public. The testimony of the four witnesses other than Railey at the "fact-finding grand jury" contained the real shockers and converted what had been local scandal into a national scandal, especially the testimony of psychologist Dr. Lucy Papillon.

On Friday, July 31, both *The News* and *The Herald* ran front-page stories with leads that focused on the relationship between Railey and Papillon.

"The Rev. Walker Railey's failure to tell police he spent time with a female psychologist on the night his wife was attacked was a discrepancy authorities had hoped to clarify through a grand jury investigation, a prosecutor said Thursday," wrote Olive Talley.

"The Rev. Walker Railey and Dallas psychologist Lucy Papillon had discussed marriage during romantic encounters before the near-fatal choking attack on the minister's wife in April, according to a source familiar with Papillon's testimony before a grand jury this week," wrote Davis and Needham.

Although Papillon's lawyer, Phil Burleson, had said that there was no romantic involvement between his client and the minister, the source said Papillon testified that she and Railey had kissed in the Presbyterian Hospital suite where Railey was staying. Papillon further told the grand jury that she had accompanied Railey on a number of trips, including a vacation in England; she had met him in London after he had attended a World Methodist Council meeting in Nairobi, Kenya, in July of 1986. Railey had left the Council meeting several days early, after he had been photographed with South African Archbishop Desmond Tutu.

One person who was shocked, but then again not really surprised by the revelation of the affair between Walker and Lucy, was Maxie Hardin. The Sunday evening after the attack on Peggy both Maxie and Lucy had attended a career women's meeting at the church. They knew each other only slightly, but Lucy had come over to Maxie and said she was sorry that Maxie's little boy had not been allowed to come to the Yarringtons and be with Bryan.

Bryan! Maxie was stunned. It was a mistake easily made, and she hadn't supposed Lucy knew the Railey children well. As far as she could remember Peggy had never mentioned Lucy. What Peggy had mentioned was that in the threatening letters *Ryan* was referred to as *Bryan*. It was a strange coincidence.

While not nearly as titillating as the testimony of glamorous Lucy Papillon, the testimonies of the other witnesses were equally damaging to Railey.

Stephen Mbutu, an employee at Fondren Library at Southern Methodist University, testified that Railey gave him a business card regarding some reference material he had been unable to locate. According to Mbutu, Railey noted on the back of the card that the time was ten-thirty P.M. when in fact the time was after midnight.

Psychiatrist Dr. Dwight Holden, who had been ordered by the court to turn over his notes and records to the district attorney's office, testified. Reverend Howard Grimes also handed over records of a Church committee made up of his wife Johnnie Marie Grimes, Susan Sanders and Karen Spencer. These women had attempted to replicate Railey's stated movements on the night of the attack. This proved impossible. Railey simply could not have been where he was at the time he said he was.

There was doubt now even among Railey's strongest supporters. Everything the minister had done raised questions that he refused to answer. Still evading the police, Railey again appeared on television. Channel Four reporter Bud Gillett suggested that even though Railey was within his rights in not talking to the police, the serious inconsistencies in his first statement and what the police later uncovered made him seem guilty. Was he not afraid that these inconsistencies, coupled with his taking the Fifth Amendment forty-three times, could lead to another grand jury hearing and a possible indictment?

"I don't worry about an indictment because I didn't do anything," Railey replied. "There are times when I'm the only one in the world who believes that, but I'm the one who knows."

Discerning minds watching that interview wondered how a man who previously had claimed not to know what happened to his wife the night she was attacked—"I don't know. I just don't know"—could now say that he was the only one who really knew what happened that night. Some even wondered if there might be two Walker Raileys, one who knew and one who did not know.

22

THE REAL WALKER RAILEY WAS A SUBJECT THAT MANY acquainted with the senior minister now pondered. Few, however, pondered with as heavy a heart as John Yarrington, who, in his own words, had played the role of "the trusted aide in the breach." It hurt him to accept that Walker had a secret life that he, "the trusted aide," never suspected.

A number of times Walker had said, and had been quoted in the press as saying, that the closest person in the world to him was John, yet John had neither known nor suspected Walker's intimate relationship with Lucy. Clearly Walker confided in John only what he wanted John to know. If Walker could conceal adultery for over a year, what else could he conceal?

The success and ease with which Walker lied astounded John who worried that Walker visited his children less frequently than in the days immediately following the attack.

It also bothered him that Walker had taken the Fifth Amendment before the grand jury and that he was refusing to help the police with their inquiries. Even if Walker was sacrificing his own reputation to protect Lucy, he should still want to have the crime against Peggy solved. Surely Lucy herself had nothing to do with the attack on Peggy—unless, knowingly or unknowingly, she had provided Walker with a motive. Walker might bully people and commit adultery, but there was no way that John could believe Walker was a murderer. At least not the Walker John knew.

Was the one he knew the true Walker Railey? If John Yarrington didn't know the true Walker Railey, who did?

Across town from the Yarringtons, in Highland Park in a sixty-year-old red brick cottage a few blocks from SMU, Howard Grimes is dying of lung cancer. The house where Howard and Johnnie Marie live seems morbidly appropriate. The Grimes have barricaded themselves from unwelcome intrusion. On the windows are black iron burglar bars. The front door has a second black barred door which makes the house seem like a prison or a South Dallas drug house.

After some forty years of marriage, the Grimes still seem an oddly matched couple. Although their appearances belie it, Howard is more than twelve years younger than Johnnie Marie, a solidly built woman with red hair and freckles. Johnnie Marie spent most of her working life as private secretary to Dr. Willis Tate, a former president of SMU for over twenty years.

Recently Howard has had a recurrence of cancer. Three years ago he underwent an operation for colon cancer. This time the cancer is in his lungs. It is inoperable, and he knows that he has only a few months left to live. Before the Railey debacle, Howard's cancer had been in remission. If Railey had not betrayed his own ideals and discredited the Church, Howard believes his cancer would not have returned.

Until a few weeks ago Howard thought the greatest tragedy of his life was the death from cancer of his only child and legally adopted son at the age of twenty-one. Now Walker, who calls Howard his adoptive father, is an even greater sorrow. Howard's true adopted son had led a good life, but Walker has two opposing sides to his personality. Howard believes that the cruel, dark side of Walker has prevailed. While there may be forgiveness, Walker cannot be redeemed.

Having awakened from his afternoon nap and taken his medication, Howard shuffles along the narrow hall from his bedroom to the living room. The house has the odor of moth balls and dried flowers. Howard is helped by a wooden cane with a polished brass, duck-head handle. In the living room he lowers himself into a straight back chair, leaning heavily on his cane. He can't get Walker off his mind.

Even though it is September and the outdoor temperature still in the eighties, Howard shivers and pulls his brown cardigan tightly across a heavy gray shirt buttoned to the collar. He has lost weight; his clothes hang loosely. Sitting in his gloomy living room, locked from the outside world by the black iron bars, he shifts uncomfortably on the low Victorian chair. His feet in thick gray socks and fleece-lined brown house slippers are cold. Most of the time he is in pain.

For a long while he has known that Walker and Peggy didn't have a happy marriage. He thought probably they didn't have a satisfactory sex life and had come to an arrangement about their relationship so that on the surface, at least, the marriage worked. He remembered a day some six years ago, shortly after Walker had been appointed senior minister at First Church. Walker had dropped by Howard's office at Perkins to have the kind of "father-son talk" Walker frequently initiated, even though Howard did not have such fatherly feelings toward Walker.

Howard was aware that Walker also called another minister, three bishops and two ordinary Christian laymen "fathers." No doubt he intended adoptive parenthood as a compliment, though Howard didn't appreciate it and sometimes wondered if the others did.

Actually Howard didn't much like either Walker or Peggy, though he believed Walker possessed charisma while preaching. Six years ago in Howard's office, Walker had asked Howard if he thought his career would be helped if he had children. Howard replied that he thought Walker's career would indeed be helped. Children gave a special purpose to one's whole life. Shortly thereafter Peggy had an operation and immediately became pregnant.

In retrospect it seemed to Howard that Walker hadn't wanted to have children to fill a need in his life but simply to enhance his career. Lucy, as Walker's wife, could also enhance Walker's career far more than Peggy. Not only was she the daughter of a popular, nationally recognized bishop, Lucy had "class." Howard couldn't think of a less snobbish way to describe it. Lucy's family was upper-class with an established place in the community. Lucy wore expensive, sophisticated designer clothes; Peggy enjoyed sewing her own dresses. When Lucy made an entrance, men stared at her admiringly. She was, in the slang of the day, a knockout and a perfect trophy wife for an ambitious minister in Manhattan. Peggy would dislike Riverside Church even more than First Church. But Lucy would adore it.

Howard had seen the sexual attraction between them that evening when Lucy came to the hospital with a red rose. Howard regretted introducing Walker and Lucy but more for Lucy's sake than Walker's. Even though Walker might never be made a bishop it would have been better for him to divorce Peggy and marry Lucy. Whether marriage to Walker was the best choice for Lucy was another matter. Howard suspected that Walker's being senior pastor at First Church, following in the footsteps of Lucy's father, was his chief attraction. Lucy would always be her father's girl.

Though Howard could believe and forgive Walker his affair with Lucy, he had not believed Walker capable of murder. When Howard formed the ad hoc committee of Johnnie Marie, Susan Sanders and Karen Spenser to recreate Walker's movements on the night of the crime, he had hoped to vindicate Walker's story to the police regarding his whereabouts. Johnnie Marie and Susan and Karen loved Walker and believed in the truth of his mission. It had frightened them when nothing checked out as Walker had claimed. When Howard testified before the grand jury, he felt he had made a moral choice in favor of the truth. And the terrible truth had brought back the disease that eventually would prove fatal to him.

Jo Ann Hill was not in the least surprised by the news of the Walker and Lucy affair. What surprised and bothered her was Walker's taking the Fifth Amendment. Jo Ann believed there could be only one reason for that—he was guilty of the attack on Peggy.

Jo Ann is a large woman in her late forties. She wears her heavy, blue-black hair in a casual, straight bouffant style.

Her very white skin is sometimes described as alabaster, and she possesses an exotic gypsy look. She is a public relations consultant and has attended First United Methodist for many years. For almost ten years she has been Lucy's friend and consultant. In her own words she had "helped Lucy shape her image, getting her to reconcile her glamorous physical appearance with the intellectual image she wanted to portray."

Jo Ann sits at her desk in her office, looking at glossy photos of Lucy and Walker. Outside it is hot. Her feet hurt and her ankles are swelling, so she kicks off her shoes.

To Jo Ann, Lucy is "a sweet, loving, feeling person—but a needing person." Over and over again Jo Ann had asked her if she wanted to be Marilyn Monroe or a doctor of psychology. Of course Lucy wanted to be both—but the images were difficult to blend.

Walker is a different type of person. For four years Jo Ann had worked with him on the television show "Faith Focus." She wrote his scripts, and once a week he and Jo Ann drove to Fort Worth together to do the show. Walker intimidated people a lot, not Jo Ann, of course; but most of the crew on "Faith Focus" kept their distance.

Jo Ann looked at a photograph of Walker that she recently had commissioned to be taken at the Church. She had told him she wanted him to look really good. She asked him to think of Peggy. He had smiled. But later, at the Church when she showed Peggy the pictures and said they were good because Walker was thinking of her, Peggy had replied: "You don't know him."

At the time, three months before the attack, the remark seemed strange to Jo Ann. Now it seemed even stranger. From her experience in the business of image making she knew that people were seldom what they seemed.

Despite his self-assurance and his sometimes bullying manner Walker had been victimized. As a child he had been psychologically abused by alcoholic parents. In his sermons Walker frequently referred to his mother's and father's drinking and fighting on weekends while young Walker longed for a parent who would take him by the hand and walk him to Sunday School. Jo Ann believed that what Walker wanted more than anything in the world was a loving, caring family. Lucy was foolish to have become involved with him.

Reverend John Thornberg, was pastor at Greenland Hills and had been an associate pastor at Christ Church when Walker was there in the late 1970s. He told his congregation: *"Walker Railey is now mired in a tragedy of his own making, but the sermons he preached are among the finest that have come from any American pulpit, and the advice he gave to young ministers and his own parishioners is still valid, even with what has transpired."*

Thornberg's statement provokes debate. If pure evil exists, might it not be most cleverly concealed in a Christian sermon? On the other hand, is it not true that lives may be saved by a gifted surgeon who himself has incurable cancer? If evil is not something tangible that can be examined in a scientific manner, should it be compared with a physical or mental disease? Can a person become evil by living within a particular environment or by being exposed to someone who is inherently evil?

The subject of human evil is, like death, one that few people today feel comfortable in discussing. Evil is ugly. It destroys and murders. Its existence is denied by many who believe in God. Yet, as Hannah Arendt noted in her book on the trial of Adolf Eichmann, "the banality of evil" makes it easy to deny its existence and to overlook its danger. On an individual basis it is small and tawdry. On a group basis it is mesmerizing and powerful. Builders of medieval cathedrals placed gargoyles upon the buttresses of their cathedrals to ward off evil spirits, for they believed that evil tended to hide in the cloak of the goodness and respectability of religion.

Many people who had known Walker over a period of years would have assumed that, next to John Yarrington, Reverend Dudley Dancer was Walker's closest friend. Ten years older than Walker, Dancer was an extroverted "Hail, fellow, well met!" sort of man, who was nearly as energetic and hyperactive as Walker. Whereas Walker was frequently sarcastic and provocative, Dudley was a conciliator, turning a sensitive or controversial issue into a joke. Clever, affable and quick-witted, Dudley had been the senior associate at First Church when Walker had been a junior assistant and when Ben Oliphint, now bishop of the Texas Conference, centered in Houston, had been the senior pastor. Dudley remembered the three of them being a close team and working well together for four years. They did a Sunday night radio talk show from ten to twelve on WRR.

"Walker would turn off the 'nuts.' He could take a nutty question and run with it," Dudley said.

Dudley, Walker and Ben also developed twelve or thirteen sermons they did together. And Irby-Mayes, an exclusive menswear store, whose owners were members of First Church, gave the three of them matching suits.

The ministers were a team. Ben managed them, but it was a shared ministry, and Walker accepted that. Ben was another of Walker's father figures.

In the early 1970s, the three ministers had frequently played handball together. Walker played to win. If he wasn't winning when it was time to quit, he insisted that they continue playing until he was winning. Dudley thought it amusing and sometimes let him win just to be able to quit. Walker was always serious about winning.

In 1974 Dudley and his wife Sally were sent by the Church with Walker and Peggy to Edinburgh where they stayed for three weeks in dorms at the university. There the two couples became good friends. On weekends they drove around Britain, staying at bed and breakfasts and playing golf.

Dudley remembered playing golf with Walker on a course where there was a water trap. Walker hit a whole bag of balls in the water trying to get the ball across the trap. He was very determined.

Like most ministers, Walker had a big ego, which Peggy occasionally felt the need to squelch. Peggy was intelligent, caring and laughed a lot.

When Ben Oliphint was made Bishop and Walker succeeded Ben as pastor at First Church (and Dudley succeeded Walker as senior pastor at Christ Church) the relationship between Walker and Dudley changed. They didn't get together so much. All of a sudden it seemed as if Walker had no peers. Yet, if there *was* a change, it was more in Peggy than in Walker. Dudley thought it was the strain of being the pastor's wife in a big church that was constantly in the limelight.

Since Walker had become senior pastor at First Church, Dudley hadn't seen him over four or five times during the past seven years. Walker was in the fast lane. Dudley wasn't. Despite the hurt of this realization and despite the credibility of Walker's suicide letter, Dudley could not believe that Walker had attempted to murder Peggy.

From Houston Bishop Oliphint said: "It is a great and continuing tragedy—I don't have any proof of what has happened and I'm not making a judgment."

While hardly enlightening, at least one bishop was speaking with the media.

23

AFTER THE GRAND JURY HEARING AND THE COMMUnity's shock at the minister's taking the Fifth Amendment, the focus of the crime shifted. The sad truth is that the public's interest in the damaged life of the victim soon diminishes. Because of contradictory desires to punish or to rehabilitate a general interest in criminals continues to fascinate. The media inevitably refer to a crime by the name of the criminal, not the victim, unless of course the criminal is a nobody and the victim a superstar—the Lindbergh kidnapping, the Kennedy assassination—but these superstar crimes are rare. Superstars are seldom victims, and criminals, not victims, sometimes become superstars. There is a fine but distinct line between famous and infamous.

Dallas was titillated by the revelation of a minister's extramarital affair. Many Church members fell into a state of denial. As unambiguous circumstantial evidence mounted, their feelings that Walker simply could not have done this solidified. If he had committed such a heinous crime as attempted murder, how could any of them have thought he was the most wonderful man in the world? Losing faith in Railey meant not only losing faith in the Church but in themselves as well. The need for a scapegoat emerged. Lucy, "the other woman." Whispers of more "other women" grew louder. Janet Marshall, who was frequently seen with Walker, was mentioned most often.

On Sundays Janet ate lunch with the Railey family in the privacy of Walker's Church office. Anyone who saw her with Walker could tell she was in love with him. Peggy and Diane Yarrington joked about a clerical romance and teased Walker who was sometimes testy about it. But Lucy Papillon was no joke. In her own kitchen, Diane Yarrington confronted Walker directly. "Is it true that you have been having an affair with Lucy Papillon?"

"Yes."

"Walker, you've violated everything you've preached."

He nodded, not meeting her eyes.

"I don't want that woman ever to come in my home again," Diane spoke loudly. "So don't you ever bring her here because she *is not welcome!*"

"I hear what you're saying," Walker replied softly.

But did he really hear? Did he understand that Diane's rage focused on Lucy because Diane, like half the membership of First Church, simply could not accept Walker's culpability? Lucy *had* to have seduced Walker. He could not have initiated anything immoral. Others, more tolerant of sexual peccadillos, wondered aloud why, with all the shocking revelations, Railey had *not* been indicted by the grand jury. While there was still a chance that he was not guilty of the attack on his wife, he certainly was *not* an innocent man.

Norm Kinne patiently explained to Olive Talley that "Walker Railey is a liar. He has been cheating on his wife. On the night of his wife's attack, he was not where he said he was at the time he said he was. But none of that makes him a strangler. When a judge asks me, 'Mr. Kinne, where is your evidence that this man strangled his wife?' I have to say 'I simply don't have any.'"

Kinne acknowledged that other cases had been won on circumstantial evidence, but in this case he feared an indictment could be too easily dismissed on summary judgment. On appeal there could be a directed verdict. The decision would then be reversed, and Walker could never again be tried for the crime, even if evidence *proving him guilty* turned up later.

The last time Olive Tally had been to a service at First Church, she was conscious of people staring at her with unfriendly expressions. She overheard herself referred to as "the woman who wrote about Walker and Lucy." Walker had told several members of the Pastor-Parish Committee that Olive was a traitor to him, a traitor to the Church and a traitor to God. Because of personal discomfort, Olive felt she could no longer go to First Church to worship. Now the Church was simply an institution on her beat, a suspicious element in an ongoing, unsavory story, yet, perhaps containing the solution to the unsolved crime.

The abuse Olive encountered at the Church was mild, however, compared with the hostility met by Lucy Papillon. Speculation about her lifestyle and her adulterous sins almost relegated to second place the discussion of whether or not Railey had attempted to murder his wife.

One Saturday evening Lucy attended Temple Emanu-El and was standing in the receiving line. When Sheldon spotted her, he exclaimed: "What on earth are you doing here?"

"I thought anyone could come," Lucy said, backing off.

"Of course, of course," Sheldon mumbled, ashamed of his abruptness.

The Judaic-Christian tradition has never been as fair to women as to men. In what had now almost become a cliché case of a minister committing adultery and consequently suffering a flip-flop in all his moral behavior, Walker Railey was compared with Elmer Gantry and Reverend Tinsdale. Lucy was Sadie Thompson defiantly wearing Hester Prynn's invisible Scarlet A on her ample bosom.

Indeed it seemed that many members of First Church's congregation were suggesting that Lucy was responsible for Walker's fall from grace. Some even suggesting that Peggy herself was so cold and disagreeable that she had forced loving Walker into another woman's arms, thereby provoking the attack upon herself. Other older members said that a good man trapped between two malevolent women had surrendered to the human foibles of illicit sex and violence.

Bishop Russell refused to discuss this unpleasant, ecclesiastical scandal. As far as he was concerned the more it was discussed, the more harmful it was to the Church. Some Methodist ministers believed the opposite—the public deserved some response from the Church.

The Bishop's silence and failure to call meetings of the ministers to discuss the tragedy left them without any clue as to how to answer their parishioners' questions. Absence of an official position resulted in confusion. Many ministers felt that Bishop Russell and Bishop Stowe knew more than they were telling.

Less than two weeks after Lucy Papillon's revelation to the grand jury that she and Railey had "dated" for a year, taken trips together and discussed marriage, eighteen Methodist ministers in the North Texas Conference signed a letter to Bishop Russell calling for an investigation of the allegation that Railey had an extramarital affair with Lucy

Papillon. They felt it was time "to clear the air" regarding this allegation and others against him.

According to *The Methodist Book of Discipline,* a man may remain a pastor if he is *accused* of murder, but if it can be proven that he has committed adultery, he must resign from his Church. Actually, of course, an ecclesiastical court has jurisdiction only over violations of Methodist rules of moral and ethical conduct. State or federal courts determine if a crime has been committed against an individual or against society.

Bishop Russell issued a four paragraph press release that stated that "actions are being considered" following requests for an investigation into allegations of Walker Railey's immorality.

In an article by Olive Talley published in *The News* on August 16, 1987, Bishop Russell was quoted as saying:

> "The district superintendent of the North Texas Conference and I are seriously concerned about reports of alleged ministerial misconduct on the part of Walker Railey. The Book of Disciplineship [sic] of our denomination carefully outlines the appropriate process of review and investigation of ministerial misconduct.
>
> "In keeping with requirements of the Book of Discipline, various actions are being considered at the present time."

Observers of and participants in Methodist politics suspected that the only action being considered by the bishop was how to avoid action. This cynicism was confirmed when the ministers calling for an investigation were told by Bishop Russell that their request was rejected. He cited "lack of evidence" without which an investigation would be "a violation of church law."

In an article with the headline, BISHOP: FACTS DON'T MERIT RAILEY PROBE, Helen Parmley attempted to clarify the bishop's response by quoting him more fully. *"An investigative committee,"* the bishop explained, *"can only be called on the receipt of written accusations against a clergy, accusing that person of a chargeable offense."*

With the utmost sincerity he then told Helen: "I couldn't call an investigative committee just to investigate. We have to begin with a written accusation."

Thus, ecclesiastical law followed the precedent of government law. If there was not concrete evidence, there was no investigation and therefore no trial.

The last thing in the world the Church hierarchy wanted now was an ecclesiastical trial with all the attendant publicity.

Four of the ministers who had signed a letter to the bishop formed a committee representing all who had asked for an investigation and, coincidentally, most of the other ministers in the North Texas Conference. The committee visited the bishop in his office at Highland Park Methodist Church.

"This Railey scandal is simply not going to go away. Most of us think it may get a lot worse before it gets better," the spokesman said. "If there can't be an investigation, then you simply *have to say something."*

"But what can I say?" the bishop agonized.

"It doesn't so much matter *what* you say, as long as you say something," a quick-tempered Oak Cliff minister told him. "As long as you remain silent, there is no official Church statement. We have no guidelines to talk to our parishioners."

"Sometimes it is best to remain silent," the bishop said mildly.

"Not in this case!" the four ministers replied in unison.

Still two weeks later no official statement was issued from the bishop's office.

Walker Railey made certain that he would not face an ecclesiastical jury. He would *not* be judged by his peers. If he could not with certainty avoid forever a criminal trial, he could with certainty prevent an ecclesiastical trial. He could return his credentials and resign. A man who is no longer a minister cannot be examined or accused in an ecclesiastical court.

August 20, 1987

As Chairman of the Pastor-Parish Committee Ralph Shannon telephoned Walker at a home where he knew he was staying. At the end of August Railey would receive his last pay check from First Church. Shannon wanted to be certain that Walker remembered this and that he understood that expense-account privileges ended, too. Walker said that he was going to the Church to do some work.

Ralph, too, was going to the Church. When he arrived, he met Susan Monts who anxiously told him that Walker was in his office writing to the bishop a letter of resignation as a Methodist minister.

Ralph was stunned. This was one thing he had not anticipated. Walker's entire ego was bound up in being a minister, in being the very best minister in America. Without being announced he walked into the senior minister's office.

"I've decided to resign my ministerial credentials, Ralph," Walker said.

"Walker, this is not a wise move," Ralph said firmly. "So far you've not been indicted for anything, nor are you being investigated by the Church. Your whole life has been the ministry. By handing in your credentials now, you'll be losing everything and gaining nothing. You'll be endangering your wife's insurance."

"Let the bishop take the heat for a while," Railey said coolly. "I'm writing a letter of resignation, which I'm going to deliver personally."

Ralph, John, Susan and Karen accompanied Walker to the bishop's office in Highland Park Methodist Church. Ralph drove and John sat in the front seat beside him. Walker sat in the back seat between Karen and Susan, his Deacons and Elders certificates, which he had removed from their frames, rested on his knees. No one attempted to make conversation.

With tears in his eyes Bishop Russell met the five of them

outside his office. There were also tears in Walker's eyes as he handed over the certificates.

The following Sunday Bishop Russell announced Railey's resignation from the pulpit at First United Methodist Church. And, in a prepared statement for the press, Railey said:

> "Over the past four months, the burdens upon me have been tremendous, as have the complexity and confusion of the situation surrounding my life . . . I will cherish forever my twenty-two years under (ministerial) appointment of a bishop and look forward in the future to serving God, however that may be."

24

September 1987

BILLIE JO AND BILL NICOLAI WERE EXPECTING AN afternoon visit from their son-in-law. Instead of meeting at The Clairmont Nursing Home, Walker was coming to the Nicolais' house.

Today's meeting, which Walker had initiated, was not of a family gathering to comfort one another in tragedy but a business occasion. Billie Jo knew clearly now that her role in life was to nurture her child and to see that she was well taken care of for the rest of her life. Though she would never cease to pray for Peggy's recovery, she had to accept that this might not be God's will. She had to make arrangements for Peggy's future as an invalid, and this she was prepared to do. She hated to admit that money was so important, but, in this instance even now, and certainly after her own death, it was everything.

Walker had always been ambivalent about money, on occasion wildly extravagant yet at other times parsimonious almost to the extent of lacking Christian charity. He told them that he knew that he had heavy obligations toward his wife and children and that he wanted to find a job, maybe teaching or writing. The two books he had been working on had been cancelled, as well as his participation in "The Protestant Hour" radio series. He said he hoped to liquidate his assets and to gather enough money to pay off some debts and to provide for himself until he could get his life back together. Both Bill and Billie Jo wondered if getting his life back together included Lucy. They wanted to know the truth about their son-in-law's relationship with Lucy Papillon and whether this was in any way connected with what had happened to Peggy. But they were afraid to ask. It surprised them to realize they were actually afraid of Walker. It was an unspoken fear they shared but had never discussed before.

Since the Nicolais had returned to Texas ten years ago, an undefined, unmentioned tension prevailed within the family. When they had lived in Milwaukee and only saw Peggy and Walker once or twice a year, Billie Jo had believed that Peggy was happy and that Walker was a special person. He was still special, but for years Billie had sensed in him a cruel, chilling deception that she did not know how to combat. She was fearful in his presence, yet she was more afraid to speak critically of him to Peggy. Her daughter immediately became defiant and defensive, closing her out and reinforcing Billie Jo's suspicion that a dark secret existed between Peggy and Walker.

Bill collected his courage. "What about Peg?" he asked.

Walker replied that she was covered by the Church insurance.

"Only for two years," Billie Jo said. "Her coverage was dependent upon your being a Methodist minister."

Walker told her that the Church would always take care of Peggy, that she was deeply loved by that congregation and by the entire North Texas Conference. Tears came to his eyes when he told them that they could be assured of the continuance of the Church's love and Christian charity.

"And what about you, Walker?" Billie Jo asked.

"I know my responsibilities," Walker said flatly. "There are community property laws in Texas. Half of everything is Peggy's. I have put the Trail Hill house on the market, but in order to sell the house, someone besides myself needs to sign for Peggy. Half of the equity in the house and the furniture and the savings accounts belongs to her."

"You mean that you want *me* to become Peggy's guardian?" Billie Jo asked.

Walker said that was *exactly* what he wanted. He reminded them that they were the ones who were with her daily. He had to work. His voice was almost pleading when he said that if Billie Jo looked after Peggy's interests, writing checks and managing her account, no one could suggest that he had not been absolutely fair to Peggy.

"I don't believe we can just agree among ourselves for me to become Peggy's guardian," Billie Jo said. "Some people might suspect that I am just anxious to get my hands on my daughter's money."

"Oh, no!" Walker exclaimed.

"Some legal contract has to be drawn up and approved by a judge," Bill said. "Otherwise Billie Jo will have the money and you will still be responsible for Peggy's debts and welfare."

Walker asked them to have a lawyer draw up whatever contract was necessary. He rose to his feet and then bent down to kiss his mother-in-law. "We are all still family."

On September 23, 1987, Billie Jo Nicolai filed a petition in a Tyler probate court seeking appointment as legal guardian of her daughter and her daughter's estate. Attached to the petition was a sworn affidavit from Walker Railey in which he "waives and renounces the right to be appointed guardian" of his wife in favor of his mother-in-law, Billie Jo Nicolai.

Ten days later Tyler Judge Larry Craig approved the

petition, and Billie Jo Nicolai became legal guardian of her daughter and her daughter's estate. A week later on October 30, 1987, a Dallas judge gave temporary legal custody of Ryan and Megan Railey to Diane and John Yarrington, who told reporters that there had been no attempt on their part to gain *permanent* custody of the children. "I resent the idea that either Walker is dumping his children or that we're taking his children away," Yarrington said in an interview with newspaper reporters.

There was no FOR SALE sign on the front lawn of 9328 Trail Hill Drive, but since July 18 the house had been listed for $269,000 in the Board of Realtors' Multiple Listing Service. Houses in which a crime has been committed are notoriously difficult to sell. Peggy Jones, the realtor who had sold the house to the Raileys in December of 1985 and now relisted it, knew that there were a lot of gossips, amateur sleuths and idle sensation seekers who had no intention of buying the house but who were simply curious to see it. Ms. Jones screened her clients carefully and asked other realtors to do the same.

The Railey family no longer seemed to anyone ever to have been the ideal American family. Assigning to his mother-in-law and to his friends the custody of his wife and children was to many members of First Church the final disappointment. Not even Walker's strongest supporters wanted to defend him. Following the example of the bishop, most of them refused to talk. Gordon noted that there were few contributions to the four trust funds set up for the Raileys. It seemed to him that Church members felt not only disappointed but somehow cheated. People who feel cheated don't contribute.

Although investigative reporters, including Mike Cochran of the Associated Press, who was stationed in the offices of *The Fort Worth Star Telegram*, were tracking every lead, a strange event occurred that was not noted publicly by the press or by the police.

Janet Marshall died.

That Janet loved Walker and that he considered her a part of his family was common knowledge. Jealous and protective of her relationship with him, Janet hadn't even liked the Yarringtons' sharing Sunday lunch in Walker's Church office.

While she appeared healthy, Janet suffered from lupus, a hereditary disease from which her twin sister had died several years earlier. Janet took medications regularly and was occasionally hospitalized.

Her final hospitalization, which was sudden and lasted only two days, came exactly six months after the attack on Peggy. At the time neither police nor press questioned her seemingly hasty death. She died quietly, without fuss.

The service for her was held in Dickerson Chapel of First United Methodist Church at seven o'clock on a Thursday evening before the burial the following day in her home town of Waxahachie, an hour's drive from Dallas. Just before the service Walker appeared at the administrative office with a prayer he had written for Janet. Howard Grimes agreed to read the prayer for him. As the service was about to begin, Walker slipped quietly into the chapel and sat in the back row.

Howard watched him from the chancel. Walker was not really grieving for Janet. He averted his eyes when mourners entered the chapel, probably, Howard decided, because he was uncertain now how they felt about him. Poor Janet. Even at her funeral she was taking second place to Walker. Howard was convinced that the shock of Walker's possibly being a murderer had hastened Janet's death.

After Janet's service Dede and Gordon Casad went to Northwood Country Club where the main dining room with its gold and white walls, brass chandeliers and Williamsburg furnishings is quiet and relaxing.

They were both tired. Dede wore her navy linen funeral suit and Gordon his black "C" suit—cocktails, church, cemetery. Both of them were disturbed by Walker's presence at Janet's service. Of course the church, God's house, should be open to everyone, mourners and sinners. It was just that Walker's unexpected appearance seemed to have an ulterior motive.

"I still can't help but think that Janet was somehow involved with the attack on Peggy," Dede said pensively.

Gordon took off his glasses and rubbed his eyes. "Now, Dede, let the poor woman rest in peace."

"Janet would have done anything in the world that Walker told her to do," Dede said, "particularly if she thought she might become the second Mrs. Railey. She adored Walker, and she loved those children."

"Dede, Janet was a sick woman. She knew that she didn't have long to live."

"All the more reason for her to take risks," Dede persisted, "for her to grab for whatever chance for happiness she thought she had. Besides there has been a lot of progress in medical research recently. People with lupus live longer than they did in the past. And there aren't those awful side effects from the new drugs."

"Well, there is no way now of knowing what Janet really felt or knew," Gordon said in the tone of voice that meant that he was ready to change the subject.

"Maybe they were both in it together?" Dede suggested.

Gordon was shocked. "Dede, there is no reason to believe that Janet disliked Peggy—or, for that matter, that Peggy disliked her. She had a special relationship with the family. She was their baby sitter."

Dede was silent. Then she said: "There is just something strange about that relationship."

"Dede, it makes no more sense to me than it does to you, but I can't believe that Janet hurt Peggy."

"Well, if she *was* his accomplice on the night of the attack, then Walker is home free," Dede said. "She can't speak up from the grave."

The Nicolais, the Yarringtons, the Hardins and the Grimes could have told both Gordon and the police that Janet was seldom the Raileys' baby sitter and that the Raileys would not even have been in need of a baby sitter during that weekend after Easter. They had decided to take the children with them to San Antonio.

Billie Jo also could have told of a conversation she had witnessed between Walker and Peggy in which Walker had said: "You don't get on with your sister, and I don't get on with my sister; therefore, the children won't have an aunt. So Janet Marshall is going to become their aunt." Billie Jo then remembered that Janet had collected Ryan and taken him to the Ice Capades.

The Yarringtons could have told the police that their daughter Julie, a senior in high school, was the Raileys' regular baby sitter, and that Peggy would never go out of town and leave the children with anyone but her mother. Billie Jo could confirm this.

The press never disclosed that between calls to Lucy on the night of the attack, Walker indeed had telephoned Janet from his new mobile phone. And, in her only interview with the police, which had seemed merely routine, Janet had explained that Walker had telephoned her to ask if she would stay with the children for a week while he took Peggy on a holiday. Someone, or perhaps even two people, was lying. But the significance, if any, of this lie was buried with Janet on a hot, windy day in September after Howard had read the prayer Walker had written on her death.

As with so many circuitous digressions in this tragedy, what at first appeared irrelevant or even illogical often was the exact opposite.

25

IN THE METROPLEX THERE ARE TWO WIDELY READ regional magazines, *D* and *Texas Monthly,* admired for their watchdog attitudes on shady shenanigans and for their willingness to chronicle colorful Texas scandals. The lead story in the October issue of *Texas Monthly* was on Bishop Finis Crutchfield and was headlined THE GAY BISHOP.

The October cover of *D* Magazine had a portrait of Railey in his ministerial robes, looking as evil as the picture of Dorian Gray in the latter stages of dissipation; the title of its lead story was THE SILENT SPRING OF WALKER RAILEY.

Journalist Mike Shropshire, who wrote the article on Railey, disclosed that though Railey spends most of his time alone, he did play golf once at Northwood Country Club with Doug Mulder and retired District Attorney Henry Wade. Shropshire also wrote:

> The talk of Railey's driving ambition began as far back as 1980. Railey was barely installed in his lofty perch as the young senior minister at First United in Dallas when suddenly he was on board the private jet of Houston oil man Eddy Scurlock, flying to Houston at the behest of the late Bishop Finis A. Crutchfield. Railey, it developed, had been hand-picked by Crutchfield to take command at St. Luke's United Methodist in Houston.

Railey was already in enough trouble without the revelation that he had been "hand picked" by a gay bishop who *"had stayed [as bishop] an extra month or so specifically so he could appoint Railey at St. Luke's."* The implications were made worse by revelations in Emily Joffe's article in *Texas Monthly* which reinforced the idea of Crutchfield having been the leader of a closet community of gay Methodist ministers.

> *By day he was a Methodist bishop. By night he was Jimbo, patron of gay bars. Only after his death from AIDS were the two halves of his life finally joined.*

Walker Railey also appeared to live two lives. By day he was a Methodist minister. By night he was Steve, allegedly seen in bars. An Oklahoma woman claims that she met Walker-Steve in a hotel bar. He told her that he was a history professor from Vanderbilt. One Sunday morning several weeks after the evening with the "history professor," the Oklahoma woman turned on her television and was startled to recognize her professor preaching a service in Dallas as the senior minister of First United Methodist Church.

There had been great national interest in the moral misbehavior of TV evangelists Jim Bakker and Jimmy Swaggert. Here was a story even more shocking.

A mainstream minister in a mainstream community was being investigated as a suspect in the strangling of his wife. This suspect had national credentials and spoke from the pulpit of one of the largest Protestant churches in the country. He preached in a city that was a major center not only for Methodism but for many of the old Protestant denominations that had helped shape the country. The moral values of Christianity and of America were being put on trial.

November 1987

OLIVE TALLEY PURSUED THE STORY WITH A PERSONAL dedication that, like Walker Railey's sermons, "grabbed you in the heart, the head and the gut." She had a proprietary feeling about the story. Nothing could sidetrack her from following both the crime and its consequences for the citizens of Dallas.

On Sunday, November 15, she wrote an explosive article that partially revealed the "unresolved discrepancies" between the story Railey initially told the police and what the police had later called "irrefutable evidence." Since Railey, who was within his legal rights *not* to talk to the police, refused to answer questions, at least the public would know what some of those questions were.

Olive's front page article had a large six column headline: RAILEY GAVE WRONG TIMES IN CALLS ON NIGHT OF ATTACK.

Forty minutes before Walker Railey reported finding his wife unconscious on the floor of their garage, he left a message on his home answering machine that cited an erroneous time and suggested that his wife lock the garage door for her safety, The Dallas Morning News *has learned.*

Olive reported that while the time Railey stated on his mobile telephone was 10:30 to 10:45, the actual phone records showed the time to be 12:03. Had the time he claimed been correct, it would have distanced him from the attack. This difference in the time Railey stated and phone company records typified major unresolved discrepancies.

Two taped messages left by Railey for his wife on the night of the attack are also included among the discrepancies. His failure to mention time spent with Lucy Papillon that night, his telephoning his wife on the public line with the answering machine, which the family rarely used; his informing his wife that he was not wearing a watch, when it was generally known that he never wore a watch; his telling his wife to go into the garage and lock the garage door because he would park in front of the house (when he did drive to the garage) and his refusing to tell the grand jury about his relationship with Dr. Papillon were just a few of the inconsistencies about which investigators would like to question him.

The story concluded that Railey was looking for a new home and a new job and was expected to move to California.

Neither the Nicolais nor the congregation at First Church were surprised by the revelation that Railey intended to move to California. The police replied they were not overly concerned about the move as they didn't even know where he was in Dallas.

Two people who *were* surprised and concerned, however, were Diane and John Yarrington. Diane had been angry with Walker for several weeks now. Several people reported seeing him at a Starplex outdoor concert with a cousin of Craig Holcomb and a niece of Ad Oakley. Walker and Lucy had been seen several places together, one being the opening of a play at the Majestic Theater. The Yarringtons were learning a lot of things they had not known before about the man who supposedly was their closest friend.

Determined to clarify the situation, John asked Walker if they could get together in private, and they agreed to meet late in the afternoon in a large parking lot in front of a K-Mart store in East Dallas.

Dressed in a blue, short-sleeve, cotton-knit shirt and khaki pants, John looked over the half-empty parking lot while he waited for Walker. His allergies were bothering him, and he sniffed a lot. When he saw Walker's tan Honda whip into the parking lot and stop abruptly about twenty yards from John's car, John did not move for a couple of minutes, making sure Walker had not been followed. Then he opened his car door quickly, got out, and hurried to Walker's car.

The atmosphere between the two men was strained. John had compiled a list of questions to ask his friend, yet he didn't want to offend him. He told Walker that several issues troubled him, but that he wanted answers not only for himself but also to respond to others who were expressing doubts.

Walker said he understood.

John's questions were the same that other people had. Why had he told Peggy to go into the garage when he knew that the garage was the only place not covered by the security system? Why had he driven to the back of the house when he left a message on the recording machine saying he would park in front? And why, if he really wanted her to hear the message, had he left a message on the recording machine, instead of calling on the private, unlisted number? Why did he give the wrong time on the answering machine? And why was the security system turned off?

Walker replied that he could appreciate John's confusion and concern. He explained that the digital clock in his car was wrong because the wires had been disconnected when the cellular phone had been installed earlier in the day. He said he hadn't really wanted to awaken Peggy with a message, but had she awakened or had to get up with one of the children he didn't want her to be worried or frightened by his absence. His driving to the back instead of the front was nothing but forgetfulness. He almost always drove to the back whatever the hour. It was habit.

At the time Walker seemed to have answers for all of the puzzling discrepancies, yet, later, when John repeated the conversation to Diane, some of Walker's statements seemed less logical than they had earlier. John grew increasingly irritable, lethargic and depressed. There were so many questions without any satisfactory answers about the crime. How had the attacker entered the garage? Walker had told the police that when he last saw his wife she had been working on the garage lock with a bar of soap. Why then did the police find no traces of soap on the lock when they examined it? And why, especially since her children were at home with her, had Peggy failed to fight her attacker?

Why had Lucy Papillon told the grand jury that she and Walker had been "dating" for about a year when Walker took the Fifth Amendment on the same question? Several of Lucy's neighbors were aware that Railey was living at Lucy's house a great deal of the time. In the mornings Lucy would drive her Volkswagen close to the back door where Railey would run out, frequently with his jacket pulled up over his head, get into the car and slouch over so that he could not be seen. In the afternoons or early evenings, Lucy would sometimes drive the car to the back of the house, let Railey out, then reverse so that she could leave the car on the drive at the front of the house; she would unlock the front door and enter the house alone. Why, for heaven's sake, was Walker playing this childish game of hide-and-seek?

In November Walker left Dallas permanently and drove to San Francisco. Associates at First Church said that in San Francisco he intended to contact a former classmate from Perkins, the Reverend Cecil Williams of Glide Memorial Church, an inner city church with a transient, heterogeneous congregation. Williams, one of the first black graduates from Perkins, was considered even more liberal in his theology than Walker.

Walker had spent part of Thanksgiving with Ryan and Megan and the Yarringtons; then he went to the home of his adoptive parents, Adeline and Knox Oakley. What neither the Yarringtons nor the Oakleys nor any of Walker's other friends knew was that Lucy was making the drive with him.

Ad Oakley is a staunch Methodist. Friends, including Bishop Slater, say that she is a truly Christian woman. When she was a student at SMU more than fifty years ago, her roommate, who has remained a life-long friend, was Thelma Quillian who became the wife of Robert E. Goodrich, Jr., and the mother of four children.

Childless herself and the stepmother of Knox's son from a previous marriage, Ad had always had a particular fondness for the Goodrichs' second child Lucy. When Lucy was a little girl, she called Ad her "second mother." As with Ad and Walker the affection was mutual. Though Ad did not introduce Lucy to Walker, she recently had included Lucy with the Raileys at family gatherings in her home. When Thelma was out of town and Lucy's two sons were spending Thanksgiving of 1986 with their father, Ad asked Lucy to her home for Thanksgiving dinner along with the Raileys and her stepson and his family. Then Lucy was invited with the others for Christmas and for the infamous Easter of 1987. Jack Taylor, an astute reporter for *The Times Herald* observed that the Oakley house was used as a rendezvous for Walker and Lucy. Both came and went frequently, and Ad often brought Ryan and Megan to her home. She also saw Thelma Goodrich regularly and kept in touch with Billie Jo Nicolai.

What baffled observers most about Ad was whether *she* was being used by Walker and Lucy or whether (for reasons no one could imagine) she was using them. This was just one more block in a puzzle where none of the pieces seemed to fit.

The loyal young ministers whom Railey had selected and brought to First Church, and who were most personally affected by Walker's situation, were gradually leaving to assume positions in other churches or to work in related areas.

Over the past year Joe Poole and Hugh Clark, whose wife Lisa had been one of Peggy's doctors at Presbyterian Hospital, had left, not at the same time, but at intervals of two or three months. Farewell parties were given, and the congregation seemed neither surprised nor disturbed by their departures.

What did surprise them, however, was John Yarrington's taking a three month leave of absence because of severe depression. To most of the staff, the choir and the congregation, he and Diane symbolized the steady, ideal nuclear family, selflessly assuming the care of the children of a seriously troubled friend. The stress of suddenly leading a public life, of being father to two more young children and, most of all, the stress resulting from the mysterious turmoil surrounding the man he *thought* was his best friend were certainly enough to depress any man.

Almost everyone both in the media and in the community at large was sympathetic. A few people, including some members of First Church, weren't so sure. When a member of the Men's Bible Class asked John if he didn't think forty-seven was rather old to be taking on raising a two-year-old, John snapped that he hadn't noticed anyone else offering to take on the responsibility. Several other Church members noted that John seemed nervous and irritable these days, which was a big change from his usual affable, easygoing personality. A few cynics wondered if here again was another man with another life that was not what it appeared to be. There is only so much shock and disappointment people can accept without emotional harm to themselves. Churches and ministers are no exceptions.

In August John Yarrington resigned his position as Minister of Music with the explanation that the stress he had been under, from the restructuring of his family combined with his heavy work schedule at the Church, made it necessary to change jobs to regain his good health.

The resignation triggered off another spate of rumors. There was no doubt in the minds of Church members that John was (or had been) Walker's closest friend. Was Walker the real cause of his resignation? Had the Church forced his resignation? Or was John genuinely disillusioned with his best friend and burned out with his work at the Church? Indeed, now that Walker had left for California with Lucy, what *was* the relationship between the two men?

Helen Parmley interviewed him and wrote in *The Dallas Morning News*:

> . . . *Yarrington has been widely known for years as a musician and composer. His religious music is used*

extensively by many denominations in worship services and in hymnals . . .

Yarrington and his wife have legal custody of the Raileys' two young children and were featured in many news media reports—including a national television program—about the Railey case.

After 'a year and a half of our life being so public,' Yarrington said, he decided to leave the Church and pursue another career.

President of the Fellowship of United Methodists in Worship, Music and Other Arts, a denominational organization with three thousand members, Yarrington said that during his leave he had done some composing and was completing revisions on a book about youth choirs. He planned to remain in Dallas and to continue his work as an adjunct professor at Southern Methodist University while he considered other careers.

That Yarrington would leave a lifelong career for an unknown future at a time when his responsibilities and expenses had increased troubled some Church members. It appeared, and indeed was true, that the Church was covering up another scandal. If few in the Church knew of Railey's personal problems, a great many knew of Yarrington's alleged emotional problems.

Two families with sons in the youth choir reported to Hal Brady and Gordon Casad that Yarrington had engaged in "inappropriate behavior" with boys in his choir. The families of the boys wished Yarrington dismissed from the Church but did not want to press charges with the police. They believed that exposing the boys to testifying at a trial would bring further harm to them.

Both Hal and Gordon were astounded, and both feared that the revelation of the Yarrington trauma would exacerbate the pain of the Railey situation. More complaints were voiced against Yarrington.

Dr. Brady and the Church staff hired a psychologist and for over two years sponsored a counseling service for members and their children. Yarrington was hired as director for the adult choir at Pulaski Heights Methodist Church in Little Rock, Arkansas.

Less than a year after Yarrington resigned, Susan Monts requested a sabbatical to perform ministry in England.

With the departure of Monts and Yarrington, ministerial colleagues, who in the past had been reluctant to comment negatively about Railey, now spoke as if the gates to a secret hell had suddenly been unlocked. Jo Biggerstaff, an associate minister who earlier had refused to be interviewed, described the relationship of the staff with Walker as "terror."

"The power he held over us was frightening. He had the power to make or break a career. His need for perfection and his intensity made most of us feel something was wrong with us. He had the ability to make a person feel valueless. In staff meetings he would choose one person to belittle. It was painful for everyone. He was not always like that. In the past year or so he changed. And so did Peggy. She was more withdrawn."

Howard Grimes agreed. He felt that Walker was under such great stress during the year or so before the attack that he took out his frustration by humiliating members of the staff with abusive language. "He seemed to gain some sadistic satisfaction out of the abuse." A former minister at First Church who had requested a transfer when Walker was first appointed senior minister (and who prefers not to be identified) admitted to an instinctive fear and dislike of him. "It was not just that Walker was self-centered, hypocritical and manipulative—there was something truly evil about him." It was an inbred evil and not the sort of criminal personality that is developed within a deprived environment, though he was smart enough to use poverty and abuse as explanations. 'My parents were alcoholics, you know.' That was just about the first thing he told everybody."

Another former member of the Church staff recalls a weekend retreat for the choir that Walker joined. "He spoke of his love and friendship for John Yarrington in such an emotional manner that almost everyone there was embarrassed. It didn't sound like the usual Christian brotherly love type of feeling. Many of us wondered about Walker's emotional stability—if, maybe he was having some sort of nervous breakdown."

A year after the attack it appeared that Walker had had many admirers but few close friends. Associates who said they never really knew him well mentioned that Dr. Dudley Dancer of Highland Park Methodist, Reverend Milton Guitierez of Oak Lawn Methodist and Reverend Justin Tull of Walnut Hill Methodist were thought to be his closest friends among his colleagues. Both Reverend Guitierez and Reverend Tull refused to speak about Walker.

Some of his fellow ministers still combined compassion with objectivity. Gordon Casad could not accept that Walker was inherently evil, born with a demon inside, yet neither could he believe that he was an innocent man. Towering ambition coupled with a lust for power had brought Walker to the abyss of sanity. Whether he had fallen or still clung to the edge, Gordon didn't know. To him Walker was a living textbook example of a man through whom God had spoken, but who was now speaking and acting as if he had become God. Walker was a man who already had done and given so much and who could have done and given so much more had he not possessed to a pathological degree the fatal combination of ambition and arrogance. Gordon truly grieved for those who had placed their faith in a preacher instead of in God.

The Church membership grieved in much the same manner as the clergy. One who bonded even closer with the Church and whose belief was strengthened was Mary Ruth Leavell. Her feelings reflected the ambivalence and sadness of many longtime Church members. "Perhaps Walker changed or perhaps he wasn't ever the person I thought he was—but he didn't write those sermons by himself, you know. God spoke through him."

A persistent rumor is that Walker has a group of friends who are Methodist ministers in an area outside Dallas. Supposedly they have knowledge of his role in the attack on his wife and have banded together to protect him. Various investigative reporters have attempted to track down this report and failed. Either the stonewalling tactics are working or else there is no truth in the story.

Many of the former "new power structure" Church members were disillusioned. Some now attended other churches or else diminished the role of religion in their lives. Ken Menges said: "I no longer want to discuss it (the Railey tragedy)." Lynn Menges said: "It was sad to be at First Church. There was no more Camelot."

Craig Holcomb did not withdraw his membership but he no longer attended services. First Church was not the same. Privately he said that Walker deserved to be left alone, that someone in the Church wanted to stop Walker from having an affair, which was why Peggy was strangled. *Who* in the Church knew of Walker's affair and wanted to stop it? And *why* would strangling Peggy (instead of Lucy) achieve this goal? In the slang of the day, Walker and Lucy were still "an item."

27

IN THE METROPLEX, AS IN ALL URBAN AREAS, THE local newspapers are highly competitive. This was true of *The Times Herald* and *The Dallas Morning News*, which had a much larger circulation than *The Herald* and a more conservative editorial policy.

Recognizing the need for a single investigative voice that

the public could follow, *The Herald*, like *The News* six months earlier, selected a newcomer to the paper. Laura Miller, an ambitious dark-blond young woman, came to *The Herald* as a columnist from the *New York Daily News*. She is imaginative and writes quickly or, as Texans say, "as fast as a New York minute." She had told her editor that she wanted to write a column on the Railey story from the point of view of Peggy Railey's family—a facet of the story that had received little coverage.

The Nicolai family had said that they were private people; they did not want to talk with the media. Apart from an occasional telephone call, the media so far had respected their wishes.

Having located a listing in the Tyler telephone directory for Nicolai, Laura Miller drove to Tyler. The phone number and address were for a different Nicolai family. Next, without success, she searched through the telephone directories of nearby small towns. Then she went to the county tax office where she learned that Peggy's parents were on a rural postal route in Flint, Texas.

Luck was now with her. Leaving the building, she met the postman who had the route. He told her how to locate the house. Late in the afternoon she boldly knocked on the door of the Nicolais' yellow cottage.

She was met by Peggy's eighty-seven-year-old grandmother who politely told her that the family had agreed not to be interviewed. But Laura talked her way into the house by saying that after driving around for several hours she was tired and thirsty.

Ella Renfro invited her to come into the house and sit down at the kitchen table. Soon the two of them were chatting over tea and cheescake. Half an hour later Bill Nicolai came home and joined them. Laura was getting her interview. They had visited for three hours when Billie Jo arrived. She was furious with Ella and Bill for talking with anyone from the media. But she was polite to Laura, although she asked her to leave. Laura didn't mind. She had enough material for several columns.

Laura's first column appeared on January 25, 1988 with

the headline: HOW PEGGY RAILEY'S FAMILY SEES WALKER RAILEY NOW.

> *Most people think Walker Railey did it.*
>
> *But then, most people aren't in a good position to think that: They aren't on the inside; they don't know the details of the police investigation. They rely on the newspapers. They listen to the gossip.*
>
> *Ella Renfro and Bill Nicolai don't have to rely on secondhand news. They're family . . . They know things most people don't know. They have a direct pipeline to the police. They sit right at Peggy's bedside. They mourn.*
>
> *And they think Walker Railey did it.*

She went on to say that the Nicolais had never before talked with the press about their feelings and that Walker's telling a magazine reporter that he and his in-laws are still good friends is a lie. They spoke of Walker as "a pathological liar, egomaniac, a fake, Satan himself, a real S.O.B." Peggy's grandmother believes that the police should have arrested Walker when he left the grand jury room.

Bill Nicolai suggests that Railey *"orchestrated the assault, but didn't commit it. He didn't wrap the wire around his wife's neck. He didn't watch her staring at him, wild-eyed, knowing, clutching for breath, slipping into permanent senselessness. He's too much a coward to do it himself."*

Billie Jo was upset with her mother and her husband for talking with Laura Miller. The three of them and Ted and Linda had agreed not to talk to the press. Billie Jo wanted their lives and Peggy's life to remain as private as possible. She could not see that their giving interviews to the media would help the police solve the case. Nor would it help if they broke off all contact with Walker, making him think that they believed him guilty.

Reverend Jim Reaves was especially outraged because he felt Laura Miller had taken unfair advantage of the kindness of Ella Renfro and Bill Nicolai. Jim believed this was the worst sort of publicity possible for the Church. Most church-going Methodists agreed. The result was a backlash against the press.

Even though Laura Miller had presented the Railey story in a different manner, all reporters, whether newspaper, wire service, or television, were lumped together as untrustworthy hustlers. By word of mouth, the press was, so to speak, getting bad press. Clergy from all denominations wanted to suppress the story. Within the general public there was a split between those who thought Miller's column a moral effrontery and those who thought opinionated gossip was now respectable because it had appeared in print. There was also an anomalous group of angry people who preferred to read only nice stories about nice people.

A large number of people turning against the press is hardly an unusual happening. Centuries before Christ ancient rulers killed messengers who brought bad news. Railey himself denounced the media for persecuting him, yet, at the same time he continued to grant interviews and issue statements to the press.

Laura Miller's second column was even more of a scorcher than the previous one. The headline was NO WALKER IN WHAT'S LEFT OF PEGGY'S LIFE.

> . . . who could have guessed that Walker Railey could go so low as to abandon his own children? Who could have guessed that it was all hogwash last summer when Walker tearfully told reporters that he had come to terms with the fact that his in-laws were moving his wife to Tyler. 'They will have Peg closer to them so I can have Ryan and Megan closer to me,' he said. 'It's going to take all I have to be Mommy and Daddy to them.'
>
> A mere five months later, suitcases packed, he had apparently given his all.

Allegedly infuriated by Laura Miller's columns, Railey was even more furious with Olive Talley. Railey had an irrepressible need to have an open line through which he could speak to the world. He could still telephone Helen

Parmley, whom he called a saint, and offer her a story without fear of his reputation being blackened further.

"Walker Railey says he did not leave Dallas last month to avoid the speculation of 'sidewalk psychiatrists,' but rather to build a new life away from the despair that has haunted him since the attack on his wife in April," Parmley wrote. *". . . while I am relocating, looking for work, financially strapped, not knowing where I'm going to end up or what I'm going to be doing, everybody involved in this drama believes that at this point in time in their lives, the most stable, loving, Christian environment they [Ryan and Megan] can be in is where they are."*

Many people had begun to notice how frequently in newspaper quotes Walker referred to his life as "a drama." It was as if he were alone in a darkened theater directing himself in a play that resembled a Wagnerian opera.

28

December, 1987

WALKER RETURNED TO DALLAS TO SPEND CHRISTMAS with the Yarringtons who had agreed with the "20/20" news show to film their family Christmas with a hand-held video camera and to give "20/20" the film to incorporate in a program next spring.

The Yarringtons, their four children, Diane's parents, Ryan and Megan and Walker, in a blue velour warm-up suit, were all exchanging Christmas presents. Walker, who was attempting to hold a twisting Ryan on his lap, said to Megan who was carrying a present larger than she: "Let Mommy help you open it."

The two-year-old ran to Diane and hugged her. Clearly, to

213

Megan, Diane was now Mommy. But what most viewers remembered of that Christmas morning film was not happy children absorbed into a new loving family but five-year-old Ryan squirming to escape from his father's kiss and his unyielding grasp.

While Walker continued to appear in the media, a new senior minister quietly arrived to take up his appointment at First United Methodist Church of Dallas. His name is Hal Brady. He is nothing at all like Walker Railey, yet he has some of the same talents that Railey has. In a homiletics examination, Brady would certainly excel. In selecting Railey's successor, the committee knew it had to find a man who projected the opposite personal image from Walker yet who had Walker's gift for rousing the emotions with almost evangelical style preaching. The one thing Walker's successor could not be was boring. Hal Brady is not boring.

He is an attractive, well-mannered Southern gentleman, some ten years older than Walker. He is tall and slender with wavy, gray-white hair, a thin face with an aquiline nose, clear blue eyes and a relaxed manner. Having come from Atlanta, where he was preaching at Glenn Memorial Church, he possesses a refined, naturally appealing Georgian accent.

Gordon Casad and Ralph Shannon had told him that there had been a tragedy in the life of the former minister; the congregation was still grieving. Hal had read about the Dallas minister who was the chief suspect in a failed murder attack on his wife, but it was a brief article and of little interest to people in Atlanta.

When he received the telephone call offering him the position, he knew his initial role would be that of healing the wounds. But he had no idea how deep those wounds were, how obsessed both the Church and the city of Dallas had become with the Railey case and how the crime persisted in unravelling more and more shocking secrets that would keep the mind of the public on the mystery of the crime rather than on the mysteries of God. His ministry at First Church had to be one of reconciliation and liberation.

To a member of the Church, he said: "In spite of people experiencing great hurt, the purposes of the Church are reaffirmed in a magnificent way. Jesus Christ and the Church are our hope. In the final analysis, it is God's faithfulness to us that matters. The Church depends upon the faithfulness of God. Period."

There were three pastoral aims he set for himself: to try to hear what members of the congregation are really saying; to minister to them at the point (on the spiritual journey) where they are; and to keep the Church in the purposes of God as best we understand these purposes.

Although he did not officially assume his position as Senior Pastor until January 1, 1988, Hal Brady preached his first sermon "On Facing the Future" at First Church on Sunday, December 13, 1987.

". . . Some time ago, I was reading about a well-known minister who was having a conference with some of his associates. They were sitting around a rather long table, and one of his associates said, 'What do you think about the political situation in America today? What do you think about the credibility gap in government? What do you think about inflation? What do you think about the depression some people say will hit this country? What do you think about the rising crime rate and AIDS and so forth?' That minister said he thought long and hard before he answered. He said, 'I am very concerned about the things you are talking about. But I am not remotely concerned about holding them in my mind until they get on top of me, because you see, these things are not my source. These things are not stable, they change. God doesn't change. God is constant. God is always the same.' And then he said, 'God is in the now.' I like that. God is not just in the past or in the future, but God is in the now. Isn't that what his book tells us over and over again? Place your confidence in God . . .

"Place your confidence in God. Step forward in

courage. The last thing is this—remember this—you really can make a difference. . . ."

The sermon was delivered well. It was easily understood and it contained a reassuring message. *You can make a difference.* First Methodist was back in the traditional middle lane where it had always been. Many members of the staff and the Pastor-Parish Committee heaved a sigh of relief. *Hal Brady would make a difference—a difference that was greatly needed.*

29

February, 1988

IF RAILEY THOUGHT HE COULD START LIFE IN SAN Francisco free of the problems that had plagued him in Dallas, he greatly underestimated the tenacity of the media.

Norman Kinne told a reporter he couldn't just telephone the Nicolais and suggest what they ought or ought not to do. But, if someone like Ted Nicolai were to come to him for advice, he would be happy to give him the name of someone who could give him legal counsel. Later Ted Nicolai telephoned Kinne who referred him to Bill Arnold.

Norman Kinne and Bill Arnold had been colleagues in the district attorney's office. They agreed that Peggy Railey needed money and that a civil trial might provide her with money, if there was any money to get. A civil trial might also uncover information useful for a criminal case.

When Arnold received a call from Ted, he was surprised by the name Nicolai. The media always used the name Railey, partly because of Walker's prominence and partly because the Nicolai family persistently refused to be interviewed by the media.

"Peggy Railey's brother," Ted explained to Arnold. "Norm Kinne suggested I telephone you to see if you might be able to help us."

"Oh yes," Arnold said. "I'm not sure that I can be of help, but I'd be happy to get together and discuss the situation."

They agreed to meet for lunch at a chain restaurant in Arlington, a community between Dallas and Fort Worth. Arnold knew that if he took this case it would be his alone; the hours could not be billed to the law firm, and he would be working a lot of hours overtime. With a young family he was not sure that this was something he wanted to do. Yet his wife Carol was in favor of it. They could all put up with a little inconvenience for a few months.

Bill and Ted, who were both thirty-four years of age, liked each other immediately. Ted explained his frustration and concern that Walker had some influence somewhere in the system and that nothing was being done to help Peggy. Bill told Ted that his wife had been a student at Ursuline Academy in the early 1970s when Peggy taught there. After half an hour Bill agreed to drive to Tyler the following weekend and talk with Ted's parents.

Attorney Arnold met with the Nicolais at their home in Flint. He explained to them that he was a civil lawyer, not a criminal lawyer, but that it *might* be possible to bring a civil suit against Railey that would get Peggy some money.

Bill Nicolai questioned if it was right to sue his son-in-law after they had already agreed to divide what assets Walker and Peggy had. Billie Jo wondered how they would find enough money to retain Arnold, who quickly assured her that that was something that didn't matter right now.

Before his drive back to Dallas, Arnold followed the Nicolais in their car to The Clairmont Nursing Home. The sight of Peggy Railey propped up on pillows in the standard plastic oak nursing home bed, her bloated body grotesquely twisted, saliva foaming at the corner of her mouth and the occasional, almost inhuman howl that she emitted, horrified him in a manner for which he was completely unprepared. This poor, wretched creature sharing the room with an aged, partially paralyzed woman was unrecognizable from the woman whose photograph had appeared so frequently in the newspapers. This was a tragedy worse than death. If the family agreed, he would take this case and he would do his best to win it.

"I haven't said this before," Billie Jo told Arnold, with tears clouding her brown eyes. "But, after all that has happened in the past few weeks, I've changed my mind. I agree with Ted. Walker *did* attempt to murder Peggy."

Walker and Lucy signed a one-year lease on an apartment in an old Victorian house at 1808 Broadway in Pacific Heights, a couple of miles from the San Francisco Bay. Investigative reporter Jack Taylor of *The Dallas Times Herald* was the first Dallas reporter to publish Railey's address in California. He had never interviewed him face to face, but he knew he would recognize him. He'd looked at his picture in the newspaper almost every week for the past nine months.

Taylor is a large, heavy-set man in his late forties. He has heavy eyebrows and thick, bushy, brown hair. A family man with seven children and strong opinions about what is right and what is wrong, he loves his job. Big enough not to be intimidated by tough guys, he can be brusk and confrontational himself. He is not above shouting, blocking a doorway or outrunning a suspect for an interview; but, there is also a gentle persuasive side to his personality.

Staking out Railey's house one afternoon, Jack saw him walk up the steps to his front door. Casually Jack went over to talk to him, pleasantly, not identifying himself and not saying anything threatening.

"You've got the wrong guy," Railey said and went into the house.

Next Jack telephoned the owner of the house. His secretary said he had no idea of Walker and Lucy's background. It was not a neighborhood where sensational things happened.

The apartment in fashionable Pacific Heights where Railey had been seen moving in furnishings had prompted the trip by Taylor and Bud Gillett, KDFW-TV television reporter. Also, allegedly Railey was attending church in San Francisco at Glide Memorial and had applied for a position on the staff there.

Photographs of the three-story Victorian building appeared in *The Times Herald* and on channel four. Gillett reported that the rent was sixteen hundred dollars a month, somewhat steep for a man who claimed to have no job, no assets and no independent income from any source.

Olive was chagrined that Taylor, who was one of the most respected senior reporters in the business, had scooped her. But at least he hadn't interviewed Walker or photographed him in San Francisco. Walker had simply disappeared again. Both Olive and her editors felt that eventually he would return to his apartment, and Olive wanted to be there to interview him when he did.

On February 2, 1988, Billie Jo Nicolai, guardian of the person and estate of Peggy Nicolai Railey, and plaintiff, filed a petition in the Dallas County District court, against Walker L. Railey, defendant, who *"intentionally, knowingly and brutally attempted to strangle his wife, Peggy Railey, to death. Thinking Mrs. Railey was dead, he left her on the garage floor of their home. Thinking only of himself and callously leaving his two precious children, Ryan, five years old, and Megan, two years old, in the house alone with a comatose mother, Walker Railey then drove to the Fondren Library at SMU in a clumsy attempt to conceal his actions and to establish a false alibi.*

"Because of Mr. Railey's intentional and knowing attack upon his wife, Mrs. Railey has suffered serious bodily injury. She will probably be unable to take care of herself or her children for the rest of her life.

"Mrs. Railey is entitled to recover judgment against Walker Railey for damages resulting from the malicious attack of Walker Railey upon his wife . . .

"Punitive damages requested are in excess of the minimum jurisdictional limits of this court."

Mrs. Nicolai's lawyer Bill Arnold said, "We hope to get money to take care of Peggy's medical expenses now and in the future. We also hope that something may be uncovered in the civil trial that will help the district attorney's office in building a criminal case against Mr. Railey."

"Well, the mud has finally hit the fan," declared Olive as she read the petition at her desk less than an hour after it was filed.

She finished writing the petition story and had her bag packed to leave for San Francisco that day with a copy of the petition for Railey. Now she figured he might be angry enough to make some comments about his in-laws. She would spend a week in San Francisco investigating anything she could find.

She arrived in San Francisco at almost midnight, rented a Hertz compact car and registered at a Holiday Inn in Union Square. At dawn she headed for Pacific Heights to locate Walker's residence. About three hours later she saw Walker's Honda with the Texas license plates park on the closest side street. Olive drove around the block, then parked her car on the same side of the street about half a block from 1808 Broadway. She wondered if he had been served with the subpoena to answer the accusations against him filed in a petition by his mother-in-law. She also wondered how he would respond when he saw her.

She had waited only half an hour when Walker suddenly appeared, dressed in casual clothes and carrying a lumpy, black garbage bag. He headed for the tan Honda. Olive had an immediate decision to make—should she confront him now or follow him and perhaps discover where he was working, what he was doing and who he was seeing? Gambling on the long shot, she made the wrong decision, losing him in the heavy traffic of the unfamiliar area. She cursed herself for not jumping out of the car and facing him when they were alone in the middle of the street.

It was an even more unfortunate choice because again Railey did not return to his apartment, which Olive continued to watch for the next two days.

She knew that he was avoiding the process server and

probably had no notion that she was out here. To escape the process server, he probably wouldn't be back for days, maybe even weeks. She telephoned her editor who told her to investigate the area and discover what, if anything, there was to be discovered.

Studying a map of the area, and using 1808 Broadway as the center of a square, she marked off four blocks on all four sides of the center. It was mainly a residential area. Methodically she rang every doorbell and knocked on every door in each block. If no one was home, she would jot that address in her notebook and return. No one knew of anyone named Walker Railey, nor did anyone remember seeing a man or woman who looked like the newspaper pictures she had of Railey and Lucy. Even the other residents of 1808 Broadway couldn't identify Railey for certain. A middle-aged couple who lived next door had seen a man occasionally coming in and out of the apartment, but they had not met him. They were nervous at being interrogated by a newspaper reporter. They didn't want to make trouble for a neighbor or become involved in a scandal. There was even some disagreement between them as to whether he was the man in the picture.

Every place she went Olive left her card, jotting down her San Francisco telephone number as well as the Dallas number. If anyone saw Walker or Lucy or heard anything about them, please telephone her. She must have left at least sixty or seventy cards. She spent the most time and left the most cards with the merchants in the area, the gas station attendants, the cleaners, the grocers. Surely if he lived in the area, these are the places he would frequent. All of the merchants politely took her card and promised to call, even though none of them recognized the photos.

Not since that first morning when she had seen him had Walker returned to his apartment.

Each day she drove through the area where she had followed him and lost him; no place seemed plausible for him to stop. She went to Glide Memorial Church, but Cecil Williams refused to see her. A spokesman for him said that

Walker occasionally attended services there but that he had not been hired on the staff of the church nor would he be hired in the future. Olive left him her card.

She was depressed and still angry with herself for letting that one opportunity slip away. Exhausted after six days of pounding the pavement and accomplishing nothing, she decided to take the last day of the trip as a vacation and see something of the Bay Area with which she was unfamiliar.

A couple of miles from the apartment on Broadway was the Marina district. Dressed in jeans, Nikes and a casual shirt she drove to Fisherman's Wharf off Ghiradelli Square. After a brief tour of the boat museum, she stepped outside and shivered in the cool morning air. Seeing a sidewalk shop on the square with souvenirs and sweatshirts, she bought a black sweatshirt with the skyline of San Francisco on the front. Pulling it over her head, she felt like a real tourist.

All around the square were restaurants, gift shops, fishmongers, bars, arcades with pinball machines and more clothes' vendors. What caught her attention next, however, was a woman setting up a card table and three chairs on the sidewalk just off the square. The woman was in her mid-thirties. She was thin and her brown hair was pulled straight back and fastened with a clasp at the nape of her neck. She wore an oversized dark sweater and a fully gathered dusky print skirt.

Olive watched as she placed a fringed, Persian-design cloth of dark reds and blues and browns over the table and then spread out a deck of oversized cards, which even at a distance Olive knew were Tarot cards.

Olive didn't believe in that sort of thing. Fortunetelling, whether horoscope, crystal ball or cards, was a rip-off. Still, she continued to watch the woman settle herself in a chair facing the street, flipping over the cards, one by one and then moving them face-up either to the right or the left. Some she turned back over and stacked beside her. For a few more minutes Olive observed her. Then abruptly she walked in the opposite direction. Twenty minutes later she had passed the woman again, turned and was heading back toward her car when they made eye contact. The woman didn't look kooky.

Olive crossed the street and approached the table. "I don't know if I want to do this," she said. "How much does a reading cost?"

"Twenty-five dollars."

"How long does it take?"

"It can't be done in five minutes," the woman said. "Somewhere between twenty minutes and half an hour."

She seemed genuine. Olive had nothing else to do. Maybe it would make her feel better, a positive memory of San Francisco.

"Okay," she said. "Read my cards."

The woman smiled as she shuffled the deck and asked conversationally, "Where are you from?"

"Dallas."

"Are you out here on vacation?"

"No. I'm here looking for someone."

"A man?"

"In San Francisco?" Olive smiled. "You've got to be kidding!"

The woman laughed as she began turning over cards. "Are you a police officer?"

"No." Olive said surprised. "Hey, aren't you supposed to be telling instead of asking?"

"Seriously," the woman said. "You are here trying to find a particular man, aren't you?"

"Yes."

"Well, maybe I can help you. Maybe I know him."

"You wouldn't know him," Olive said. "He's a preacher."

Poised with a card in her hand, the woman looked straight into Olive's eyes. "Are you looking for Walker Railey?"

Olive nearly fell off her chair. "Jesus," she said. "How would you know about Walker Railey?"

"I read his cards and Lucy's, too."

"When did you read their cards?"

"A couple of months ago, when they were looking for a house."

Paradoxically Olive was becoming more impressed yet, at the same time, more skeptical. She wondered if the woman had read about them in the newspapers and simply made a lucky guess.

"Thelma Jean was with them," the woman added.

Olive was positive that Thelma Jean had never been mentioned in any of the printed stories. The woman continued to stare at her.

Olive took a business card from her handbag and slid it across the table. "Can you tell me what Walker's cards said?"

"Just like lawyers and doctors, readers have professional ethics, a confidentiality of clients. So, shall we look into your future now?" The woman was confident she had made an impression.

Olive listened to the good and the bad in her own personality, to the frustration she felt in her professional life now, to the conflicts within her family.

"Most of what you've told me is right," she said. "I just wish you would tell me some more about Walker and Lucy. I mean are they somewhere around here?"

"I can't talk about clients to each other."

"Do you expect to see Walker again?"

"Perhaps."

"I really need to interview him," Olive said. "I can understand your not telling me what you know or feel about him personally. But—well, you have my business card, and if you do see him again or talk with anyone who knows where he is, I really would appreciate your telephoning me."

The woman put Olive's card in her pocket, but she made no commitment. "I'll think about it," she said shuffling the cards.

Absorption with the Railey case had now spread beyond Dallas and Texas. Producer Janice Tomlin of "20/20" wanted all of America to know what had captivated the citizens of Dallas, and she wanted the "20/20" investigative team to reveal some as yet undisclosed information about the crime. What the police and the district attorney's office had not made public were the complete messages Railey had left on his answering machine the night Peggy was attacked and the text of his suicide letter written a week later.

What previously had been whispers and speculation would soon become one large chorus with the single face of tragedy chanting "guilty, guilty, guilty."

PART III

A Cloud of Witnesses

"Wherefore seeing we also are compassed about with so great a cloud of witnesses, let us lay aside every weight, and the sin which doth so easily beset *us,* and let us run with patience the race that is set before us."

Hebrews 12:1

30

A WEEK AFTER OLIVE HAD RETURNED FROM CALIFORnia to Dallas, her editor left a message for her to come to his office as soon as she returned from lunch.

"We've got a tip from California," he said. "Walker Railey is staying at La Quinta Inn in South San Francisco near the airport."

"He was probably there all the time I was in San Francisco," Olive groaned.

"We've already booked you on a flight back to San Francisco tonight. Evans Caglage is going with you to take pictures. I'm sure the two of you will bring back a front page interview this time."

Evans Caglage is one of the best photographers *The News* has. Of medium build and about the same age as Olive with light brown hair and a hairline receding like Walker Railey's, Caglage is an easy companion.

They arrived in San Francisco after midnight. Both were tired, yet after they had rented a car, they drove to La Quinta Inn. Sure enough Walker's car was there. Olive wanted to begin the stake out then, taking turns sleeping in the car. If she lost Walker a second time, she would be too embarrassed to face anyone at the paper; but Evans finally convinced her that Walker wasn't likely to leave in the middle of the night. They both needed comfortable beds, a place to clean up, change their clothes and grab some food so they would be in good shape the following morning.

Reluctantly Olive agreed that this was the more sensible plan. She also suspected that she was becoming neurotic about this story. It probably was good that Evans was with her.

To make certain they were not discovered by Railey before they found him, they drove to another motel a couple of miles away. By seven o'clock the following morning they were back in the parking lot of La Quinta Inn with Walker's car in clear view, yet they were far enough away from it not to be recognized.

Prepared to wait as long as necessary, they waited only an hour before Walker came out the front door and headed in the direction of his car. Quick as a pair of greyhounds Olive and Evans were running toward him.

Walker saw them, recognized them and abruptly halted, waiting for them to reach him. He was dressed in a tan velour warm-up suit, a camel-colored cap and running shoes. He hadn't shaved; his eyes were bloodshot, and he looked tired and seedy. When he remained where he was, Olive and Evans stopped running and walked toward him at a more normal pace.

"Don't shoot until I give you a signal," Olive muttered to Evans who now let his camera hang casually around his neck.

"Oh—uh, I have no comment," Walker said to Olive when they were about ten feet away from him.

"How do you know until you hear what I'm going to ask you?" Olive said in a calm, friendly voice.

"I don't want to be interviewed," Walker said tonelessly.

Olive suggested that his situation would seem worse if he were photographed looking scruffy and running away from her. She offered to respect the parameters he wanted to set and give him an opportunity to be photographed more presentably in the lobby of the motel, where they could talk in a civilized manner over a cup of coffee.

Walker was hesitant. "I'm not sure that I want to talk."

"It'll look worse if you don't," Olive said. "You need to respond to some of the statements and accusations against you."

Walker shrugged and said, "All right." The three of them went into the motel lobby, where Evans joked with Walker about both of them wearing English wool sports car caps that were the same color. While Olive and Walker talked, Evans unobtrusively took pictures of Walker.

The interview lasted two hours and was far less dramatic and confrontational than Olive had anticipated. In the last few weeks Walker's pugnacious arrogance had dwindled, but not his self-confidence, even though she observed that his hands were shaking, perhaps from the chill of the morning or perhaps from anxiety.

In the first of two copyrighted articles, Olive reported that Railey had told her he was not trying to be a fugitive . . . but that he felt like he was being hounded by the press. He resented reporters sitting in front of his flat.

"I didn't run away from my children. I didn't run away from anything," Railey said. "That's been terribly distorted in the press."

Having said he had not received the civil suit subpoena, he declined to read the copy which Olive had brought. He told her that he wanted to discuss it with Doug Mulder first.

"I won't respond to what the [Nicolai] family has said. But in the last ten months of my life I've done the best I could do . . ."

The second of the two-part series Olive wrote appeared the following Sunday, Valentine's Day. The main subjects of the article were Walker's search for inner peace through a new life in the Bay Area and his resentment at what he perceived as "the pain of public scrutiny" into his private life.

The tone of his statements to Olive was resentful and self-pitying, as if *he* were the only one suffering.

> *"I'm in a situation where my silence makes people wonder and, when I talk, the way it's used [in the media] also makes people wonder," Railey said.*
> *"I'm kind of between the devil and the deep blue sea. And in a situation like that, it's hard to know what is the best, most honest and responsible way to respond . . ."*

No grief was expressed for his wife or children. He said that he was optimistic about making a new life unless he was *"publicized to impotence."*

He was resentful of the way the media had publicized his problems, and he refused to talk about the night his wife was attacked or about his relationship with Lucy Papillon. He deemed that the media already had tried and convicted him. But, in spite of negative attitudes toward him, he was confident that good fortune lay ahead and repeated the ministerial cliché that there was *"hope beyond the darkness of despair . . . I will let the world judge me any way they [sic] want to . . ."*

Surely it was presumptuous to imagine that he could do anything else. To almost everyone he was incomprehensible. Probably even to Lucy he was an enigmatic valentine.

31

ONE MAN WHO WAS BETTING ON RAILEY CELEBRATING Valentine's with Lucy was *The Times Herald* reporter Jack Taylor. Having read Olive's Saturday article, Jack's editor telephoned him at home and told him to fly out to San Francisco that afternoon.

Jack called Bill Arnold and offered to be of help. "I'm going to San Francisco by myself," he said, "and I need to be in two or three places at once because I don't know where Railey is now; and I don't suppose your process server does either. But if you'll give me his name I can watch one place while he watches another. If I find Railey, I'll let him know. If he finds him and serves the papers, he can let me know where he is."

Arnold said that sounded okay to him and told Jack that the process server, a young man named Steve Adams, had been watching the Glide Memorial Church where there were persistent rumors Railey had been going. Jack told him that he would be staying at a hotel in San Francisco near the church and that since Railey had left La Quinta Inn, where Olive had interviewed him, Jack had received a couple of tips that Railey was staying in a downtown San Francisco hotel. Arnold said he certainly hoped Jack could find him soon and that Steve would serve the papers. Arnold had been trying to get those papers served for over a month now, and the costs were getting a little expensive, especially since he was paying the bills himself.

Jack said he'd do his best, and Bill said he'd telephone Steve and give him Jack's name and hotel. They would work as a team.

About nine o'clock that evening, after he had settled into his own hotel and met Steve, Jack started calling other hotels in San Francisco. He didn't locate the right one until about midnight, but Railey had checked out earlier. Jack arranged to come to the hotel and talk to the clerk about five A.M., before the front desk got busy. Steve went home to get a few hours of sleep before returning to watch Glide Memorial.

At five A.M. Jack told the young desk clerk in the empty lobby that he wanted to look at Railey's bill so he could check long distance phone charges.

"Well, we don't normally do that," the clerk said, "only for federal officials or police officers."

Jack said he wasn't a police officer, but he reached in his

pocket and pulled out a small plastic billfold case which contained his membership card in an Indian tribe issued by the Interior Bureau of Indian Affairs. The clerk watched him fold a fifty dollar bill and put it behind the card before handing it to him.

The clerk left the desk and came back with a photostated copy of Railey's bill.

"I brought you a list of calls he made from the hotel," the clerk said, passing over a couple of sheets of paper along with the plastic card that was missing the fifty-dollar bill.

"Thanks."

Back at his own hotel, Taylor studied the list of calls noting that most of them were back to Dallas.

From his hotel room where he had stayed February 8 through February 11 Railey had telephoned Jim Singleton, his banker in Dallas, the Yarringtons and an investigator who worked for Doug Mulder. Five calls to Lucy Papillon at different locations were also on the bill. Then Taylor noticed that there were three calls made to resorts in Northern California.

It was Valentine's weekend, and a number of men went to these resorts with their mistresses. The first two calls were brief, but the third one, to the Albion River Inn in Mendicino County, lasted nearly five minutes. Taylor figured he'd made a reservation and that was where he and Lucy were now.

"Steve, I'm going to drive to the Albion Inn and check out my hunch," he told the young process server. "It's a long drive and I'd be glad to have some company if you want to come with me."

"I'll have to call Bill Arnold," Steve said. "He's paying me twenty-five dollars an hour, and there will be a number of hours when we're just riding back and forth in the car. I don't know if he wants to pay me that money."

"Use my telephone and find out," Jack said.

Steve asked the operator to ring Arnold's number in Dallas. Jack listened to Steve's explanation of the situation;

then in the background, he overheard Bill's wife Carol saying, "Go for it."

"Go for it," Arnold repeated. And twenty minutes later Jack and Steve were on their way north to the Albion River Inn in Jack's rented car.

It was about two o'clock in the afternoon when they reached the Albion Inn, a beautiful resort on a small inlet in the rocky coastline. Jack and Steve casually drove through the resort, which has a big U-shaped drive. And there sitting out in the sun and watching the shore was Walker dressed in slacks and a patterned sport shirt. Beside him was Lucy wrapped up in a big, long, white terry-cloth robe, as if she had just stepped out of the jacuzzi. They were drinking beer.

In the event Railey wouldn't give him an interview, Jack wanted to get a picture before Steve served the papers.

Steve replied: "Yeah, you can do that. Now that we've found him, he's not going anywhere."

Jack had two cameras, one that he always took on surveillance and a borrowed one with a telescopic lens. He gave Steve his camera, and the two of them left the car and walked along the rim of the cliffs about fifty meters from Walker and Lucy. They pretended to be tourists, but they weren't dressed for it. Steve had on a jacket and Taylor was wearing a pullover sweater and loafers, which, by his own admission, made him look more like a house detective than a tourist.

Moving closer and closer to the cottage where Walker and Lucy were sitting in the sun, they snapped pictures of the ocean and of each other. As soon as Jack turned toward Walker and Lucy, they jumped up and ran into the house.

Jack cursed himself. Like Olive he had made the mistake of wanting too much. Instead of grabbing the moment and running up to them while Steve served the papers, Jack had wanted a full-page story with photographs. Steve was the one who should have been disappointed; he was the one who represented the law and who could have completed his job if he hadn't been nice to Jack.

"You were the one who located him," Steve said kindly. "Now we know where he is. There's only one way out. So it's just a matter of waiting."

For the next twenty-two hours they waited. It was cold and Jack was tired and feeling sick. He sat in the car most of the time while Steve hid in the bushes. A couple of times Jack went into the motel office and telephoned Railey's room, but each time Railey hung up on him. Steve knocked on their door once, but they didn't answer. Then he went to the manager's office and explained he was there to serve papers, but the manager, a man in his mid-forties, wasn't sympathetic.

A few hours later the manager, who was also the owner, came out and asked Jack and Steve to leave the premises.

"Several of the guests have detected that something is wrong," he said. "It's not good for business."

Steve stood on the edge of Highway One at the entrance. It's a narrow road, not much of a shoulder, while Jack backed his rental car into a sheepherder's driveway across the road. He explained what was going on to a woman who had a house on the property, and she gave him permission to stay there. He was shivering and feeling worse by the hour. He was hungry and sleepy and sick with the flu, but he felt sorrier for Steve who had to stand on the highway with nothing to protect him from the cold.

At two o'clock in the afternoon, twenty-two hours after they had arrived, they saw a porter knock on Railey's door, collect luggage and put it in the back of a car parked in front of the rooms. Lucy came out wearing a big green straw hat and got in the car behind the driver's wheel. As soon as she had started the car, Walker ran out of the motel holding a windbreaker over his head. Lucy backed the car out of the parking lot, and Steve jumped a fence and ran to the passenger side of the car. Lucy swerved the car, making a big U-turn to get to the exit. Steve ran behind them, and when Lucy slowed down to turn right on Highway One, he threw himself on the hood of the car, slapped the papers under the windshield wiper, and yelled: "Mr. Railey, you're served!"

Somehow the papers stuck, Steve slid off the car, and

Lucy turned south on the narrow, two-lane highway. She roared past Jack with Walker slumped down on the passenger side. Jack had his motor running, ready to give chase, but he had to wait until Steve could jump into the car.

Highway One winds and curves around the coastline and the traffic is heavy at any time. Jack drove about a hundred miles, but they never did catch them. They didn't even see them again. Finally Jack asked Steve to drive. He climbed into the back seat and lay down, knowing he had a miserable case of the flu and a second rate story; but, at least he had helped Steve serve the papers. Bill Arnold ought to be pleased. He wondered if he were getting too old for this job, but this was one case he really wanted to crack. What innocent man would refuse to help the police find his wife's attacker and then abandon his children? This man was as amoral as they come. Jack felt an instinctive revulsion. Huddled down on the back seat of the car and covered by his rain coat, he wasn't sure if he was shivering because of the flu or because of the near encounter with a man who he believed was truly evil, a man who may have attempted to murder his wife. Nothing could be more evil than killing or destroying another person. Jack wondered if Railey felt any guilt or remorse. From his actions it appeared he felt none. Railey had taken the law into his own hands, and he shouldn't get away with it. He *shouldn't* get away with it.

32

March 1988

❧ ON FRIDAY, MARCH 11, WHEN ABC AIRED THE Railey story on "20/20" at nine P.M. Central Time, *The Dallas Morning News* ran a banner headline across the front page: "RAILEY CALLED HIMSELF 'LOWEST OF THE LOW.' " Opposite a photograph of the final paragraph excerpted from Railey's suicide letter, was the subheading: "SUICIDE LETTER, PHONE TAPE RELEASED." Olive Talley's article began:

> In a desire to "fill in the blanks" of the stalled investigation into the nearly year-old choking attack on Margaret 'Peggy' Railey, a Dallas prosecutor Thursday released a phone tape and suicide note left by Walker Railey, the chief suspect in the case . . .

The article went on to say that Kinne publicly played a tape of two messages Railey left on his home answering machine shortly after midnight on the night his wife was attacked. Kinne pointed out inconsistencies in the tape and Railey's failure to explain them. The calls were made to the Raileys's publicly listed phone answered by a machine, though the Raileys used a private unlisted phone line for their personal calls.

> "'Hi, Babe' Railey began the first message. 'I'm calling you from my mobile phone. Peg, it's about, oh, I don't know, I don't have a watch. It's somewhere between 10:30 and 10:45.'"

Phone records show the actual time of the call was 12:03 A.M.

Olive reported that Railey went on to say on tape that he would finish his research at the SMU library and be home around one A.M. He further told his wife to go ahead and lock the garage door and that he would park out front. Witnesses at the library cannot account for Railey's presence during the entire time he says he was there. One librarian said Railey gave him a business card after midnight with a note written on the back stating the time as 10:15.

Railey mentioned the incident in the second message he

left on his answering machine about ten minutes before he says he arrived home at 12:40.

> "*Everything really went well. I got a lot accomplished. I had to leave my card with the reference librarian because there was one deal I couldn't quite work out. I'm not calling on the private line because I know you're already asleep, but in case you get up with the kids, I just wanted you to know that I'm on my way home. It's 12:29. I'll be home about 12:45. Love you, dear. Bye-bye.*"

The Assistant District Attorney revealed that Railey's five-year-old son Ryan had told police that he saw who attacked his mother but that his statements were inconsistent and thus "practically of little value." Also, Kinne disclosed that another discrepancy was Railey's failure to tell police that he spent time that night with Lucy Papillon who had told a grand jury that she and Railey had been romantically involved and had discussed marriage.

Kinne emphasized that neither he nor the police wanted to drop the case but that more evidence was needed to move the case forward. The prosecutor said: "It appears to me that at this point in time the investigation is stymied . . . I feel like this may very well be the last anyone is hearing of this and I want to fill in the blanks as much as I can."

This statement appeared to be a shocking reversal of Kinne's attitude towards the case. But, what distressed Methodist ministers and Walker's former congregation was not so much Kinne's suggestion of closure or the inconsistencies in Walker's account of his activities on the night of the attack but the suicide letter.

The confession of a demon inside his soul, of being possessed by a malignant, supernatural being contradicted modern Methodist beliefs. That the demon, the personification of evil, was not only alive and well but had actually won the battle with God for the soul of one of Christianity's most popular standard bearers was incredulous and ruinous.

In Olive's lengthy article was a reproduction of Railey's four-page handwritten suicide letter. The text was also printed in ordinary type-face:

Bury me quietly at Sparkman-Hillcrest Cemetery. Among any participants someone chooses, get Bishop O. Eugene Slater and Rev. Don Waddell (Fayetteville, Arkansas) if either is willing. Have Sparkman [sic] pick up my life, too.

There is a demon inside my soul. It has always been there. My demon tries to lead me down paths I do not want to follow. At times that demon has lured me into doing things I did not want to do.

For almost 40 years God has been struggling with my demon and eventually God always prevails. My demon is working inside my soul again, filling me with despair and taking away my hope. My demon has finally gotten the upper hand.

All of my life people have seen me as strong. The truth is just the opposite. I am the weakest of the weak. People have seen me as good. The truth is just the opposite. I am the baddest of the bad. People have seen me as virtuous. The truth is just the opposite. I am the lowest of the low.

For 22 years God's grace has flowed through me. In spite of me, God's strength has somehow seeped through my weakness. God's immortal Word has been made flesh in spite of my mortal ways.

I have never stopped struggling w/my demon, and God's "Everlasting Arms" have never turned loose. My problem today is not that God has let go of me, but that I have grown weary of holding onto God.

I have received more in this world than I have been able to give, but for some reason it just has not been enough to defeat the demon inside my soul. I have not given up on God; I have just given up on me. This is still God's world and God's will still triumphs. It is simply time for me to get out of God's way.

It pains me beyond description to think of what this

might do to Ryan and Megan, but they have people much better than me to take care of them. 'Pa Bill' and 'B', Ad and Knox, John and Diane can do for them what I could never do at all. If God's healing works enough, Peggy can do more than all six.

I beg forgiveness from First Church, Dallas for doing this because I have preached just the opposite for the last seven years. The people in that congregation are the greatest and most loving on earth, and they have made the Word become flesh for me in an abundance of ways. I can only pray they will see beyond this drastic action to the God whose love never ends.

I love John & Diane Yarrington and feel closer to him than any man on this earth. He is the older brother I never had. Please forgive me, John, for letting go.

Ad, my mother, will never understand this. I can only hope her love is strong enough to remember the hope of the past and not be sidetracked by despair of the present. I pray the same for Knox, and especially for Billie Jo and Bill.

I would like to list thousands of names here, but I would omit, in error, someone significant. If you are really close to me, you know already how I feel. If you are not really all that close, words are not adequate.

Pray for Peggy, take care of my children and forgive me for the pain I inflict on so many. I have finally made the decision to take care of myself. I have grown weak. God has remained strong. Therein lies your hope. I have none.

Walker L. Railey

Was this confession of a despairing soul also the confession of a man who had attacked his wife with the intention of murdering her? He has not admitted to the attack, but neither has he expressed compassion for Peggy. In what he surely thought were his final words, he mentions her only twice: in the context of "if God's healing works enough" and in his request to "pray for Peggy."

Whether the letter is genuine or faked, there is no declaration in it of love for his wife, his children, his mistress or his God. As far as his love is concerned, he writes: ["I love John & Diane Yarrington and feel closer to him than any man on this earth."] One would suppose that if anyone understood Walker, it would be John.

Almost all of Dallas, half the state of Texas and quite a few people across the country watched the "20/20" television show on Railey titled "A Fall from Grace."

Photographed in the sanctuary of the church, Ralph Shannon said: "Railey was the ultimate preacher. Someone has said he didn't preach a sermon, he preached a drama . . . I think it was assumed by most members of the Church that whoever wrote the threatening letters was also responsible for the attack."

Only later did a few thoughtful observers question why Shannon felt this obvious assumption worthy of a sound bite—unless he suspected the two events a coincidence. Though Spurgeon Dunnam had hinted at it in his interview with *Newsweek,* this was an hypothesis no one before had implied.

Diane and John Yarrington said that Peggy would not have gone in the garage, the one place unprotected, alone at ten P.M. Nor would she let into the house anyone she didn't know. Either Peggy Railey knew her attacker, or else the attacker knew the code to the alarm system. The odds of guessing the combination are more than a million to one.

Diane Yarrington said: "To even think that he could be a suspect was so foreign to everything I knew and believed that I just couldn't deal with it. But that was seven months ago and since then we've learned a lot of things we didn't know at the time. But, I cannot, no matter what else he has done, conceive of him [sic] doing that to her."

What, beyond the affair with Lucy, were the things about Walker that the Yarringtons had learned over the past seven months? The two couples knew far more secrets about each other than anyone else knew. They shared the same code to their alarm systems, the number of the church on Ross Avenue.

Assistant District Attorney Norman Kinne questioned if the suicide attempt was not a deathbed confession. But, a confession of what? Certainly not his affair with Lucy who is not even mentioned. Nor is the letter a confession of the attack on Peggy. The letter focuses entirely on his feelings and his struggles, none of which are specific.

Kinne also points out the inconsistencies in time when Railey said he telephoned his wife and when the mobile phone company recorded the times.

"He calls his wife and says, 'Hi, Babe. I'm doing this that and the other.' He tells her it's somewhere between ten and ten-thirty and that he doesn't wear a watch. Well, everyone knows that he doesn't wear a watch. This isn't a message he need necessarily deliver to his wife. And when he calls a second time, he knows *exactly* what time it is. It is 12:29—well, has he suddenly acquired a watch in the past two hours?"

When asked if he thought Railey was guilty, Kinne looked straight at the camera. "God and Reverend Railey know that," he said. "Not me."

"This must leave you a very frustrated man," the interviewer concluded.

"Frustrated, yes," Kinne paused. "But I'm also a patient man."

Surely saying he was "a patient man" contradicted his statement to the press earlier that same day—"this may very well be the last anyone is hearing of this and I want to fill in the blanks as much as I can." The television interview was taped weeks before the last announcement to the press. Had something occurred between the two interviews to convince Kinne of the futility of patience? Why were these antithetical quotes not taken up and debated by the media?

Almost all who had been skeptical of Railey's suicide attempt in the hospital read the letter in *The News* and decided that it seemed sincere; while those who had always

believed the suicide attempt was sincere were hardly grati-
fied by its contents. That a Methodist minister would speak
of a demon inside his soul, a demon who had always been
there and with whom God had been struggling for almost
forty years, was incredible. If what he had written in what he
believed to be the last hour of his conscious life was true, he
had never been the man his followers and associates had
believed him to be. Nothing inside him had suddenly
snapped; there had always been a "demon" inside him. The
life he had pretended to live was a lie.

A Baptist minister who had attended an interfaith council
meeting at which Railey spoke, remembered driving back to
Dallas with Railey and complimenting him on being such
an inspiration to his colleagues.

Railey had replied sarcastically: "Surely you don't believe
in all that crap? You don't really believe in God or Jesus
Christ, do you?"

The Baptist minister had been too shocked to give a
coherent reply. This was heresy. Was Railey challenging him
to defend Christianity, or was he revealing his own lack of
faith, usually concealed by an actor's skill?

Spurgeon Dunnam felt confirmed in his statement:
"We're dealing with a person who is fundamentally ill. You
have to throw out the rational. Whatever the truth is, it is
not rational." A number of other ministers subscribed to
Dunnam's statement.

Howard Grimes, who hadn't believed Walker's suicide
attempt was sincere, now believed that it was. He recalled
Walker's calculated cruelties not only to himself but to other
members of the staff. In particular he couldn't put out of his
mind the staff meeting about three months before the
attack. Walker was angry and emotional. He had those
glazed, flinty eyes and that rapier tongue. "John
[Yarrington] and I have a special relationship, which we
have tried to conceal, but I think the staff ought to know
about it." He then spoke of how close he and John were and
that no one else on the staff could ever be to him what John
was. "If any of you don't like it," he concluded, "that's too
bad because this is the way it's going to be." At the time

Howard had thought someone on the staff had made a smirking comment about John, which had infuriated Walker. Now he believed that there was a demonic side to Walker that often prevailed over the good.

Diane Yarrington was now more wary about talking to the press, not so much because she believed her comments would be distorted but because her own beliefs kept changing. What she believed when she made the "20/20" tape was not the same as what she believed when it was aired. And six months from now, she might not believe what she believed now. There was so much talk about Walker's being schizophrenic or totally evil that she was forcing herself to remember the good things about him—and there were some good things. It was generous of him to give her Peggy's car. She remembered how he asked James K. Wilson, an exclusive menswear store, to telephone John and ask him to come to the store and select a suit that was an anonymous gift (though Walker later let it be known he was the giver). John had inquired in what price range to choose. The salesman had said there was no limit, to select whatever he wanted and to choose several shirts and ties to go with the suit.

Cynics said that Walker hadn't spent his own money but had taken money from the senior minister's discretionary fund and had undoubtedly added to his own wardrobe as well. Then, there was the flip side, the stingy side, the almost kleptomaniac side to Walker's personality. His attitude about watches was bizarre. Refusing to wear a watch of his own, he would borrow one from one of the other ministers just before he gave his Sunday sermon. After the service he would pocket the watch and apparently forget to return it.

If they inquired about it a day or so later, they would find Walker had either lost it or misplaced it. Most of them then took to wearing cheap drugstore watches.

On April 22, 1988, a year to the day after Peggy Railey was attacked, Walker failed to appear in a state civil court to respond to the lawsuit filed by his in-laws.

State District Judge Whittington issued a preliminary

civil judgment holding Railey financially liable for the attack and injuries to his wife, Margaret 'Peggy' Railey, and because Railey never responded to the lawsuit filed by his in-laws, Whittington adopted as legal "fact" the allegations that accuse him of "intentionally, knowingly, maliciously and brutally" attempting to strangle his wife and establish a false alibi to cover his actions. The Judge set the date of October 3, 1988, for a jury to determine the financial amount Walker Railey owes his wife for damages resulting from a failed murder attempt.

Within a week after the civil judgment the police turned over their files on the Railey case to Bill Arnold who had subpoenaed them. Since Arnold already had a guilty verdict against the elusive Railey, he issued a subpoena for him but didn't bother actively to pursue him. Instead he concentrated on gathering depositions from witnesses of two sorts: those who could testify to the hopelessness of Peggy's present condition in contrast to her previously bright future, and those who, willingly or reluctantly, could cast aspersions on the character of the former pastor. The most interesting witness would, of course, be Lucy Papillon. On April 29, she was subpoenaed to testify and to produce documents about her relationship with Walker Railey. (These would include personal correspondence as well as a wide range of business papers, such as the lease she had signed with Railey on the San Francisco apartment, hotel bills and credit card statements substantiating her continued relationship with Railey.) Through her lawyer Phil Burleson Lucy asked Judge Whittington to nullify the subpoena on the grounds of the damage done to her after her grand jury testimony was reported by the media and the "additional publicity will exacerbate damage already done to her personal and professional reputation and disrupt and injure her ability to earn a living."

Arnold opposed the motion, saying that Lucy Papillon "is one witness who has knowledge of the underlying facts on the night of the assault, as well as the motives."

Judge Whittington sided with Arnold and gave Lucy seven days to produce the records and give the deposition.

Arnold told the press: "When you compare Peggy Railey lying in a coma in Tyler, Texas, to a witness being inconvenienced, I think Ms. Papillon's concern about inconvenience in the judicial system kind of pales to insignificance."

33

ON THE MORNING OF DECEMBER 5, 1988, A HALF dozen people arrived before eight o'clock in Judge Whittington's courtroom. They anticipated a full house and no available seats by ten o'clock when the judgment hearing was scheduled.

The courthouse had been built in the early 1930s and has the kind of dignity associated with the handing down of justice. The judge sits elevated behind a dark mahogany desk with old-fashioned globe lamps at the front corners. The desk is much larger than a pulpit, with the American flag at one end and the Texas state flag at the other. A corner room, seating about two hundred in oak pews, there are two sides of the room with high Georgian windows.

Another wall of the room, leading into a wide hall where the public enters and leaves, has two equidistant doors, one at the front of the room, one at the back. Tall, evenly spaced doors also are behind the judge's desk, one directly facing the prosecutor's table and the other the defender's table. Over the doors leading to the judge's chambers and to the lawyers' waiting room are two art deco, Depression-era paintings. One with the feminine figure of justice blindfolded and the other with the same figure balancing the scales of justice.

At five minutes to eight Wayne Lee Gay, a young writer from *The Ft. Worth Star-Telegram,* spoke to a couple of TV cameramen in the hallway near the back door. A large man, tall with curly hair and a full black beard, he entered the courtroom and saw a young woman dressed in jeans with a brief case and a brown bag lunch. She introduced herself as a reporter from *The Houston Chronicle*. There was an elderly woman, to whom she was talking, who said she was from First United Methodist Church. She was carrying a canvas carry-all that held her knitting, an apple and a couple of bananas. Wayne hadn't had breakfast and didn't feel much like talking. He went back into the hall and leaned against the wall, pensively watching the cameramen set up their equipment.

A few minutes before ten he was still in the hall, which was now packed with reporters and court house hangers-on. The courtroom itself was about two thirds filled. Suddenly there was a flurry of chatter, a shout of "here they come" and the sudden illumination of the television lights, as Bill Arnold and an assistant led Bill and Billie Jo, Ted and Linda and two women whom nobody could identify, into the courtroom.

Wayne had heard that Lucy would not appear until after lunch, so he slipped in the back door and sat on a back row center aisle seat.

The perfectly balanced neo-classical room seemed suddenly off-balance with the Nicolai family seated on the front row behind the rail that separates the lawyers and court officials from the public. They were behind Bill Arnold, his assistant and his secretary Janice at the table for the prosecution. On the side for the defendant there was no one on either side of the rail.

The bailiff asked those in the courtroom to rise when Judge Whittington entered. Having instructed that no pictures be taken in the courtroom, the judge then called upon Mr. Arnold to present his evidence regarding the life and future that might have been anticipated by the plaintiff had she not suffered the physical and mental damage inflicted upon her by her husband, and also the extent of the brain damage and physical impairment, pain and incapacity the plaintiff has suffered and in all reasonable probability will continue to suffer for the balance of her natural life.

There were two television sets in the courtroom, one for the benefit of the judge and the other facing the courtroom benches so that the family of the plaintiff, the media and the public could see some of the depositions that had been videotaped.

The first video deposition was that of Charles Massoud, who testified that on the night of the attack he had observed that Railey had been drinking and that he did not touch his wife nor cover her with a blanket. He did not believe that Railey was genuinely upset by his wife's injuries.

The principal of Ursuline Academy was then called to take the stand in person. She testified to Peggy's competence as a teacher, that had she remained at the school she could have been anticipating a salary of twenty-seven-thousand dollars annually with periodic raises. She could have remained at Ursuline as long as she wished, since there was no established retirement policy, and that some of the teachers remained there well into their seventies.

Dr. William Parker, the director of the Baylor Rehabilitation Clinic, took the stand next. In response to Arnold's questions, he explained that Peggy Railey suffered brain damage because oxygen was cut off from her brain when she was choked. The odds are virtually nil that she would ever be able to identify her attacker. She exists in what is medically known as a permanent vegetative state, and in this condition she might well live another thirty or forty years.

Linda Nicolai took the stand next and told of an episode at the rehabilitation center when Peggy had become agitated after she saw a man exercising with an elastic cord in the physiotherapy center.

The next witness was Diane Yarrington on videotape. Having been sworn under oath as if she were testifying in an actual court of law, she was asked by Arnold about her friendship with Peggy.

"We were soulmates. We had been through a lot of the

same things. We had shared a lot of the same experiences. We'd both had to have the same operation so that we could have children. And we'd found that our tastes were identical. Before we even knew each other, we had selected similar china patterns and similar stainless steel."

"What sort of interests did Peggy have?"

"She was very interested in her children and doing things with them."

"Was she a good wife?"

"Yes."

"How was she a good wife?"

"She was very intelligent. She clipped articles from the newspapers that she thought might help Walker with his sermons. She read his sermons, and if he had mispronounced a word during a sermon, she corrected his pronunciation, writing it out on a piece of paper and sticking it on his bathroom mirror so he would find it the next morning when he was about to shave."

"Did she have any other interests apart from her children and helping her husband with his sermons?"

"She was very musical, but my husband can tell you more about that than I can."

"Anything else?"

"She loved to swim. She swam daily. The pool was one of the main attractions to her about living in that house. And she sewed and embroidered. She made clothes for herself and the children, and she helped a friend from Christ Church who made stoles for the ministers and liturgical banners. She enjoyed doing things like that."

"Did you see her often?"

"We talked on the phone a lot, but our children are different ages. My oldest daughter Julie was the Raileys' baby sitter. And mainly, when we were together, it was the four of us."

"The four of you?"

"My husband John and I and Peggy and Walker. We had a continuing joke among the four of us. The men always made us sit in the back seat. Peggy was a better driver and had a better sense of direction than Walker, so sometimes she would call out to John: 'Tell the bishop to make a right at the next corner.'"

"Did Walker have ambitions of becoming a bishop?"

"I think he probably did. Because we were like one family, instead of two, we sometimes worried about being separated if Walker were to be transferred—but then Walker had told John that if he went somewhere else there would be a place there for John, too."

"Some people in the Church have said that Peggy wasn't very friendly and that over the past year she had practically ceased coming to the Church at all."

"I don't think that's a fair criticism. Peggy did a lot of things. She sang in the choir. And she was shy—she just didn't do things that drew a lot of attention to herself. And during the past year she hadn't been well—she had allergies and problems with her eyes and then she had a really bad case of pneumonia that she just couldn't shake. Her mother had to come from Tyler to look after her and the children. She stayed a couple of weeks."

"You said earlier that she was shy and didn't draw attention to herself—was she more or less willing to defer to Walker and not voice her own wishes or opinions?"

"Oh, no, not at all. She could be very strong-willed and determined. She was not beyond showing her temper or arguing with Walker when she thought he was wrong or maybe acting conceited. I remember once she got angry and threw a book at him—but that was unusual. That sort of thing didn't happen all the time."

"When was the last time you saw Peggy Railey before the attack on April 21?"

"On Easter Sunday. At Church. My mother was ill and I had to drive to Oklahoma that afternoon. I came back late Tuesday. She had telephoned that afternoon to ask about my mother. Julie had spoken with her. And I was tired, so I didn't call her back."

"Have you been to the nursing home in Tyler to see Peggy?"

"Yes."

"How would you compare the person you saw on Easter with the person you last saw in Tyler?"

"They just can't be the same person. That just isn't Peggy anymore."

Next was a video of a harpsichord recital that Peggy had given at the Church a few weeks before the attack. It showed her as gifted, accomplished and attractive. The tape was, however, some forty-five minutes long. The judge was fidgeting, swinging slightly in his chair. Finally he asked Arnold how much longer the tape was. Arnold replied twenty minutes.

At this point the Judge declared an hour and a half recess for lunch. The court would convene again at two o'clock.

At two o'clock there were more people in the public seating area than there had been during the morning session. Everyone there seemed to know that now to come were the most important witnesses—Lucy Papillon and Peggy's mother.

Someone in the press had been given a tip that Lucy would be brought to the courtroom by a back elevator from which one could walk to the lawyers' chambers down a back corridor without passing through the hall that was the main entry to the courtroom. The media waited at the elevator.

Suddenly the few spectators in the courtroom were startled to see Lucy Papillon walk into the room alone. She seemed shy and uncertain about what to do. Looking quickly over the public section, she slipped into the unoccupied second row on the defendant's side of the aisle. She was dressed conservatively, wearing a beige dress with a turtle neck collar and an overblouse, gold jewelry, beige handbag and beige shoes. She sat staring forward, not turning her head, her face expressionless, her hands folded in her lap. The Nicolais, who had entered just before her and returned to their seats, did not alter their positions to look at her, nor did she look at them. For almost five minutes, there was absolute silence; then all four doors opened at once, officers of the court entering from one door, Bill Arnold and his associate entering from the lawyers' room, and most of the media, looking confused, pouring in from the two hall doors. Following them, with a smug expression was Lucy's lawyer, Bob Baskett, who had waited with her in the empty courtroom across the hall. When the media moved around the corridor to the back elevator, Lucy had simply stepped across the fifteen foot hall to the courtroom door opposite.

Baskett took her by the arm, guiding her from the public section through the inside arena to a table that was at a right angle to Arnold's table. Though she was seated close to the witness box and the court reporter's desk, it was difficult for those in the public area to see her.

The bailiff called for order. Everyone rose as the judge entered. The final twenty minutes of the videotape of Peggy Railey playing a Bach cantata was completed.

Then Arnold showed an hour videotape of a day in the life of the nearly comatose Peggy in the Tyler nursing home. The woman lying in the bed was hardly recognizable as the young woman who had played the harpsichord.

Wearing a shapeless hospital gown that opened down the back, she was like a rag doll propped up on pillows. The metal bars of the bed were lifted so she could not slide off the mattress. Her hands and thin fingers were bent and twisted, incapable of grasping anything. Her face and throat were unnaturally white and bloated. Her eyes tracked movement but showed no comprehension. She drooled, emitting gurgling groans and occasionally howling an eerie, almost inhuman sound.

The Nicolai family showed no reaction, but several spectators found the tape so disturbing that they left the courtroom.

Arnold called to the witness stand Dr. Lucy Papillon. The judge cautioned that he would tolerate no outbursts or comments from the spectators.

Billie Jo was seated on the front bench of the public area exactly opposite the witness stand. There was about twenty feet between them. It was the first time each had seen the other in person. Billie Jo's dark eyes fixed upon her, but Lucy did not meet her stare.

Arnold asked Lucy if she and Walker Railey ever traveled together prior to April 21, 1987?

"Yes."

"Would you recall these trips for the court?"

"I will as nearly as I can remember," Lucy answered softly and politely.

"Perhaps I can refresh your memory. I have with me copies of hotel bills and credit card bills."

For the next fifteen minutes Lucy confirmed that between June of 1986 and April 21, 1987, she had either travelled with or met Railey in London, Atlanta, Wichita, Austin, Little Rock, San Francisco and Conway, Arkansas. On each occasion it was a "Dutch treat." Lucy paid for her travel, hotel and restaurant expenses, while the Church paid for Walker's.

Lucy seemed hardly nervous at all. Her manner was soft-spoken. She admitted to having a sexual affair with Railey over a period of ten months and that Railey had said he would kill himself if anyone at the Church found out about their affair. She admitted that on the night of the attack on Peggy Railey she had spoken with Walker on the telephone four times and that he had visited her somewhere between nine-thirty and ten. He had seemed "stressed out" and lay down on her bed for about forty-five minutes.

"Did you and Walker ever talk about getting married?"

Lucy thought carefully before answering. Then she said that before the attack, they had discussed marriage in "a hypothetical way." They spoke of the present minister at Highland Park Methodist who had divorced his wife, remarried and held on to his pulpit. They thought it might be difficult for a divorced man to become a bishop, although they believed that their relationship would be a permanent one and that if Walker left Peggy, he would also leave the children. They would not take the children with them.

"Did you expect Walker to divorce Peggy and marry you?"

Again they had discussed their relationship only in "a hypothetical way," but they had agreed that there were four possible scenarios to the relationship: they would end their affair; they would continue with the liaison as it was; Walker would divorce Peggy and then they would marry; or Peggy might die and then they could marry.

There was a gasp from the public area and the judge hammered his gavel. Arnold studied his notes; then he asked Lucy: "How often did you and Walker Railey meet and have sexual intercourse when you both were in Dallas?"

"Two or three times a week."

"Where did you meet?"

"Usually at my house."

"At what time?"

"Around two to four in the afternoons."

"Did you have drinks on those occasions?"

"Yes. We sometimes drank champagne."

"Did you ever take drugs together?"

"No."

"Did Walker ever talk to you about Peggy?"

"Not much."

"What did he say when he did talk about her?"

"He said she was a good mother and a good musician."

"Is that all?"

Lucy hesitated and looked at the ceiling. She chose her words cautiously and spoke slowly. "He said that they did not have a good intimate relationship, but that they had a practical arrangement for living together that worked."

"Did he say he had missed having a good, intimate relationship?"

"You don't miss what you've never had. He hadn't had a satisfying sexual relationship until he met me."

Again there was a gasp from the public area and the judge hammered his gavel. Lucy was genuinely convinced of Walker's love for her and that their love was worth any sacrifice she might be called upon to make. To her their love was a rare grand passion—a Tristan and Isolde, a Romeo and Juliet—that she took for granted the world ought to know, admire and respect. To many observers, Lucy wasn't living entirely in the real world. Was it possible that she was hypnotized by someone or something evil? Was it possible that the supposed femme fatale was also a victim?

He cleared his throat and then asked Lucy about presents Walker had given her for her birthday and for Christmas of 1987. She replied that he had given her a black sweater and skirt, a gold necklace, another cashmere sweater, a gold anklet, a hat and—that was all she could remember.

Arnold asked if she was aware that Railey had sent no Christmas present to his wife who lay comatose in a nursing home. Lucy said she was not.

"Are you and Mr. Railey still continuing your relationship?"

Lucy's lawyer objected, noting that the parameters of two years—the middle of 1986 through the middle of 1988—had been established for the questioning. The objection was sustained.

Arnold asked if Lucy would explain to the court why she had changed her name to Papillon.

Clearly Lucy had anticipated the question and was prepared. "Papillon is the French word for butterfly. It meant something symbolic to me."

"Could you explain how it was symbolic to you?"

"Well, to me it means changing and becoming free, a kind of metamorphosis."

"You mean like the metamorphosis of a caterpillar to a chrysalis to a butterfly?"

"Yes."

"Do you feel that you have undergone such a metamorphosis?"

"Yes."

"Dr. Papillon, I want you to look at three pictures of Peggy Railey."

He picked up a poster on which were mounted three large photographs of Peggy—one taken before the attack, one taken by the police photographer when she was in the Presbyterian Hospital emergency area and one taken recently of her in bed at the nursing home. The poster was purposely held facing the spectators while Arnold walked toward Lucy. Then suddenly he flipped the poster around so that the photographs were at eye level with her and no more than two feet away. Lucy gave a start, moving back from the poster.

"Dr. Papillon, would you say that Peggy Railey has experienced a metamorphosis in reverse?"

Lucy's posture stiffened. Her cheeks and throat flushed, as she averted her eyes and looked down at her clasped hands.

"I—I don't know what to say," she whispered hoarsely. "I just don't know."

It was the most dramatic moment of the hearing.

Billie Jo was the last to take the stand. With sad resignation on her face and in her voice she told of the routine she and Bill had established at the nursing home, of how she needed to believe Peggy would recover so that she could get through each day. She answered questions about the cost of Peggy's medical care and of the nursing home. She said that they were not wealthy people, living off Social Security and a pension her husband had from his former employment. She explained that so far they had not been able to get Medicaid for Peggy and that because Walker was no longer a minister, the Church medical insurance extended only until September, 1989, ten months from now.

Billie Jo said that she went to court because she wanted to make certain that her daughter would be cared for financially after her death and the death of Peggy's father. Tears filled her eyes. "Bill has passed seventy and I am sixty-eight. We are not going to be here to give her that care, and we want to make sure that she is cared for."

In his closing statement to Judge Whittington, Arnold began: "Peggy Railey's life as she knew it came to an absolute end on April 21, 1987. The world in which she now exists is a living hell."

It was almost five o'clock in the afternoon. The winter sky had become darker, and sounds of the heavy rush-hour traffic were more audible in the courtroom, which, too, was darker. Television reporters put on their microphones. Everyone in the courtroom, including Judge Whittington, was visibly moved as Arnold spoke of the tragedy that not only affected Peggy, but her parents and also her children.

He pointed to the bare table of the defense counsel and the empty chairs. Railey had ignored the law. He hadn't shown up for the trial or the judgment because he didn't want to answer questions under oath. "He's a cold, cold, cold person—Walker Railey is as cold as cold can be. It's obvious why he doesn't want to help the police. He doesn't want to incriminate himself under the Fifth Amendment."

Judge Whittington ruled that Walker Railey should pay his mother-in-law Billie Jo Nicolai the sixteen million dollars requested for actual and punitive damages in the near strangulation of his wife and that he would allow Attorney Arnold also to include an estimated amount for inflation that Arnold calculated to be over two million, making the final judgment against Railey eighteen and a half million dollars.

Asked by a journalist if she did not feel that the ruling was a vindication of her daughter, Billie Jo replied: "Nothing will ever vindicate Peggy."

34

THREE DAYS AFTER THE CIVIL TRIAL THE TELEPHONE awakened Billie Jo around eleven at night.

"The last thing I needed now was an eighteen-million-dollar judgment against me," Walker told her. "I'm broke. I can't even pay my bills."

"Walker, we are trying to take care of Peggy's future," Billie Jo replied. "We don't have much money either."

Walker said he had called because of the time-sharing property in Arkansas on which he was unable to pay the taxes. He would lose the property, which the Nicolais had given to him and Peggy, if he didn't pay the taxes he owed for the past two years. He would appreciate it if Bill and Billie Jo would pay them.

Billie Jo said she would. The conversation ended. They had nothing more to say to one another. But Billie Jo could not get back to sleep. She was thinking about the way they had planned the declining years of their lives and how different now it all was. Why should she care about the property in Arkansas now? Peggy would never enjoy it. She was angry with herself for agreeing to pay the taxes. That was a mistake. She would only be helping Walker, which was the last thing she wanted to do. She didn't care if the property in Arkansas was reclaimed. If Walker telephoned again, she would tell him that they weren't going to pay the taxes. She had changed her mind.

In the year that Hal Brady had been senior pastor at First United Methodist in Dallas, very little had happened that he had anticipated. The departure of John Yarrington had created emotional conflicts in the Church that were not easily or quickly resolved. There was no simple or quick conclusion to the shock and pain that came with another betrayal and loss of trust. Even more surprising to Hal was the continuation of the Railey tragedy that simply would not end. When new events, such as the civil judgment against Railey occurred, the congregation became obsessed with looking backwards.

No matter how much Hal wanted to move the Church forward, the focus of the congregation was still looking backward. New shocks were preventing the wounds from healing. Until the series of tragedies finally ended, the grieving process would continue. What was happening to Walker was of more concern than what was happening at the Church. No one could explain why, and neither minister nor bishops could eliminate the mourning process. Hal and his wife Myron decided to put together a jumble sale to raise money to help pay some of the expenses for Peggy. Myron had never run a jumble sale, but she was energetic and well-organized. To help Peggy would bring together the clergy, the Church and the local community.

On the thirteenth of December, a week to the day after the civil trial, Bill Arnold called a press conference in the panelled boardroom of the Northpark National Bank where he announced that a new trust fund was being established for Peggy Railey. He predicted that this fund would be more successful than the fund set up at First United Methodist shortly after the attack because in the event of Peggy's death, Walker is the beneficiary of the Church fund. In the new Northpark fund, Ryan and Megan are the beneficiaries.

Seated at a long table with Arnold were bank officers and Bill, Billie Jo and Ted Nicolai. A reporter asked Billie Jo if she thought the eighteen and a half million dollars awarded in the civil trial would assist in bringing a criminal suit.

"We did not go into this primarily to recover punitive damages," she replied. "We went into it to see if there's some help down the line."

Another reporter asked Arnold if he thought that Railey had eighteen and a half million dollars. Arnold replied that he did not know how much money Railey had but that he did expect to collect some money from him.

Mrs. Nicolai, who was rumored to be ill, was then asked if she was in good health. She answered: "I'm sure our life span has been shortened by this. Not just by the shock but by the hours we willingly put in at the nursing home."

Several reporters shouted questions at her at once. Arnold took back the table microphone, asking for one question at a time. Reporters then raised their hands, and Arnold nodded at Olive who asked Billie Jo what she thought about Walker now. Arnold shoved the microphone back to her. Tears surged to her eyes, but her voice remained steady. "It would be difficult for me to forgive him now," she said, "so I try not to think about him. If I thought about him it would create some negativism, and I don't want to take that into Peggy's room."

Arnold nodded to Wayne Lee Gay from *The Ft. Worth*

Star Telegram who asked if Peggy had known about Walker's affair with Lucy. Billie Jo responded that if Peggy had known she had never given her any indication of it.

A couple of the more cynical reporters silently wondered if Billie Jo had known her daughter as well as she had thought, but no one cared to push this subject farther. The media were unanimous in their sympathy for the Nicolai family. After Arnold concluded the conference, several of the reporters, including Olive and Wayne, came over to the Nicolais and expressed their sympathy.

The past year that Walker had spent in California was far from the new life he had hoped to find there. He had *not* been offered a position by Cecil Williams at Glide Memorial Church in San Francisco, nor had he been able to find another job suited to his skills. It was expensive living in San Francisco; Lucy was spending most of her time in Dallas, and Walker felt he was being harassed by the press, both from Dallas and San Francisco. It was not a conducive environment in which to live or find work.

In the early spring of 1988 he simply disappeared, got in his car and headed south, staying in fleabag motels that were ten or fifteen dollars a night. He looked for work and some place that wasn't too expensive to live. All he found were odd jobs, mowing lawns, painting a house, delivering telephone books. When there wasn't any money coming in, he joined the ranks of the homeless and slept in his car. The Oakleys, the Flahertys, Roberta Crowe, Willis Tate and other friends in Dallas sent him money from time to time. He had withdrawn all of the money in the trust fund established for him by the Church. He had no friends in California, and his only acquaintances were people he met while looking for work or killing time in a bar or eating in a fast food restaurant. In Long Beach he met someone who introduced him to a Mr. Cedillos who was president of a small defense contracting firm. Cedillos said all he really needed in help was a Kelly girl. Walker replied that he could type, and if Mr. Cedillos would let him use an office over the weekend, he would teach himself to use a computer. Cedillos gave him a job as his assistant at a salary of $24,000 a year. He rented a one bedroom apartment for $450 a month in Long Beach, a few blocks from the water front near where the Queen Mary is docked. He was seeing a therapist outside Pasadena once a week and paying $400 a month in child support, which was approximately the same amount that his expenses exceeded his monthly take-home pay. He owed money to his psychiatrist in Dallas, his therapist in California and his lawyers. To make ends meet as nearly as possible, he paid cash for his daily expenses and borrowed $400 a month on his credit cards for the child support. It was a situation that couldn't last forever, but it bought time, though time for what was another mystery.

On Friday, March 18, Walker was picked up at DFW Airport by Ad and Knox Oakley who took him to their home, where he would be spending the weekend. He would also be seeing the Yarringtons and his children. Detective Silva also received a call on Friday from a woman who did not identify herself but who said that Railey could be found at the Yarringtons the following day.

On Saturday morning, March 19, in front of the Yarringtons' home as he was putting his children in a car, Railey was served with a subpoena by Private Investigator Mike Holland. In an interview given to Olive Talley by Bill Arnold later the same day, Arnold said that Railey had been "definitely upset" by the subpoena but that he put up no resistance.

"It basically orders him to be at my office at ten A.M. on Tuesday and bring financial documents for the last two years showing his income, expenses and assets. It's a subpoena and it's issued under Texas law," Mr. Arnold said. "If he does not show up, we'll go back to court and issue a warrant for his arrest."

On Sunday, Walker flew back to California and collected what papers he had. Borrowing money from Cedillos for another round-trip plane ticket, he returned to Dallas the following day.

35

THE MONTH BEFORE THE METHODIST CHURCH HAD its 1989 General Conference, press releases were sent out about the North Texas Conference dividing into two Conferences. The new Conference, about a fourth the size of its parent Conference, would have its headquarters in Fort Worth under the leadership of Bishop Russell. He was being replaced in the North Texas Conference by Dr. Bruce P. Blake, formerly of St. Louis. Bishop Blake is a bulldog of a man with no more sensitivity toward the rights of the media than his predecessor.

The newspapers dutifully printed the Methodist press releases. No one in the media was particularly surprised, and no one who was not a Methodist and active in the North Texas Conference was particularly interested. Denominational politics are not engaging to those uninvolved, however absorbing they may be to the few who are involved. On May 23, Laura Miller fired off another rocket at the Methodist Church. This time nobody thought it was in bad taste. And this time hardly anyone, who was not a Methodist minister, disagreed with her.

The column was titled: WILL CHURCHES TAKE CARE OF PEGGY RAILEY?

It's not over 'til it's over. Which means there are 13 days to try to convince the United Methodist Church to change its mind about Peggy Railey.

Miller reported there had been a short, three paragraph press release from the bishop's office announcing that as of

September 2 there would be no more Church insurance for Peggy Railey. No more extensions on the group policy, no more exceptions to the rule. Bishop Blake hoped that Medicaid would take up where the Church left off and he hoped that individual Methodist congregations would continue to give money for Peggy's care. Voluntary donations would replace insurance coverage. Bishop Blake had told the Nicolais of the change.

The columnist then suggested two alternatives, noting that there were three hundred and sixty-nine churches in the Conference with a combined annual budget of fifty-one million dollars. Peggy Railey's medical costs could be covered by an annual gift of $97.56 from each church.

The churches in the North Texas Conference currently give six million dollars a year for joint expenses such as insurance, pensions and missionary work. Thirty-six thousand dollars a year for Peggy's medical expenses deducted from the pension fund would hardly be an inconvenience in such a substantial budget.

> There already has been one minister to shirk off responsibility for this woman. And that was her own husband. Perhaps now, when there is so much at stake and so little to have to sacrifice, the Methodist ministers of North Texas will shine.

Laura Miller was not the only columnist to criticize the Church. On Saturday, May 27, 1989, Diane Winston of *The Dallas Times Herald* wrote a column titled: DECISION ON PEGGY RAILEY PUTS CHURCH IN BAD LIGHT.

> . . . While some were surprised by the termination of financial support for the comatose woman, the announcement didn't shock me. The church had already voted to end the insurance. The ministers didn't want to pick up the tab. The consensus was to forget the whole Railey mess . . .
>
> Real religion focuses on righteousness, justice and charity. Jesus loved the forgotten ones. The prophets

wept for the helpless. But it's hard for a bureaucracy to focus on one person's pain. A denominational conference may be made up of many sterling ministers, but their "group think" is likely to focus on perpetuating their own well-being.

This sin, this missing the mark, pervades all institutions. The human concern for power and the politics of survival dominate the schools' desire to educate, the hospitals' call to heal, the government's mandate to lead. Good-intentioned people may fill the institutions, but something has gone awry.

The contradictions seem most glaring in the churches . . .

In some ways, Peggy Railey has nothing to do with the church. But, the real question is what does the church have to do with a helpless woman?

Their answer says volumes about the present state of God's people in the world.

Ministers of all denominations were furious with the press. How dare journalists presume to criticize those struggling to do God's will. Even clergy who felt that the Methodist Church had behaved stupidly, ineptly, selfishly and in an un-Christian manner toward Peggy Railey felt that they, too, had somehow been placed on the side of the demons. And this made them angry and uncomfortable.

To no one's surprise, however, *The United Methodist Reporter* reported the annual session of the North Texas Conference in an entirely different manner from the rest of the media. The headline was CHURCHES SUPPORT TRUST FUND FOR PEGGY RAILEY. A subheading was CONFERENCE PASSES RESOLUTION OF COMMENDATION AND CONCERN.

On Tuesday, June 6 at 4:30 in the afternoon, the following resolution was presented by the Rev. Spurgeon M. Dunnam III and affirmed as conference members stood, and were led in prayer by Bishop Bruce P. Blake.

Dunnam's resolution stated that Peggy Railey was the innocent victim of a physical attack and also the innocent victim of her spouse's surrender of his ministerial credentials. He commended the Committee on Insurance, as well as the former Episcopal leader of the North Texas Conference Bishop Russell and the current leader Bishop Blake *"for their diligence and steadfastness in seeking to assure continued high quality health care for Peggy Railey . . . Be it further resolved that the North Texas Annual Conference requests that Bishop Blake keep members of the conference informed regarding Peggy Railey's continuing health care needs and the adequacy of her social service benefits combined with the trust funds raised for meeting those needs."*

Olive Talley read the article at her desk in the News Room, tossed it in the waste paper basket and remarked aloud: "Bullshit!"

The second anniversary of the infamous Easter service and the tragedy that followed arrived with the police seemingly no closer to solving the crime than they had been a year ago, or for that matter, two years ago. Public interest had not lessened; public criticism had intensified. Walker, Lucy, Peggy, Kinne, Mulder and some members of the Church were as familiar and persistently topical as characters in a soap opera.

"What bugs me is how can Railey just thumb his nose at the law?" Will Lieber said to Bobby Eubank as they waited for their golf foursome to be called at the Brookhaven Club. "The police want to question him, and he runs away. The court serves him with a summons, and he just doesn't show up. He's been doing things like this for two years. I just don't see how he can get away with it."

"I don't know whether it's true or not," Bobby said, "but Betty told me she heard he wasn't even paying child support."

"That's terrible," Will said. "If anything would convince me he's capable of committing any crime it's his not looking after his kids."

When Walker gave permanent custody of his children to John and Diane Yarrington, they had requested that the court documents be sealed from public scrutiny, explaining that the children had been through enough of an ordeal over the past two years. KDFW-TV filed a lawsuit seeking public access and won. In an interview, KDFW's attorney said: "The children are not really a part of this. This is about what this court is doing to ensure that Walker Railey, a public figure, who did occupy a position of power in Dallas, is discharging his obligations to his children."

The agreement between Railey and the Yarringtons was that Railey would be allowed to see the children four times a year, for two four-hour visits. Later the visits would be extended, and eventually he would be able to take the children with him for weekend trips.

Soon after all arrangements with the Yarringtons were announced, the Nicolais received a registered letter from Railey's California attorney informing them that Railey was seeking a divorce from Peggy "because of irreconcilable differences."

Billie Jo forwarded the document to Bill Arnold to handle. "I don't have any feeling about it one way or the other," she said. "I can't speak for Peggy, and she can't speak for herself."

When the Nicolais came to Dallas to discuss the divorce papers Arnold immediately suggested a countersuit. Even though Walker had been convicted by a civil court for damages he was unable to pay now, he might be made to pay monthly alimony just as he had finally agreed to pay monthly child support. Arnold telephoned Los Angeles Attorney Stephen A. Kolodny who agreed to take the case.

Billie Jo was worried, but Arnold assured her that they would countersue Walker and would win again. For Billie Jo there was one shock after another. Every day it was becoming harder to take the days one at a time.

36

WALKER'S COMBINED ACTIONS OF GIVING UP HIS CHILdren and filing for divorce from his helpless wife gave a bigger boost to the Peggy Railey Rummage Sale than all the advertising and public relations efforts.

Trammel Crow, one of the city's prominent real estate developers, lent a warehouse for the three-day sale. Manufacturers and retailers as well as individuals donated merchandise. There were dozens of new furniture items—over twenty sofas, and lounge chairs, bedroom suites, dining room suites; new gift items including brass candlesticks, Chinese porcelain lamps, appliances new and used. There were forty new bicycles. There was clothing, some donated by stores and some slightly worn—two hundred pairs of blue jeans at a dollar a pair, neckties at ten cents, children's shoes at twenty-five cents a pair. Twelve fur coats on a rack in a separate area were auctioned. New hardback books sold at a dollar each, and all paperbacks were a dime each.

Over three hundred volunteers came, worked for weeks collecting and organizing and pricing and, on September 8, the first day of the sale, they worked as salespeople, packers and cashiers. When the sale opened, there were five hundred people waiting to enter and buy, people from all walks of life. Despite the lack of air conditioning in the building and temperatures that were close to one hundred degrees, people remained polite and patient. The people who came and bought felt that they had not only acquired some extraordinary bargains but that they had personally done something worthwhile for someone whose need was greater than their own. Practically everyone checking out told the cashiers to keep the change, which in some instances was more than the value of the purchases.

By the middle of the afternoon of the first day, nearly two-thirds of the merchandise had been sold. On Friday evening trucks arrived with more donations from Dallas merchants. At the end of the three-day sale one hundred and seven thousand dollars had been netted for Peggy, over twice the goal set.

Charlotte Lieber, Betty Eubank and Ann Nichols went to the sale. It was the first Church activity Charlotte had attended since Easter two years ago.

"She can't resist a bargain even if it's against her religion," Betty teased.

"It's not *against* my religion. It's *for* Peggy Railey, and that's a cause to which I am willing to contribute."

"So am I," Ann said. "I hope I can get all of my Christmas shopping done. That would really make me feel in the Christmas spirit."

"Me, too," Betty agreed.

"If you two buy all your Christmas presents now, eight months from now you won't remember where you hid them," Charlotte said.

"In the laundry room," Betty replied. "Nobody in my family ever goes in the laundry room but me."

Graphoanalyst Jane Buckner was reading in the newspaper about the success of the Church sale for Peggy Railey when the telephone rang. It was Norman Kinne whom she had not seen or spoken with since the day before the grand jury *didn't* indict Walker Railey.

Kinne told her that a *Times Herald* reporter who had a sample of Lucy Papillon's handwriting would probably call her. Kinne had told him about her analysis of Walker's handwriting.

Jane had barely hung up the phone when it rang again. It was Jack Taylor who said he would like to meet with her and show her Lucy's handwriting. He said he would also like a copy of Jane's report to Kinne on Railey. They agreed to meet the following morning for breakfast at Denny's, a chain restaurant, on Coit Road.

Jane was surprised when she saw that Jack had brought a camera. Graphoanalysis had received bad publicity in news stories where reporters had confused it with graphology. Now she was on her guard with any journalist. She allowed him to take her picture on the condition that he permit her to see the article before it was published. Jack said he would let her know when it was going to appear and read it to her over the telephone but that he couldn't guarantee it would appear exactly as he said because editors frequently changed copy. He shoved across the table a Xeroxed copy of a crumpled sheet of paper that had been smoothed as neatly as possible. On it was written:

Walker, I need to say a few things to you. I really care about you and appreciate all the work you have done and are doing. I needed your understanding about my struggle on Sunday morning. I really did. I stated it was my struggle, but I needed your help. I am sorry that because of my need, I wasn't what you wanted me to be. I would appreciate your calling at 4:30 Dallas time today. It is eleven o'clock now.

"Where did you get this?" Jane asked.

"Trade secret."

"Well, it's hard to analyze writing that has been duplicated, and also it's such a small sample and the sample was crumpled."

"I think that it's a draft of a message to be left on an answering machine."

Jane looked at the page in her hand. It smelled like the ink in a copy machine. There was something familiar about the writing, as if she had looked at it before, which, of course, was impossible.

"I can leave it with you," Jack suggested. "Did you bring me a copy of the report you wrote for Kinne on Railey?"

Jane reached in her briefcase and pulled out the report. "I

think I ought to explain to you about graphoanalysis," she said.

Jack replied that he could get that information from her later after he'd studied the report and heard what she had to say about Lucy.

"I told you I might not be able to be so accurate about Lucy."

"Whatever you can come up with will be fine," Jack said. "I'll give you a call in a couple of days."

Jane was apprehensive. She feared he might be one of those reporters who wrote funny stories about astrology and reading palms and crystal balls. She decided not to tell him that she had looked briefly at Peggy's handwriting and that when he called, she would say she had been too busy to get around to studying Lucy's handwriting. This wasn't too far from the truth. She was busy.

Two weeks later he had not called her back. She thought that the story might have been postponed or cancelled. She could even have misplaced Lucy's writing. She was only sorry that she had let him take her picture. She was still willing to put her professional credentials on the line to prove that what she had written about Walker Railey was true.

37

Winter 1990

OLIVE TALLEY WAS SITTING AT HER DESK IN THE CITY room, working on a story about fraud and corruption in the town government of Plano, when the paper's travel reporter dropped some photographs on her desk.

"I was in Santa Cruz last week doing some winter

vacation stories when I drove past this corner where there is a display window with a complete computer printout of the face of Walker Railey. It covered an entire corner of a picture window. I was so shocked. I nearly wrecked the rental car," the reporter said. "Then just to be sure I hadn't lost my mind, I got out of the car and took these photographs for you. I don't know what these red and blue salamander-looking objects are."

Olive glanced at the four pictures casually tossed on her desk. "I don't believe it!" she exclaimed, picking up one of the pictures. "Can this be for real?"

"Here are four different angles," the travel reporter said, showing the corner where the shop is with the street names at the intersection, two wide angles, and the front of the building with the sign A-OK DNA LABS—SCIENCE IS OUR BUSINESS. I'm sorry that the pictures aren't better. Part of the light is reflection, but at least you can see I wasn't hallucinating."

Olive took the pictures to her editor, wondering if it was worth another trip to California. Her editor suggested that she telephone the Santa Cruz police instead and ask them to check it out. In four or five hours the police called back with information that the small one-story building on the corner of Pearl Street and East Cliff Drive was not a business but a residence. There was no picture of anyone in the window. There was no sign over the entrance that said A-OK LABS, and the house, which was in a semiresidential area where hippies hung out, seemed empty, though it was difficult to tell.

Olive hung up the receiver. What the police had said seemed like an entirely different place from the picture she held in her hand. Perhaps the occupants were aware of being photographed and simply packed up and left, the way hippies frequently did. But that didn't explain why the huge computer printout was the face of Walker Railey or why, as the police had told her, there was no telephone listing for A-OK Labs. Maybe Walker was starting his own new religion with some sort of special interest, like the Church of Religious Science, known for performing gay weddings.

Olive had other things to do now and would have to pursue it later—exactly how she wasn't sure.

On January 29, 1990, Walker Railey and his lawyer Margaret Brewer, a tall, blond woman around Walker's age, who was from Jacoby & Meyers Law Offices, entered the Los Angeles law offices of Stephen A. Kolodny on the twelfth floor of the Maxxan building on Wilshire Boulevard. The large reception area was carpeted in gray and decorated with dark traditional furniture. On behalf of Kolodny, who was involved in another case, Attorney Jill Greenspahn, a handsome woman in her mid-thirties with straight, black hair, took Railey's deposition. He had brought his bank statements with cancelled checks, phone bills, credit cards and income tax records. The three of them went into a contemporary style conference room that had a glass wall overlooking the city. The room had the same gray carpet as in the reception area but with a maroon border. The conference table had a dark marble top and was surrounded by six modern black leather chairs.

The usual opening questions were asked, and Railey answered politely. Ms. Greenspahn then asked him about the court order for child support payments and when and where the order was entered. Railey replied in early July in Dallas.

"And who do you send these payments to?"

"I send them to the Dallas County Child Payment Services Department."

"And are they forwarded to someone else?"

"That's correct."

"And who is that?"

"John and Diane Yarrington."

"Who are they?"

"They are the persons who have custody of the children; they are the godparents of the children. He is my closest friend . . ."

"When you arrived in San Francisco, where did you reside?"

"On Broadway . . ."

"When you left your apartment in San Francisco, did the reporters follow you?"

"They tried to."

"How did you get away from them?"

"Because I was smarter than they were . . ."

"The furniture put into your apartment in San Francisco . . . went into storage and remained there [until] in summer of '89, you personally moved it from storage in San Francisco to Laguna Beach?"

"That's correct."

"And this Catalina Street, whose residence is that?"

"That's Lucy Papillon's residence."

"To your knowledge, how long has that been her residence?"

"To my knowledge, less than a year . . ."

"You had a personal relationship at some point with Lucy Papillon; is that correct?"

"That's correct."

"When did that personal relationship commence?"

Railey's lawyer immediately objected to the question on the grounds that it was irrelevant. Attorney Greenspahn told Railey that he could still answer that.

"I can, but I won't."

"Are you refusing to answer that."

"I'm refusing to answer that . . ."

"You have had no contact with her since Thanksgiving of 1989 . . ."

"That's right."

Railey and Attorney Margaret Brewer left Kolodny's office late in the afternoon to drive back to Long Beach. They were prepared. They had no reason to suspect any problems.

38

$\mathcal{D}$ TOWARD THE END OF FEBRUARY, OLIVE HAD A lengthy conference with her Metropolitan Editor. Both were aware that in two months Easter and the third anniversary of the attack on Peggy Railey were coming. The paper wasn't interested in another "here's how the Church is doing three years later"—another "well folks, after three years, Walker Railey has still evaded indictment."

What the paper wanted was for Olive to come up with a major story giving *new* information, or, at least information that had not been revealed before. Olive asked what sort of information existed that hadn't been revealed.

After brainstorming for an hour or so, they came up with two ideas—one was the lives of Peggy and her parents now, photographs of her in the nursing home. Since the stories by Laura Miller, the family had refused to give interviews, unless scheduled by Bill Arnold.

The second known information that had not been revealed was Peggy's journal. The police and the F.B.I. had had it for nearly three years. Surely if there were revelations in it crucial to solving the case, they would have done something with it before now. But, there had been a number of changes in the police force, and on the Railey case in particular; Billy Prince was no longer Chief of Police. Lt. Ron Waldrop had been promoted to Assistant Chief of the Homicide Unit and Rick Silva had been transferred to another case. Detective Stan McNear was working on the case alone and now reported to Deputy Chief Ray Hawkins of the Criminal Investigation Department, Crimes Against Persons Division.

It seemed strange to Olive that Peggy's journal, which the police had found the day after the attack, had been kept secret. As far as Olive knew, the only person who had seen the journal, other than the law enforcement officers and Norman Kinne, was Diane Yarrington who had gone to the police the day after the journal was found and asked to read it. Later, when Olive questioned Diane about it, she said that she couldn't remember much of what was in it—just prayers and rambling thoughts, nothing that would have any relationship to the attack.

Olive began by telephoning Bill Arnold to ask if she could go to Tyler and interview Bill and Billie Jo and then see Peggy and the nursing home.

Bill agreed, and Olive then phoned Norman Kinne who said he wasn't optimistic that anything important would come from the journal.

Olive remembered that a neighbor of hers had told her about a graphoanalysist whom she had met at a Chamber of Commerce conference on Women in the Workplace. The woman had analyzed Railey's suicide note for Kinne. Her name was Jane Buckner and Olive recalled she had been impressed with Jane's reading of Walker's character, but that she couldn't convince her editor to let her do the story. "It's like reading tea leaves," he had said contemptuously. Then she remembered that in her conversation with Jane, Peggy's journal had been mentioned and that Jane had seen it, too. Surely if the Kinne had allowed Jane Buckner to see it, *she* should be able to see it.

She telephoned Jane who said that she had looked at the journal briefly on the day before the grand jury, but she hadn't actually read it.

"Hadn't read it!" Olive was dumbfounded.

Jane explained that she hadn't read it for content because she was looking at the base line and the up-strokes for personality traits. There hadn't been time for a complete reading. Olive asked her if she would analyze it more thoroughly if she could bring her a copy. Jane said she could not only do that but that she could compare Peggy's character with Walker's and determine their compatibility. Olive suspected her editor was going to be no more enthusiastic about the handwriting analysis of Peggy's journal than that of Walker's suicide letter. Still, the newspaper certainly wanted to be the first to reveal the contents of the journal just as it had wanted to be the first to print Railey's suicide letter.

One week before the story was scheduled to run, Olive telephoned Jane, who promised she would have the handwriting analyzed in twenty-four hours.

When she sat down at her desk in the newsroom to read the journal, Olive was astonished. First, the handwriting was difficult to read, and the duplicated copy which she had been given was so faint it was impossible to read in parts. Second, the collection of twenty-two pages scribbled at random on four yellow legal pads was undated. Olive had thought a journal would be like a diary, written daily to record the adventures that had occurred on a particular day.

Peggy's journal was fragmented and introspective, the ramblings of a desperately unhappy woman—sometimes lists, sometimes prayers or dialogues with God—and sometimes thoughts or feelings noted in phrases instead of sentences.

There were many references to ministers and members of First Church, most of whom Olive did not know. Some of these people had made Peggy feel inferior, and she disliked them. There were three lists—a list of names headed by a minus sign, those headed by a circle and those headed with a plus. There were only three names on the plus list, two of which were Gordon Casad and John Yarrington. Diane Yarrington was among the names on the more extensive circle list. Yet, Peggy also wrote: "With Diane I can vent my anger—I value her friendship—Can we add Your dimension to it? May it be so?"

Because Olive was uncertain how she was going to handle this, she brought a copy of the journal to Billie Jo at the nursing home. "I don't want to look at it," Billie Jo said.

Olive could understand that, but, if some of this was going

to appear in the newspaper Billie Jo needed to know about it and have the opportunity to comment on it. "I think you have to look at it," Olive said, handing a copy to Billie Jo who was standing alone in the center of the reception room.

There was enough going on at the nursing home, so that there was no need to talk about the journal immediately. Olive had brought a photographer with her, Judy Walgren, a sensitive young woman, who unobtrusively photographed Peggy in her wheel chair, an afghan over her knees, a restrainer around her waist, over one shoulder and tied around the back of the chair. She wore a neck brace and a head band attached to the brace so that she could keep her head erect and at the same time turn it.

The journal bothered Olive because Peggy was so desperately unhappy that she had listed her enemies and Walker's and why she felt they were enemies. She had cruel comments about Janet Marshall, whom she considered her penance. But, yes, the diary should be made public. To know who Peggy hated and feared might give some leads as to her possible attackers.

That Peggy would write prayers speaking directly to God did not seem odd when one remembered the four years she spent in a Catholic Women's College and the five years she taught music in a Catholic Preparatory School for girls.

The frequent mention of the movie *Star Wars* in the journal and her casting various people from the Church in the roles was more like a classic tragedy with gods and demons and good versus evil. Though Peggy does say a couple of times that she is angry with Walker, she more often speaks positively, even protectively, about him. Lucy isn't mentioned at all. If Peggy knew about Lucy, would she not have mentioned her? More likely she thought Walker was having an affair with Janet Marshall. Nothing in her notes suggests that Peggy herself fears a physical attack. What she apparently feared most was emotional abandonment and loneliness.

Olive drove to Jane Buckner's apartment in Garland, a suburb in the Metroplex northeast of Dallas, and the two women spent several hours going over the notes Jane had made.

According to graphoanalysis, Peggy's faults were sensitivity to criticism, vanity, prejudice, clannishness and temper. There was some need in her, something taboo that she had attempted unsuccessfully to repress. Peggy had a strong desire to be different, to be her own person. Being a minister's wife kept her from achieving this. She had a strong ability to concentrate, which was sometimes good, as in academics and music, but at other times was detrimental as she tended to magnify everything; her hurts were the worst, her triumphs the greatest. She was highly intelligent and often felt isolated from her contemporaries. Because of her intelligence she was confident about activities and impatient with the slowness of others. "I know the way this needs to be done. My way can't be improved upon, so do it," Jane Buckner said.

Peggy was unhappy, and her unhappiness was all-consuming, a clinical depression that either exacerbated her physical illnesses or else was brought on by them. She, like Walker, had a desire for perfection. She had worthwhile goals, was able to plan ahead, and had a quick sense of humor, which was sometimes unkind. Her greatest fear was of something happening that was beyond her control.

"Which was, of course, just what did happen," Olive said. "Do you think she understood Walker?"

"Oh, yes, she understood him," Jane replied. "She saw through his phoniness and his ambition and his manipulation of people, which sometimes made her very angry. She had a temper. I think Peggy found out something about Walker, something he hadn't wanted her to know, and she was so angry that she confronted him."

There was a heavy silence. "I get more from the handwriting itself than the actual content, the way she draws those heavy circles and then puts a dot in the middle, like a bull's-eye, for example.

"You see that on page two. She is thanking God for the medical help with asthma that she has received through Dr. Gross and she's feeling better—then she says: 'Thank you,

God, for the blessing of death.' I don't know what she means by that," Jane told Olive, "unless suicide was an option."

Lucy Papillon's deposition was taken April 12, 1990, also by Attorney Jill Greenspahn in the law offices of Stephen A. Kolodny on Wilshire Boulevard in Los Angeles. On the surface at least, the past three years had left no apparent adverse marks on Lucy. Golden-tanned and several pounds slimmer, she maintained her flair for haute couture. Purples and fuscias and turquoises were favorite colors this season, accessorized with wide belts and chunky jewelry. While she still did not photograph well, in person she was as sensuously attractive as ever with the same sultry looks favored in cosmetic ads. She had no lawyer, but with her, representing the petitioner Walker Railey, who was not present, was Attorney Margaret Brewer.

The three of them went into the same conference room with the large glass wall overlooking the city, the marble table and the black leather chairs that had been used for Walker's deposition. Many of the same questions that had been asked Walker by Attorney Greenspahn were asked of Lucy, and, on many similar points, such as pressuring Lucy to give her address or phone number, Attorney Brewer objected. Greenspahn was not one to back away or to forget that the underlying purpose of subpoenaing Lucy was to acquire information for the district attorney in Dallas.

"If you are refusing to give your address, do you have a vehicle for accepting service and notice on any legal proceedings relative to this deposition?"

"Yes."

"And what is that?"

"His name is Russ Reed. As far as his address, I don't know his exact address at this point, but I know that you have it."

"Are you authorizing him to accept service for you with regards to this matter for any other motions or requests that we might have of you?"

"Yes."

"So, he's in Laguna Beach and I have—"

"He's in Huntington Beach . . ."

"From the date of the attack [April 21, 1987] until the end of the year [1987] approximately how often did you see Walker Railey?"

"I really don't recall."

"Did you have sexual intercourse with Walker Railey at any time after April 21, 1987, through the end of that year?"

MS. BREWER: "Objection; irrelevant to the dissolution action or any other action."

THE WITNESS: "Yes."

"Did you have any discussions prior to April 21, 1987 with Walker Railey about marrying him?"

MS. BREWER: "Objection. It's irrelevant to the dissolution proceedings."

THE WITNESS: "No, I don't recall any."

"When is the last time you shared a motel room with him?"

"Probably a month or two ago."

"And where was that?"

"In Ventura . . ."

"Was there ever a time that you considered marrying Walker Railey at any time that you knew him?"

"Considered marrying him? It was never a possibility. No."

"Why do you say it was never a possibility?"

"He's married."

"Did you ever discuss the possibility of him [sic] getting divorced from Peggy Railey?"

"No."

"Did he [Railey] ever discuss with you after the attack on his wife who he thought might have done that?"

"No."

"Never, ever did he conjecture to you who might have done that?"

"He didn't conjecture. I don't know."

"Have you ever specifically asked Walker Railey if he was the person who attacked his wife?"

MS. BREWER: "Objection. That is an outrageous question to ask in a dissolution matter. I think it's probably even sanctionable, Counsel."

MS. GREENSPAHN: "Okay—you can go ahead and answer the question."

"I know that he didn't do it, so I hadn't any need to ask him."

"Is the answer no, you never asked him?"

"I'd like the answer to be what I said on the record."

"Everything that is being said is put on the record."

"So the answer is no."

Lucy's deposition was over. At least one person who had been subpoenaed, possibly two, had committed perjury.

Why *were* Lucy and Walker's statements always contradictory? In this instance they were accompanied by and advised by the same attorney. Surely they could have agreed on the same or similar stories? Walker had said they had not seen each other since Thanksgiving of 1989, six months ago. Lucy had said they spent the night together in Ventura, one or two months ago. Wouldn't Walker have been annoyed at Lucy seemingly revealing more than was necessary? Or was Lucy still in conflict about her image, as Jo Ann Hill, her Dallas friend, public relations agent and image builder, had suggested? Was it possible that Lucy saw her life as a drama and was acting the role of the tragic fallen heroine? Was this why she was always loyal to her love and her lover even when it was not particularly necessary?

39

ON SUNDAY APRIL 22, THREE YEARS TO THE DAY THAT Peggy had been found unconscious in her garage, Olive's article titled PEGGY RAILEY'S ANGUISH appeared on the front page of *The Dallas Morning News* beside a five-column color photograph of Bill Nicolai with Peggy in her wheel chair. The story covered another full page, with three pictures taken in the nursing home, and printed excerpts from the journal opposite the handwritten copies. The article began:

> In the weeks and months before she was brutally attacked, Peggy Railey prayed for God's help in overcoming the conflicts tearing at her soul.
> *Father, there is great violence in my response, great anger in my being, great fear in my soul, she wrote in her private journal.*

Olive reported that family and friends believe that the twenty-two pages represent a spiritual outlet for expressing feelings she successfully hid even from those who knew her well. She was unhappy in her marriage and in her life as a preacher's wife. She was haunted by unnamed fears, and she was angry toward her husband and toward some of his demanding followers. Most of the passages are written as prayers. There seems little continuity, and, since the entries are not dated, investigators have assumed that the notes were made in the six months before the attack.

The article ended with:

Barbara Wedgwood

Regardless of the interpretation of her journals, it appears that Mrs. Railey has exchanged one sort of hell for another.

Billie Jo was ambivalent in her reaction to the article. The press was focusing attention where it should be, on the victim instead of on "the only suspect." Yet, it hurt her to see her daughter's private pain spread across the front of a newspaper. It was difficult for her to accept Peggy's unhappiness, yet it was even more painful that the whole world should know of it and analyze it. Then, too, whenever articles appeared in the larger papers, she received telephone calls from distant friends who had been meaning to call, from people who had heard of someone in the same condition who had miraculously recovered, from faith healers offering their services and from reporters with small-town papers wanting to do a similar story. Following each media event, there was at least a week of added stress. And the police came no closer to solving the crime than before.

Jane Buckner had not really expected that graphoanalysis would be mentioned and explained and credited in Olive's article. That had been several weeks ago but she couldn't get Peggy's journal off her mind, not the content but the handwriting. She had been busy with another forgery case, this time in Arkansas, but one Saturday in July she awakened at three A.M. and couldn't get back to sleep. She tossed and rolled over on her back, then again on her right side, disturbing the sleep of her cat Fisher who kept getting kicked each time she changed position.

From the depths of her subconscious came the awareness that she had not analyzed the scrap of Lucy's handwriting that she had had for two years. Why this should be important now, she couldn't imagine, yet, intuitively, she knew that it was.

Getting out of bed, she put on her robe, turned on the light, and went into her study where she kept her files. Her intuition was indeed working, but after two hours it turned out to be exactly the opposite of what she had expected.

Lucy's and Peggy's personalities as shown on a color bar chart were almost identical. Their character traits determined by what they feel inside were the same—withdrawal, objectivity, poise, sympathy, emotional responsiveness. And, both were intelligent, musical and abrasive. In Walker they had found a mirror image of their flaws, setting up a self-destructive pattern. Each is asserting her desire to be different at any cost. These two unhappy women are alike in so many ways.

"Wow, Fisher! Take a look at this!" she screamed at the gray and white cat who leapt off the desk in alarm. "Fisher, come here! Come look at this one idiosyncratic circle that Lucy has used at the end of this sentence. Never in sixteen years of graphoanalysis have I seen another like it *except* in Peggy's journal. She waved the paper at the confused cat who arched its back and meowed.

Jane looked out the window into the darkness. Her unconscious was taking over again. Speaking aloud, more to herself than Fisher, she mused: "Something is missing." Her eyes felt heavy. "Could it be true that Peggy, this reticent woman gets the last word? Could it possibly have happened that way? Fisher," she whispered to the cat who had crept back beside her feet. "Could Walker Railey really be innocent?"

Happened *what way?* What did Jane mean by "Peggy gets the last word?" Surely Peggy hadn't purposely goaded Walker into such a rage that he would kill her and then be convicted of her murder. Even though he had been stripped of his position and prestige in the community, he had *not* been convicted of murder. After three years the chances of his ever being convicted were slim. Peggy could not have been certain this would happen. Even if she truly believed death a blessing surely she wouldn't have courted a painful, violent death. Could she have attempted suicide by hanging herself in the kitchen? No. However miserable and desperate she might have been, she wouldn't have risked the children's finding her. Besides Ryan had spoken of masked robbers wrapping a blue cord around Mommy's neck and Mommy saying "Please don't hurt me." Were the robbers just intending to frighten her and then accidentally going farther than intended? Was it an accident, after all?

40

ON MONDAY, JUNE 4, 1990, RAILEY, DRESSED IN THE same blue suit and blue and white striped tie he had worn on other courtroom occasions, was accompanied by Dallas Attorney Michael Pezzulli, a small, dapper man with white hair, a thin moustache and thick spectacles. The Long Beach County Courthouse was packed.

Los Angeles Attorneys Stephen A. Kolodny and Jill Greenspahn represented the Nicolais. Lucy Papillon, dressed in a bright red, high fashion suit was accompanied by an unidentified woman friend. Detective Stan McNear and a large representation of the press crowded the hall in front of the courtroom.

Inside Railey would be defending himself because his California attorneys had withdrawn, and Superior Court Judge Pro Tem Luther Callion had refused to waive state court rules requiring parties in a divorce to be represented by California lawyers.

Before entering the courtroom Railey told reporters: "It's a shame that I'm the only attorney I can afford to hire this morning, but I'll do the best I can."

Inside the court room he didn't have the chance. Attorney Stephen Kolodny immediately brought to Judge Callion's attention that the original petition was filed wrongly. The petition and the court summons failed to list Peggy's legal guardian, her mother Billie Jo Nicolai, as a party to the suit. Because Mrs. Nicolai manages Peggy's affairs, the court papers needed to name her as well.

Mr. Kolodny said he had only become aware of the problem the night before when he was putting the exhibits together. "Oh, my goodness," he had said to himself. "We've got the wrong people named here."

There was a murmur throughout the courtroom. Reporters pulled out their pads and began taking notes rapidly. Railey appeared confused, his face reddening and sweat suddenly glistening on his forehead.

Kolodny said that he was not attempting to stall the trial on behalf of Peggy Railey because "the relationship is obviously over and Peggy doesn't care, and we've found the money he hadn't bothered to disclose earlier."

What money? There were audible whispers among those watching the proceedings. Sweat now streamed down Railey's face as he rose to his feet and asked the judge: "You're saying that the last year's effort is gone and we're starting all over again? Is that what you're saying?"

Judge Callion responded that it was "better late than never" to discover flawed legal documents. The court action meant that it would be at least another six months before a legal divorce could be granted. The aborted trial ended in less than ten minutes. Everyone except Steve Kolodny seemed stunned. This open-ended conclusion was something no one had expected, yet, like every other aspect of this case, nothing occurred in the manner anticipated.

Michael Pezzulli walked out of the courtroom building with Railey, who was mobbed with at least twice as many reporters as had been on the scene earlier. They were all shouting questions at once.

"Are you going to file again immediately?"

"Why don't you file in Texas where there aren't alimony laws?"

"Where is the money Mr. Kolodny said you had concealed?" a California reporter asked.

Olive Talley suddenly found herself shoved beside Pezzulli and Railey as they attempted to push through the crowd and leave the building. Before she could ask a question, Walker fixed her with those mesmerizing green eyes.

"I have nothing to say to you." Although he was shouting, his voice trembled. "That article you wrote about Peggy was about the lowest thing I've ever read. If there's any way I can sue you, I will!"

Olive turned to Pezzulli, stunned. "Is *he* threatening to sue *me?*"

"Now, Olive, Walker isn't going to sue you," Pezzulli said soothingly as he tugged at Walker's arm, pulling him away from her. Pezzulli, whose tiny frame is only five feet two inches, pushed his way through the line of media people like a football guard making room for his client's quarterback dash.

"Is the money deposited outside the United States?" another reporter shouted.

"Money! Where is the money? The money!" Media voices echoed like a Greek chorus.

On Tuesday, June 5, 1990, *The Dallas Morning News* ran a front page story by Olive Talley, accompanied by a photograph of Railey and Pezzulli as they left the court house. The headlines were: RAILEY DIVORCE TRIAL POSTPONED. LEGAL DOCUMENTS FOUND TO BE FLAWED; 6-MONTH DELAY LIKELY.

Olive wrote that in a legal brief filed before trial on Monday, June 4, Attorney Kolodny intended to ask for a minimum of $540 monthly alimony payments and for approximately $15,000 in community property that ex-minister Railey allegedly misappropriated. It was also stated in the brief that Mrs. Railey should receive all $22,389 retained by the Church in a pension fund for her husband.

Kolodny's brief noted that Mrs. Railey's nursing home expenses averaged three thousand, four hundred dollars a month, that she currently owed the nursing home $4,500 and that her only income was $386 a month from Social

Security. It was noted that Medicaid had not approved Mrs. Railey's application for help and that all of the donations, including those from the jumble sale and from the North Texas Conference of the Methodist Church, had been spent.

Kolodny also stated that there were considerable discrepancies in the testimonies of Railey and Lucy Papillon and that he suspected Railey of lying, in particular about being unable to find better employment because the lower his income, the lower the alimony payments to his wife would be.

The article ended with a quote from Railey. "Life is waiting. I live while I wait. I'm doing the best I can."

Two facts came out of that postponed hearing that piqued the interest of the police, the press and the public. Railey had money that he had failed to report, and there was a discrepancy in depositions between Walker and Lucy.

41

AFTER ALL THE PUBLICITY IN THE LONG BEACH papers, Walker lost his job at Cedillos. Things were not going well for the Nicolais either. Both Bill and Billie Jo knew that the North Texas Methodist Conference would once more take up the issue of Peggy. They could hardly expect First Church to hold another sale. Peggy was not like the March of Dimes or the Community Chest. Under law an individual is not a charity.

Dr. Stanley Seat, who was now in charge of the United Methodist Insurance program telephoned Billie Jo a couple of weeks before the Conference and suggested that she and Bill come to Dallas on the first day of the Conference, be introduced by Bishop Blake, and then thank the ministers for their contributions toward Peggy's care last year.

This was just the sort of thing Billie Jo dreaded. She hadn't been feeling well recently and had been diagnosed as having serious adult diabetes. Standing in front of the Conference and literally asking for charity would be humiliating, even if Peggy did deserve the Church's care and protection.

Their appearance at the start of the Conference was a surprise. Billie Jo's brief speech was received with standing applause. The Nicolais left hoping that the generosity of the Conference might continue, although as time passed they knew that younger ministers would be coming into the churches and those who had known Peggy would be retiring. Eventually it would no longer be a *personal* act of charity.

After they left Highland Park United Methodist Church, where the Conference was being held, the Nicolais drove to Arlington to visit Linda and Ted.

A month later on Friday, September 14, 1991, F.B.I. agents walked into a Long Beach real estate agency where Railey had recently found employment.

The Federal authorities presented him with a California court order requiring him to give saliva and blood samples in connection with the strangulation attack on his wife in 1987.

Appearing stunned, Railey put up no resistance and left with the agents who drove him to the Metropolitan Detention Center of Los Angeles, a Federal holding facility operated by the U.S. Bureau of Prisons, where he produced samples.

Deputy Police Chief Ray Hawkins told the reporters that he hoped to present the Railey case to the district attorney's office for reconsideration on seeking a grand jury indictment.

Hawkins declined to elaborate on what authorities hoped to gain by analyzing Railey's body fluids. "As to the nature of the direction of the investigation, I can make no comment," Hawkins said. "I don't know how long it's going to take for what we need to do to be completed."

The next day Railey was interviewed on television at his Long Beach apartment by both Bud Gillett of Channel 4 and Mike Snyder of Channel 5. Railey told Gillett that he thought that the F.B.I. picked him up just to scare him into confessing. But he would *not* confess to a crime he did not commit. He was afraid that people thought he had abandoned his children, but he couldn't have them live in a place like this. He gestured at the sleazy four-hundred-and-fifty-dollar-a-month unheated, unairconditioned apartment.

Not being a daddy to his children was the hardest decision he ever had to make, Railey told Snyder. He also said that he was no longer seeing Lucy Papillon. Getting involved with her was the worst thing he had ever done. "I will pay the price for that sin all the way to the grave."

Next, as he had done with Gillett, Railey showed Snyder pictures of his children. Then he pointed to a white ceramic figure of Christ and pictures of his adoptive parents on the top of his dresser.

Like a Rubik's Cube constantly twisted but not fitting, the Railey case again had taken another bizarre turn. How could the DNA samples be used? Would it be possible to convict a person for a crime committed two years before the forensic technique used to resolve the crime had been discovered? Would there really be a criminal trial now?

Lead Detective Stan McNear released previously undisclosed news that samples of Peggy's blood were taken at The Clairmont Nursing Home. Along with samples of Walker's blood, they were being compared with blood spots found on Peggy's clothing the night of the attack. At least the police knew some things the media didn't.

Detective McNear further said that at the time of the assault he didn't notice any scratches or lacerations on either of the Raileys but that when he first saw Railey at Presbyterian Hospital, the minister was wearing a coat that could have covered scratches on his arms.

"We think he had changed clothes before going to the

hospital," McNear was quoted as saying. "I'm satisfied in my mind that he did it. We've got some circumstantial evidence, and we've got to get some more . . . If you've got enough evidence to get [Walker Railey] indicted, he might want to make a plea bargain, and some people that know something might come forward."

Plea bargain—that *was* a surprise. To plea bargain he would first have to admit his guilt, and, having done that, what was there left to bargain? Of course, the time and cost and publicity of a trial might be avoided if he pled guilty and was sentenced by a judge. Or, perhaps, if another person was involved, he might reveal who the person was, so that he or she might be indicted, too.

There were rumors, never substantiated, that when Walker went to Bridwell Library in the theology college, he was wearing a Mexican wedding shirt. Yet, Gordon and Susan had said that when they saw him the following morning he was still wearing the same jacket and trousers and yellow tie he had worn the day before. Could he have changed clothes twice? Unlikely, though nothing in this case *was* likely. Was there more evidence that the police had but had not yet revealed? Or, as Railey himself suggested, were the law enforcement officers simply harassing him?

Eight months passed before Assistant District Attorney Norman Kinne announced that he had studied the evidence presented by the police department and the Federal Bureau of Investigation but that while the material was convincingly presented he found no new evidence that would persuade him to bring Railey before another grand jury hearing.

Perhaps what the district attorney's office says is true—that there is the opportunity and the motive but no hard evidence that would stand up in court. If that is true, it is possible that Walker Railey is innocent and is so unlucky that every action he takes makes him seem guilty.

The Nicolais were disappointed but philosophical. They are relieved that Medicaid is now paying part of Peggy's nursing home bills, and the Methodist Church, as well as a

Dallas private trust fund, has agreed to pay the balance of Peggy's bills. Billie Jo still talks to her daughter at the nursing home. "Peggy, we don't know where your soul is—or your mind or your spirit. We know only that this [Peggy's body] is the house and we're doing the best we can to take care of the house in case you ever need it again."

Ted Nicolai said: "It was a senseless crime with many victims, which was committed by Walker for purely selfish reasons." He wondered "how could a man who claimed devotion to God and his word have such a total disregard for human life?"

Others, too, wonder the same.

42

March 31, 1991

THE SUN ROSE IN A CLEAR SKY THIS EASTER WITH A fresh ocean breeze cleansing the morning air. No tall buildings obstruct the view of the Pacific, as worshipers walk to the First United Methodist Church in Santa Ana, California. It is a small church able to accommodate a congregation of only three hundred, nothing at all like First United Methodist in Dallas. Yet, today the Church in Santa Ana is completely filled, not only because it is Easter but because today Dr. Walker L. Railey is delivering the sermon.

Walker has been part of the small, primarily elderly congregation for almost a year now. Everyone likes and admires him. They think he has been treated unfairly by the Church in Dallas; the ministers and the parishioners here are filled with Christian charity. Even if Railey is no longer a Methodist minister, they are glad to have him stand in their pulpit and address their congregation.

The service is remarkably similar to the order of worship on Easter at First United Methodist Church in Dallas four years earlier. The small choir begins the processional with "Jesus Christ Is Risen Today."

Walker Railey stands at the pulpit, shoulders thrown back, complexion tanned, sun-bleached hair swept up at the sides, confidently meeting the eyes of the congregation. The title of his sermon is *"Stumbling into Easter."* He tells them that the text for the day is II Corinthians, 4:18.

. . . We look not to the things that are seen, but to the things that are unseen; for the things that are seen pass away, but the things that are unseen are eternal.

Next he refers to an article in *Time* magazine by Philip Elmer-Dewitt, which suggested that the most serious problem America faces today was not an economic depression but a clinical depression. In the past signs pointed to *better days for everyone around the corner . . . Now our spirits are low, our attitudes moody and our outlooks overcast.*

He told them that if *Time* was correct, then we would find ourselves not marching triumphantly to the tune of a glorious Resurrection, but stumbling there in a state of a clinical depression. Walker went on to tell the congregation that today was not the only time in history when Christians have endured such unsettling events that they despaired. He reminded them of the women who came to the tomb, *"with the pain of passed memories eating away at the insides of their souls . . . Do not delude yourself into believing these three women were taking lilies to the Garden of Triumph that first Easter morn. The Scripture is clear. They were carrying embalming fluid to anoint a corpse."*

Walker had not lost his power to mesmerize and then to shock. The tomb was empty. The Resurrection had taken place. What is most important in the story, he told them, is not how the body was raised or its physiological condition after Resurrection occurred. More meaningful than what happened to Jesus on Easter is what happened to those disheartened women. In the midst of the deepest depression when these women had lost their faith and their hope, God's ultimate miracle of transformation took place . . . Someone else's hands took over.

He told the congregation that Resurrection affirms that when we are most vulnerable God is most invincible. In crises our redemption is in God's hands.

"Easter Sunday is not just the anticipation of what Resurrection will produce when we die in the future. Easter Sunday is also the celebration of what Resurrection will provide while we live in the present."

Walker then referred to the text for the sermon—that the things that are seen pass away, but the things that are unseen are eternal.

"Did you hear that?" he asks his listeners in a raised voice. Then he enunciates clearly and precisely that when the hope and happiness that we *see* has left us, our true redemption comes from what we *cannot* see.

Walker had lost none of his charisma as he suggested that the life changes that cause depression may have occurred among members of the congregation today—the death of a spouse, divorce, the loss of a job, loneliness, loss of health, the loss of self-respect. Five different times after each depressing situation, he states his theme changing only one word. *"When God's hands take over, our resurrection takes place . . ."* or, *"When God's hands take over, your resurrection takes place."*

He repeats the phrases alternately, ending this portion of the sermon with a phrase reminiscent of another Easter sermon he preached four years ago, "The Conspiracy of Hope."

He tells the congregation today that hope comes only when God's hands take over, and that the only possible response to such a life-changing experience is ALLELUIA!!!

There is a personal epilogue to this Easter sermon in Santa Ana, and it touches the worshipers more deeply than the sermon itself. Walker confides in them the story of his own suicide attempt that he confesses was brought on by depression and despair. He explains that his soul was so darkened that he swallowed all the sleeping pills and prescription drugs he could find. He tells them when he awoke several days later in a semiconscious state, somebody was holding his left hand. He recalls words from his suicide note: "My problem is not that God has let go of me, but that I have grown weary of holding onto God."

He then says that while many things changed for him over the past four years, one reality has not changed: God still holds his hand.

No matter how miserably I stumble and fall on my face because the burdens of life seem too much to carry, I always land in the 'Everlasting Arms' of God. Regardless of how much life gets out of hand, God's hands are always ready to take over.

You know what that means! When God's hands take over, *my* resurrection takes place. So, if you came here this morning refusing to believe in resurrection, just take a look! And, my dear sisters and brothers in Christ, what is true for me is just as true for you. ALLELUIA! HAPPY EASTER!

The sermon is over. It has been vintage Railey. There are indeed many, many sermons left in this still young ex-minister. He appears genuinely joyful. Maybe God's hand *is* in his, and like the mythical phoenix, he, too, will rise again.

43

April 22, 1992

〰️ ONE YEAR LATER AND FIVE YEARS AFTER THE ATTACK
on his wife, Walker Railey is once more employed by a
church. He has moved to Los Angeles and is Chief of Staff at
Immanuel Presbyterian Church, an inner city church with
a nine-hundred-member congregation. He manages the
Church's finances and its seven-hundred-fifty-thousand-
dollar-a-year budget.

Former Senior Pastor Gary Wilborn said, "Walker is a
terrific addition to this staff and meets all of the qualifica-
tions of this Church."

Between October 1991 and June 1992, Railey, whom a
church official said has *not* returned to the ministry,
preached several sermons at Immanuel. His first service
there detailed for the congregation his affair with Lucy and
how she had "reached a part of him that no one had ever
reached before." Did not thoughtful people there wonder
why *his* love should be more meaningful, more dramatic
and more tragic than the affairs of other mortals?

Later wearing a black robe and red stole he delivered a
sermon humorously titled, "The World's Most Beautiful
Body." He poked fun at liposuction and tummy tucks and
his own baldness to a laughing, appreciative congregation of
over two hundred.

That Walker jokes in the pulpit and that neither he nor
anyone else has been brought to criminal trial over five years
after the attack on his wife demonstrates that justice in
America is neither swift nor certain. The law and justice are
not the same. Sometimes the law prevents justice. That is
hardly a laughing matter. In the past, Americans found the

assumption of innocence natural. Today the assumption of guilt comes more naturally. Until he is proven innocent many people will assume Walker Railey guilty. In the face of such assumptions, Walker steadfastly maintains his innocence of any involvement in the attack on Peggy.

The tragedy is Peggy's story, as much as Walker's. Her existence is, as her grandmother said, "worse than death."

She still lies in a persistent vegetative state in the nursing home in Tyler. All the artificial supports and the trachea tube have been removed. She is fed through a tube in the stomach and could live for another thirty years. While she remains unchanged, Billie Jo suffers from diabetes and Bill is not as strong as he was five years ago. Few people come to visit them anymore.

Every day Billie Jo wears her medal of Saint Jude, the patron saint of hopeless causes. It appears now Saint Jude is her only hope. At times she is fearful that one day at the nursing home she may turn around and see Walker standing in the doorway.

Lucy Papillon has closed her counseling practice in Dallas. She has bought an expensive condominium on the beach in Laguna Beach, California, where she works for a management consulting firm that conducts training programs for executives.

Whether Walker and Lucy are still romantically involved is a matter of ever-changing rumor. The divorce suit, and consequently the countersuit for alimony and a substantial settlement from Railey's pension has not been refiled.

John and Diane Yarrington send reports from Little Rock to the Dallas Department of Human Resources regarding the condition of their legal wards, Ryan and Megan Railey.

Ryan and Megan see their father for a brief visit every four months. Ryan, now ten, who suffers from posttraumatic stress disorder, is still in therapy and attends a special school. Megan, now seven, fears separation from her new family after visits from her father. The children do not see their grandparents or their mother, though they know that she is hurt and in a hospital. Ryan misses his grandfather

"Pa Bill," and Walker himself concedes that this is another tragedy for the child.

The Nicolais strongly felt their first responsibility was toward Peggy, though Billie Jo admits it may not have been the best decision. Now the Nicolais say they feel that they would only be a further complication in their grandchildren's lives. There are almost no telephone calls or correspondence between the Yarringtons and the Nicolais, no Christmas or birthday presents. One wonders whether the Nicolais are making certain they cannot be accused of influencing the children against their father, in case there is another lawsuit against Walker Railey.

In an interview given to Olive Talley and published April 22, 1992, in *The Dallas Morning News,* Assistant District Attorney Kinne said he feared Ryan might come under dual pressures to alter his account of the attack on his mother. "If it's Walker, he's going to try to convince the kid he didn't do it—and I'm also afraid there may be people trying to convince him that Walker did do it."

What does Kinne mean by this? Unwilling to elaborate further on the dilemma surrounding Ryan, Kinne still insists that current evidence does not merit a prosecution, even though he is personally convinced that Walker Railey is guilty.

On the afternoon before she was attacked did Peggy find the demon inside her husband and threaten to expose it?

Does Walker Railey now reside in an earthly purgatory between godliness and pure evil?

The association between evil and organized religion has not been overlooked in history or literature. An evil person finds a good place to hide in a church. Surrounded by goodness, evil is less apparent. Surely evil people are to be pitied as well as feared. They live in anxiety, dreading the humiliation of exposure. Christianity embraces the forgiveness of sins. But can we forgive evil? Do not those who associate with evil people become victims or else evil themselves?

Over the years ideas about God and about the devil have

come and gone, but that does not mean that either God or the devil changes. What is believed today is not necessarily truer than what was believed a hundred or even a thousand years ago. In Dallas on April 19, 1987, something demonic happened. People who were at that Easter service look back upon the day not as the affirmation of the Resurrection but as the announcement of the arrival of the Antichrist, that rough, slouching beast, "its hour come round at last."

Afterword

What can be predicted about the Railey tragedy is that it is unpredictable.

On August 25, 1992, five years and four months after the attack on his wife, Walker Railey was arrested in Los Angeles at Emmanuel Presbyterian Church by Dallas Police Detective Stan McNear. Jailed for three days in California, Railey was then extradited to Dallas—where he was indicted for the attempted killing of his wife by choking her with a ligature. Judge Pat McDowell set bail at $25,000. Representatives of Railey immediately posted the required 10 percent, or $2,500. Within a few minutes, Railey was again free—until his trial.

Not only was Railey stunned by his indictment and arrest, but he once again vehemently proclaimed his innocence. The Methodist Church and the city of Dallas were shocked. What had happened? What had changed?

District Attorney John Vance had removed Norman Kinne from the case and turned it over to Assistant Prosecuting District Attorney Cecil Emerson. Vance told the media that his office was still concerned about bringing a case that could result in an instructed verdict or a guilty verdict overturned on appeal for a lack of concrete evidence. But, Vance decided that nothing could be gained by waiting for new evidence which, at this point, seemed unlikely.

Rumors abounded. A new technology existed that could locate exact places where Railey had telephoned from his mobile phone on the night of the attack. Psychiatrists said ten-year-old Ryan Railey was now able to testify in court. Assistant District Attorney Emerson told the media there was no new evidence and that he expected to go to trial within sixty days.

The amazing facts of the Railey story reflect how fragile and uncertain beliefs are. Nothing in this mystery was, or is, entirely what it seemed. Apart from who committed the attack, other disturbing questions remain. Did the Dallas police mishandle the investigation? Would the police have been tougher had Railey and Lucy not been prominent people? Would Railey have been indicted sooner had his attorney been less aggressive than Doug Mulder? Would Railey have been indicted sooner had Prosecutor Norm Kinne not been, in his words, so morally outraged that his feelings clouded his judgment? Had Peggy Railey been found dead instead of alive, would an autopsy have revealed important clues?

A case is never shut as long as there is no final answer, and the only final answer to an attempted murder is a trial. The world doesn't pause long for attempted murders or for unsolved crimes. New atrocities occur daily. Consequences of evil overshadow its banality. Still, like a Greek tragedy with numerous subplots the Railey crime continues to fascinate.

The unanswered problems of the Railey tragedy *should* be answered at Walker Railey's trial whenever and wherever it takes place. But, Railey did not appear for his civil trial. It is possible that he many not appear for his criminal trial.

Assuming he does appear, he might plead guilty—or, a jury might find him innocent. On his own behalf he could be a beguiling witness. Despite the sincere efforts of the police, the church and the district attorney's office, justice is not certain.

You have read the facts, or what some people involved have said are the facts. You have noted those concerned and those on the periphery of the mystery who would not speak at all. You as readers may still be the only judges.